The Word of God *and*
Latino Catholics

The **Word** of **God**
and
Latino Catholics

The Teachings of the Road to Emmaus

Edited by
Jean-Pierre Ruiz and Mario J. Paredes

AMERICAN BIBLE SOCIETY

The Word of God & Latino Catholics: Teachings of the Road to Emmaus has been granted the Nihil Obstat by Monsignor Michael F. Hull and the Imprimatur by +Bishop Dennis J. Sullivan. The Nihil Obstat and the Imprimatur are official declarations that this book is free of doctrinal or moral error. No implications are contained therein that those who have granted the Nihil Obstat and Imprimatur agree with the content, opinion or statements expressed.

Library of Congress Control Number: 2011960837
ISBN Number: 9781937628086
ABS Item Number: 123312

American Bible Society (ABS) is an interconfessional Christian organization whose mission, in part, is to work with churches and Christian organizations to make the Bible available so all people may experience its life-changing message. For over 190 years, ABS has been providing churches of all Christian faith traditions with Bibles and Scripture resources needed to enlighten, inspire and enrich the lives of the people they serve. The Society is pleased to provide this collection of essays, presented at the Camino a Emaus Conference held at Notre Dame University. The conference reflects the search for God in the Holy Scriptures. Fifteen scholars explore and promote The Word of God in the Life and the Mission of the Church. We trust that Catholic readers will find The Word of God & Latino Catholics: Teachings of the Road to Emmaus useful in forming and deepening their habit of meaningful Scripture reading. Please note that the Catholic doctrinal positions presented in this manual do not reflect the interconfessional stance of American Bible Society.

American Bible Society gives special thanks to the Cushwa Center for the Study of American Catholicism of the University of Notre Dame and all who contributed to make this volume possible, in particular:

Efraín Agosto	Ricardo Grzona, F.R.P.
Juan I. Alfaro	Felix Just, S.J
Archbishop Nikola Eterović	Jaime Lara
Eduardo C. Fernández, S.J.	Hosffman Ospino
Renata Furst	Mario J. Paredes
Francis Cardinal George, O.M.I	Arturo J. Pérez-Rodríguez
Archbishop José H. Gómez	Jorge Presmanes, O.P.
Raúl Gómez-Ruiz, S.D.S.	Jean-Pierre Ruiz

Contents

～

Preface

Mario J. Paredes

〜

The account of Emmaus is found in the Gospel of Saint Luke, chapter 24—a beautiful passage.

Luke's account concerning the disciples from Emmaus is direct and easy to read, and very enlightening concerning the resurrection of Christ, while at the same time profound, theological, somewhat complicated, with some in-depth teaching that the author wants to give the reader. Let's give it our attention now. What Luke wants to show us is a critical reflection about the Christian faith.

All the accounts in the Gospel of Saint Luke are didactic. He expressly tells us this in his prologue. He wants to provide a solid basis for the teaching we have received and accepted among the faithful members of the Christian community. Through significant deeds he is seeking to teach, clarify, and strengthen our faith. And for us, providentially, what he proposes is to precisely define the radical foundation and the true nature of our faith. What is real Christian faith, and what does it imply?

Historical-literary criticism has discovered the complexity of the passage. Luke builds on an earlier narration, touches it up, and completes it with other, older narratives. The two persons of our account who are walking from Jerusalem felt deceived and sad, for their teacher had died: "They were talking and thinking about what had happened" (verse 14). (All Scripture in this preface is from the *Contemporary English Version Bible*.)

Their knowledge of the Scriptures, their personal time with Jesus, and their attention to his teaching did not help them to understand his death on the cross. Their faith in the Jesus they had known in public evaporated at Golgotha and had become instead a historical memory of a "powerful prophet, who pleased God and all the people" (Lk 24:19).

To ignore or to reject the mystery of the cross is to ignore the mystery of the universal redemption of Christ, which presupposes the mystery of human iniquity and the mystery of God's goodness and infinite mercy. There is, then, no genuine Christian faith that does not spring from the acceptance of the incomprehensible cross. But faith in the crucified one is not enough. The basis of Christian faith is Jesus crucified and risen again; it is Jesus forever alive with a transfigured body, freed from the limits of historical existence: the clarification, argument, and prelude of what awaits us in the light of his crucifixion and resurrection.

And this is precisely what the risen Jesus, when he appeared to them on the way, was explaining to the disciples from Emmaus: "Jesus then explained everything written about himself in the Scriptures, beginning with the Law of Moses and the Books of the Prophets" (verse 27). Acceptance and confession of the resurrection, according to Saint Luke, is so fundamental for the Christian's faith that, if it is absent, Christ's divinity is lost, and faith inevitably evaporates.

Even so, it is not enough to believe in the living and glorious Christ. We need to believe in his renewed presence and activity among us, a multiple and real presence. Luke explains this. As he sees it, the living and glorious Jesus is present, in the first place, wherever we are thinking about and discussing the significance of his life, death, and resurrection. And this is the case even when the discussion is dominated by doubt, unbelief, or disappointment.

Luke writes:

> [13]That same day two of Jesus' disciples were going to the village of Emmaus, which was about seven miles from Jerusalem. [14]As they were talking and thinking about what had happened, [15]Jesus came near and started walking along beside them.

The situation is clear, as is also the fact that he approaches them to converse and to clarify matters.

> Jesus asked them, "What were you talking about as you walked along?" [17]The two of them stood there looking sad and gloomy. [18]Then the one named Cleopas asked Jesus, "Are you the only person from Jerusalem who didn't know what was happening there these last few days?"
> [19]"What do you mean?" Jesus asked.
> They answered: "Those things that happened to Jesus from Nazareth. By what he did and said he showed that he was a powerful

prophet, who pleased God and all the people. [20]Then the chief priests and our leaders had him arrested and sentenced to die on a cross. [21]We had hoped that he would be the one to set Israel free! But it has already been three days since all this happened."

The combination of two different narrations or traditions is evident in Luke's account. First, as regards the empty tomb. With this, Luke wants to tell us that Christians should not seek Christ among the dead in the cemetery of those who once lived, but among those who are living and present again, although in a different way, which is where Christ is obviously to be found.

Christ is also present in a unique way in his living word, in the interpretation of the Old Testament (the preparation for the New Testament), and in the New Testament, the "Word of God made flesh." This is seen as follows in Luke's text:

[25]Then Jesus asked the two disciples, "Why can't you understand? How can you be so slow to believe all that the prophets said? [26]Didn't you know that the Messiah would have to suffer before he was given his glory?" [27]Jesus then explained everything written about himself in the Scriptures, beginning with the Law of Moses and the Books of the Prophets.

Jesus, risen and alive, is present in the event of the inspired language, questioning and teaching through his vital communication.

What a shame that the tradition has not preserved for us the sacred lesson of biblical exegesis offered to this pair from Emmaus! At twelve years of age, when Jesus stayed in the temple with the teachers of the Law, Luke mentions that "everyone who heard him was surprised at how much he knew and at the answers he gave" (Lk 2:47). The same disciples from Emmaus would say a little later, after the risen and living One disappeared from their sight: "When he talked with us along the road and explained the Scriptures to us, didn't it warm our hearts?" (verse 32).

Jesus, risen and alive, also made his presence known, according to Saint Luke, in a unique way in the breaking of bread, that is to say, in every kind of human fellowship. For several to sit at a table together and include a stranger in the ancient world was a symbolic way of defining human brotherhood. The presence of a stranger is important, an unknown guest, for it underscores that human brotherhood, in a broad and real sense, transcends the more obvious family relationships, as well as friends or neighbors.

In the light of this symbolism, the meals that the earthly Jesus had with publicans and sinners take on greater significance (compare Mt 9:11; 11:19; Lk 5:2, 19).

In times of so much isolation and social exclusion of so many human beings from the great banquet of life, it catches our attention that Luke, at this particular moment, would tell us that the risen and living Christ was not only present and active, but also recognized in the sharing of food with others, with neighbors.

Luke writes:

> [28]When the two of them came near the village where they were going, Jesus seemed to be going farther. [29]They begged him, "Stay with us! It's already late, and the sun is going down." So Jesus went into the house to stay with them.
> [30]After Jesus sat down to eat, he took some bread. He blessed it and broke it. Then he gave it to them. [31]At once they knew who he was, but he disappeared.

As in all the early Christian communities, the principal meeting over which Luke presided in the Lord's name was for the breaking of bread, the Eucharist, according to the Master's mandate on the night of the last supper with his disciples: "Do this in memory of me." It is another very special way, underscored by Luke, of revealing the risen and glorious Christ present and active among us. To express this in Luke's account, he places Jesus as presiding at the table, and he employs the words of the Eucharistic prayer: "He took the bread in his hands, blessed it, and gave it to them," sacred words that are still repeated today at the moment of consecration of the Mass.

We find the words of Luke charged with profound meaning when Luke reaches this precise point, when "at once they knew who he was" (verse 31). That is the great experience that they will joyfully share with the apostles in Jerusalem.

> [33]So they got right up and returned to Jerusalem. The two disciples found the eleven apostles and the others gathered together. [34]And they learned from the group that the Lord was really alive and had appeared to Peter. [35]Then the disciples from Emmaus told what happened on the road and how they knew he was the Lord when he broke the bread.

Introduction

Jean-Pierre Ruiz

∿

Wasn't it like a fire burning within us when he talked to us on the road
and explained the Scriptures to us?
—Luke 24:32, *Good News Translation*

It is with these words that the two disciples who encounter a mysterious
companion on the road from Jerusalem to Emmaus begin to express the
life-changing significance of their encounter with the one whom they come
to recognize as the risen Jesus when their guest becomes their host in the
breaking of the bread. Though Jesus vanishes from their sight in the very
instant that they recognize him, in that same moment their disappointment
and doubt give way to understanding and faith, and at once they return
to Jerusalem to share the Good News of the resurrection. In Luke's Gospel, Jesus' public ministry begins with his reading from the Scriptures in
the synagogue at Nazareth and announcing "This passage of Scripture has
come true today, as you heard it being read" (Lk 4:21, Good News Translation). How fitting it is that the risen Jesus makes himself known to his disciples through the Scriptures along the road to Emmaus. It is Jesus himself,
identified in John's Gospel as God's Word-made-flesh (John 1:14), the one
to whom the Law and the Prophets testify, who teaches them about himself
in the words of the Word of God (Lk 24:27).

This book celebrates two important encounters with the Word of God,
encounters that bear convincing witness that God's life-giving Word is alive
in the Church. The first of these was the Twelfth Ordinary General Assembly of the Synod of Bishops, which was convened at the Vatican from October 5 to 26, 2008, and which had as its theme "The Word of God in the

1

Life and Mission of the Church." In his introduction to the *Lineamenta* for the synod, Archbishop Nikola Eterović, General Secretary of the Synod of Bishops, expresses the hope that sustained the work of the synod fathers: "the Synod wishes to promote an inspired rediscovery of the Word of God as a living, piercing and active force in the heart of the Church, in her liturgy and in her prayer, in evangelization and in catechesis, in exegetical studies and in theology, in personal and communal life, and also in the cultures of humanity, purified and enriched by the Gospel."[1] In his Post-Synodal Apostolic Exhortation *Verbum Domini*, promulgated on September 30, 2010 (the Memorial of St. Jerome), Pope Benedict XVI writes that "the synodal assembly was a testimony, before the Church and the world, to the immense beauty of encountering the word of God in the communion of the Church."[2] Bishops from around the world "gathered around the word of God and symbolically placed the text of the Bible at the centre of the assembly," and, as the pope explains, "We recounted to one another all that the Lord is doing in the midst of the People of God, and we shared our hopes and concerns."[3] The synod fathers were addressed by the Ecumenical Patriarch Bartholomew I of Constantinople and they listened to Rabbi Shear Yashuv Cohen, Chief Rabbi of Haifa, speak to them about the meaning and the place of the Scriptures in Judaism, the first time a rabbi has addressed a plenary session of the synod.[4]

In "*Verbum Domini*," Benedict XVI suggests that

> in the Church there is also a Pentecost today—in other words, the Church speaks many tongues, and not only outwardly, in the sense that all the great languages of the world are represented in her, but, more profoundly, inasmuch as present within her are various ways of experiencing God and the world, a wealth of cultures, and only in this way do we come to see the vastness of the human experience and, as a result, the vastness of the word of God.[5]

The second encounter with the Word of God that this book celebrates took place from July 30 to August 1, 2009, on the campus of the University of Notre Dame. Several hundred participants—bishops and biblical scholars, catechists and youth ministers, diocesan directors of Hispanic ministry, and theologians—gathered for a conference entitled "Camino a Emaús: The Word of God and Latino Catholics," jointly sponsored by the American

Bible Society and the Cushwa Center for the Study of American Catholicism of the University of Notre Dame. Resonating intentionally with the theme of the 2008 Assembly of the Synod of Bishops on the Word of God in the Life and Mission of the Church, the conference explored and promoted God's Word at the heart of the Church, with a particular focus on Scripture in Latinos' lives and call to mission. More than 50 percent of all Catholics in the United States under the age of twenty-five are Latinos/as, and Latinos/as currently make up more than 35 percent of the total Catholic population of the country. In a Church that speaks many tongues, the vibrant presence of Latino and Latina Catholics in the United States is loud and clear testimony to what Pope Benedict XVI called "the vastness of the human experience," and "the vastness of the word of God."[6] Participants listened to an opening keynote address by Cardinal Francis George, Archbishop of Chicago and then President of the United States Conference of Catholic Bishops, one of the five U.S. bishops who were delegates to the synod. The General Secretary of the Synod, Archbishop Nikola Eterović, also addressed the participants, focusing on Pope Benedict XVI's contribution to the synod. Archbishop José Gómez, then archbishop of San Antonio and now Archbishop of Los Angeles—the largest Catholic archdiocese in the United States, with a Catholic population of more than four million—delivered the closing plenary, in which he reminded participants that "the encounter with Christ in the Scriptures must lead our people to bear witness to him."

The essays in this book were originally presented as plenary addresses and workshop presentations at the "Camino a Emaús" conference and revised by their authors for publication. They take their inspiration from Luke's narrative of the encounter on the road to Emmaus, exploring the rich dimensions of that biblical text and its abiding significance for the Church today. Presentations that were originally delivered in English have been translated into Spanish, and presentations delivered in Spanish have been translated into English. Participants at the conference themselves asked that the rich resources provided by the presenters be made available in print, so that, in keeping with the spirit of the synod, the Word of God might enrich the lives of Latino and Latina Catholics across the country. This book, therefore, is presented in the spirit of the first words of the First Letter of John:

> We write to you about the Word of life, which has existed from the
> very beginning. We have heard it, and we have seen it with our eyes;

yes, we have seen it, and our hands have touched it. . . . What we have seen and heard we announce to you also, so that you will join with us in the fellowship that we have with the Father and with his Son Jesus Christ. We write this in order that our joy may be complete. (1 John 1:1–4, *Good News Translation*)

⁓

Notes

1.　Nikola Eterović, Introduction to the *Lineamenta*, "*The Word of God in the Life and Mission of the Church*" (Vatican City: The General Secretariat of the Synod of Bishops, 2007), http://www.vatican.va/roman_curia/synod /documents/rc_synod_doc_20070427_lineamenta-xii-assembly_en.html.

2.　Benedict XVI, "Postsynodal Apostolic Exhortation *Verbum Domini*" (September 30, 2010), http://www.vatican.va/holy_father/benedict _xvi/apost_exhortations/documents/hf_ben-xvi_exh_20100930 _verbum-domini_en.html.

3.　Ibid.

4.　Bartholomew I, Speech at First Vespers of the Twenty-Ninth Sunday of Ordinary Time (Vatican City: Holy See Press Office, October 18, 2008), http://www.vatican.va/news_services/press/sinodo/documents /bollettino_22_xii-ordinaria-2008/02_inglese/b30_02.html#SPEECH_BY _THE_ECUMENICAL_PATRIARCH_BARTHOLOMEW_I; Shear Yashuv Cohen, "Rabbi's Address to Synod" (October 7, 2008), http://www.zenit.org /article-23837?l=english.

5.　Benedict XVI, "*Verbum Domini.*"

6.　United States Conference of Catholic Bishops Committee on Cultural Diversity in the Church, Subcommittee on Hispanic Affairs, "Statistics on Hispanic/Latino(a) Catholics," http://www.usccb.org/hispanicaffairs/demo .shtml.

Reflections on the Synod on the Word of God in the Life and Mission of the Church

Francis Cardinal George, O.M.I.

~

The topic of the synod was the Word of God in the life and mission of the Church. But it is not, certainly not in this country, just a topic for the Church, because, in the light of the Hispanic presence in the Catholic Church here, the situation of Catholicism in our country today is a snapshot of the situation of the entire country thirty years from now. What the Catholic Church looks like now, the entire United States will look like in thirty years. That's a demographic fact as well as a cultural reality that has transformed the life of the Church and is transforming the life of the United States. So I am very pleased that the University and the American Bible Society and the others who have come together to create this conference have enabled all of us to reflect again not only on the synod but on its importance for the Latino community here and, therefore, for the whole Church and our society.

I'd like to spend a moment on the nature of a synod because, while some have been there, most here have not, and it's a good thing to understand the process in order to understand the content at the end and how we get to the content at the end. The very end, of course, will be the Holy Father's promulgation of the post-synodal apostolic exhortation, which is being worked on now. Perhaps Archbishop Eterović can speak to that; but until the papal exhortation is published, the synod is still in process.

The process begins long before the 260 some bishops and the invited guests and the experts and the secretaries get together in the Synod Hall in the Paul VI Aula in Rome. It begins with the choice of the topic by the Holy

Father, after consultation with university faculties, with conferences of bishops, with people around the world who are all involved in the conversation that creates Catholic communion. When the Holy Father, on the advice of many and those most involved, particularly the Secretariat of the Council, headed now by Archbishop Eterović, decides on a topic, then a *Lineamenta* is produced—a sort of a first attempt to delineate the topic. Themes are presented and, again, the same people and more who were asked to suggest a topic are consulted. Their work goes back to the permanent council for the synod, which then produces the *Instrumentum Laboris*, the working paper. This is the document that the bishops who come, as well as the observers who can't speak, and the experts will use in order to prepare what they want to contribute to the live conversation that will take place in the Synod Hall itself. It is the working document for the synod.

The Roman Synod of Bishops meets every three years and has done so since the Second Vatican Council. Many topics that are now part of the regular conversation of the Church have become embedded in our way of speaking and thinking and our sharing with one another because they were the topics of synods. Synods as a regular practice in advising the Holy Father began in 1967. The first synod discussed the renewal of seminaries and the priesthood, a call on ministry for justice. Evangelization, catechesis, the family, reconciliation, and penance followed as synodal topics; then the various vocations in the Church were discussed: first the laity, then the priesthood and consecrated life, finally bishops. They turned next to the Lord himself and had a synod on the Holy Eucharist. The most recent synod considered the eternal Word made flesh and the inspired witness to him in human words, "The Word of God in the Life and Mission of the Church." After the conversation in every synod, an apostolic exhortation was written. Each of the synods has therefore changed the life of the Church by raising themes and topics that perhaps otherwise we might not have thought about, had we each remained immersed in our own personal struggles, or even our parishes or dioceses, or episcopal conferences.

The method of the synod is open to change from time to time. Basically, when the synodal bishops come together with the others who are invited, they meet in a hall like a lecture hall. There is always a president, of course, who is the Holy Father. But he delegates his presiding to three cardinals, who take turns, day after day, moderating the sessions. The language they use is Latin, and the manner of presiding is quite formal. There are no surprises as they moderate. The surprises come when people can speak their own languages!

The three bishops or cardinals who presided at the recent synod were Cardinal Levada of the Congregation for the Doctrine of the Faith, Cardinal Pell of Sydney, Australia, and Cardinal Scherer of São Paulo, Brazil. There was a special secretary, Archbishop Monsengwo, who is the Archbishop of Kinshasa in the Congo, and of course, there are all the secretaries who are part of the secretariat headed by our guest, Archbishop Eterović.

The key figure in each synod is somebody called the *relator*. He's the key figure because it's his responsibility to present the *status quaestionis,* the topic, before we begin to discuss. He begins after the introductory talks and after the general secretary relates the business of the synod since the last synod met. Special synods also meet; each of them is usually called for as part of the Catholic world. This fall, a second meeting of the Synod for Africa will be held. We had a synod for America in 1997, to prepare for the great Jubilee. At each synod, the *relator* is named by the pope. In this case, it was Cardinal Ouellet of Quebec, Canada. The *relator* is the key person for sorting things out in terms of content itself, not for keeping the process going, which is the responsibility of the presidents. Before the general discussion begins, the whole assembly listens to the *relato ante disceptationem.* The *relator* gives, in the light of the working paper, the outline of the subject to be discussed in plenary sessions. Then, as each of the bishops and the invited guests speaks for several minutes, he and the secretaries make note of what is said, try to put the ideas together and begin to move toward synthesis and consensus. Very often there is no continuity from one talk to another, because the bishops speak as they present their papers and do not respond directly to the speakers who have been part of the conversation before them. There is some more direct exchange at the end of each day, in an hour that is more freely structured, but basically one listens to people whose ideas aren't connected as they give them, and it's up to the *relator* to make the connections.

The *relator* listens very carefully for ten days or so, as bishop after bishop gives his individual intervention. Then he intervenes to sum up the discussion. He brings it together in such a way that when the members of the synod divide into linguistic groups, the discussion will be focused. The idea is to get as many ideas as possible into the hourglass at the beginning, and the *relator* grinds the funnel in order to come out at the end with consensus.

To achieve further consensus, the members of the synod sort out ideas in small groups with the idea of creating propositions that will be voted on at the end of the synod and presented to the Holy Father. Then he writes the post-synodal apostolic exhortation that we're now awaiting.

It's a process that is quite formal, but it works. The content is given, it's criticized, it's analyzed, it's discussed in smaller groups, and then the content issues into the propositions that are finally voted on. At each turn, it's the *relator* who is the key figure in the conversation, because after the small groups have talked and brought in reports to the full assembly, the *relator* takes the floor again to shape their reports into propositions. These are discussed for the last time in small groups, revised, and then voted on.

The synod methodology enables three hundred people from all over the world, with translations into six languages every day, to move a topic along to a revelation that enriches the life of the Church. The process can seem too formal at times, and at other times it can seem to be ineffective, but it withstands manipulation, which is important in an assembly with people from different countries. The quality of the individual interventions is, of course, as key as the work of the *relator*. The quality in this recent synod was high because many of the Synodal Fathers were themselves biblical scholars, graduates of the Biblicum attached to the Gregorian University in Rome. They could speak as experts about Holy Scripture, as well as speaking as bishops always do, as pastors. When they spoke, I found myself very enriched by intervention after intervention.

Moving from the process to the topic, the first clarification of the synod content was to distinguish the senses of the Word of God. First of all, the "Word of God" is the eternal Word of God made flesh, Jesus of Nazareth, Son of God and Son of Man, truly divine, truly human. It is the encounter with the risen Christ, the living Word made flesh, now risen from the dead, that begins everyone's journey of faith. From that living encounter with the now risen person who in his own body is immortal, with the marks of the Passion in his hands, his feet, and his side, faith is born. The body that was born of the Virgin Mary is the body that rose from the dead, a body transformed because it is now immortal and is not subject to the rules of space and time that so subject and limit our lives.

The risen Christ is perfectly free, and he wants to be with us. In their encounter with the risen Lord, people begin to think and reflect on who he really is. Touched by the witness to Christ in Holy Scripture, the Church elaborates her catechesis and doctrinal theology. Then, knowing and loving Christ, his disciples ask what they must do to follow him. Moral theology is developed to help the Church understand the demands of discipleship.

The Incarnate Word, the Word made flesh, risen from the dead, is the first sense of the Word of God.

The second sense of the "Word of God" is our own speaking about Jesus in human words. The first creed proclaimed that Jesus is Lord; he, not Caesar, is Kyrios. The Gospel was preached before it was written. The community that is formed through that proclamation and that is pastored by the apostles and their successors begins to develop its understanding of what the proclamation means and to live it truly. When the community puts its understanding in written form, the community itself discerns what is a genuine or true witness to the Lord and what is false, what is inspired by the Spirit and what is not.

The synod insisted that the Church is the first context of scriptural understanding because the biblical books are documents of faith, written by people of faith for a community of faith. While there are many levels of signification in the pages of Scripture (the literal sense in the mind of the human author, the spiritual sense in the mind of the divine author, and the cultural signification taken for granted at the time of writing), it is the Church that decides, first of all, what is the canon of Scripture, and then what it means. This is why we read Scripture preeminently as we worship God together in Christ's body, the Church.

The inspired written text is the third sense of the "Word of God." The Incarnate Word Himself and the spoken proclamation of who He is are captured in written texts that give certain witness to Christ because they are inspired by the Holy Spirit.

It is that third meaning of the "Word of God" that was most emphasized in the synodal discussions. In looking at God's Word in human words, whether spoken or written under the inspiration of the Holy Spirit, we had to keep in mind the original encounter with the Lord, that allows us to enter into God's self-revelation. Considering the "Word of God" in these various senses enables us to see revelation as a conversation that includes our participation. There are four moments in the conversation between God and the human race that He calls to eternal life through Jesus Christ, four moments that are helpful in analyzing the rich content of the various synodal interventions.

In the first moment of the conversation, the initiative is always with God. God speaks. In discussing the written human word through which God speaks, the legitimate diversity of senses in Scripture has to be allowed, and so it was.

The senses of Scripture were the subject of a number of interventions, because in recent years the spiritual senses of Scripture—allegorical, moral, analogical—were seen as *eisegesis* rather than exegesis. They weren't really in the text, but were brought to the text by the faith community, whether individually or collectively. Many of the Synodal Fathers, particularly those who were Scriptural scholars, wanted to reincorporate into the sense of the text itself the spiritual meanings that the Church has discerned, because she has the mind of Christ, as St. Paul says. These are meanings that the Lord himself intends to be read in Holy Scripture. You can't know that on your own, but you can know them through the Church, reflecting together, particularly in liturgy, on the pages of Scripture. The historical-critical method and the various instruments that it uses in order to help us sort out the meaning that is in the text were put into a larger context of the theological elaboration of Scripture. The study of the Bible and the study of doctrinal theology cannot be separated, lest Bible study become merely archaeological and theology become mere human ideation or argument.

Discussing the relationship between Bible and theology brought up the topic of inerrancy and inspiration. If Scripture is inspired by the Holy Spirit, if He is moving the human author to write in a certain way, then what is written must be true, but it is true in various ways. Scripture contains many literary forms. Some of it is poetry, some of it is homiletics, some of it is history, and each of those has a different set of criteria for determining what the truth-value of the text might be. It is a mistake to read all Scripture as if it were a newspaper—we all know that. But when the relationship between inerrancy and inspiration was debated, the topic of the fidelity of translations to the original also came up. Many linguists communicated that they don't have a complete translation of Holy Scripture, and the work of the American Bible Society in assisting translations in so-called minor languages was noted and appreciated by many in the assembly. Beyond the challenge of putting Holy Scripture into languages that have never been used to express God's Word in human words, this elaboration of criteria for deciding whether or not a translation is faithful was discussed. A translation is a good translation because it captures the meaning of the inspired text, but God does not inspire translators. No translated text is inspired in the sense that the Hebrew and Greek texts are inspired. Since we don't have absolute certitude about the original texts in many cases, the Church seeks the studies of those who are experts in the languages and the texts.

Those are the kinds of questions that arise when one starts to ask how is it that God can speak using human words to express what he wants to reveal. However, in that conversation we listen, and there were many interventions about listening in different contexts. You know that when you write a letter you take a lot of pains to see to it that your ideas are clear, but what you have to also keep in mind is, "What's the context in which it's going to be read? Will it be read on a battlefield? Will it be read in a kitchen? Will it be read in an office?" The context shapes the meaning as the person listens to or reads what has been clearly written. Often a reader or a listener can't hear the message because of the context that he brings to that text.

In the conversation that is revelation, we listen. One of the surprising developments for me in the synod was the insistence with which the personal context was so emphasized in discussing *Lectio Divina*. This is a prayerful use of the texts read for your spiritual enrichment, for meditation in the morning or in the evening. People go to Scripture in the midst of joys and hardships, and there is a system of reading, *Lectio Divina*, spiritual reading, that has been developed to help them grow in understanding of the Lord's ways. What is meant by *Lectio Divina?* We mean many things, but basically what we mean is how to use Holy Scripture, the inspired text, to pray so that the Lord can truly break into our lives. The synodal interventions sometimes spoke about the need in Catholic communities to have a Bible in every home and in every hand.

It wasn't only the personal context of reading the Bible that was the subject of interventions. What was most touching, and it always is, was when the bishops in particularly troubled lands were able to speak about the context in which their people read Holy Scripture. It's very different to read Holy Scripture among the Chaldean Catholics in Baghdad today than it is to read it in Indiana tonight. Bishops are always at their best, no matter what else they speak about, when they bring their people with them— and they always do. They are shepherds. They are concerned about their people, they love them; and when they speak, the people are always there. When they speak explicitly about the sufferings that their people are going through and the challenges of being faithful to the Lord in various parts of the world—parts of Africa, where there is civil war; in Iraq, where war continues; in this country, in a more secularized society with our own tensions—when those contexts are brought up, the contexts give new meaning to the text of Scripture. It isn't the original context, and one has to study the original context, but the context of one's own life also directs the reading of the sacred text.

In revelation as conversation, God speaks and we listen. There then comes a moment in the conversation which shapes God's self-disclosure to his people when he trusts us to speak. When we speak what we listened to, what we have studied and meditated upon, what do we say? The bishops talked about homilies, often self-critically. Catholic homilies can get quite heady and rationalistic because we have a vocabulary besides biblical vocabulary. We have philosophical vocabulary that enters into theological discourse; we use it and it is important to do so. God gave us minds to think critically. It is also a vocabulary that enables us to speak to society in non-biblical ways, which was a condition that Barack Obama said is necessary if people of faith are to participate in the public discussion that shapes society. If we have to speak in such a way that even a secularist can understand, we can't use biblical language exclusively. Maybe we make too much use of philosophical language; more than one Synod Father complained that homilies are not sufficiently imbued with the culture of the biblical world. The mind of the homilist has to be shaped not only by what he has studied and not only by his personal context, not only even by the teaching of the Church in rather abstract terms, but by the images and the various ways of relating to the world that were proper to the people who first received the Word of God, who first received God's self-revelation. Homilies were discussed, as was catechesis; the lectionary was spoken about, and some called for a revision of the lectionary.

There was a call for biblical schools and centers in dioceses so that non-professional students can find a way to study at greater depth God's inspired Word in Holy Scripture. The general diffusion of texts was mentioned, and there was even one intervention about amplification in churches. If you are going to speak, you had better be sure that people can hear, and if you don't have a good sound system, then see to it that one is put in! Likewise, several times the subject of the use of modern communications came up, of making an electronic text out of the spoken or the written text so that Scripture will be part of the conversation that now shapes our society in sometimes unexpected ways. Even in poorer countries, there is access to the infrastructure of communication; they now skip that step of telegraph wires and telephone poles because communication is wireless. God speaks, we listen.

Finally, there were a few interventions that were poignant because they raised the question: "What happens when God is silent?" And He *is* silent, or, at least, we sometimes have a very hard time hearing Him. This consideration usually arose in the prayers. Each session of the synod begins with prayer. The Third Hour of the Liturgy opened the session each day, during which one of the Synodal Fathers reflected upon the Word for all of us to relish and to inspire us for the conversations that would follow. Some of the Fathers brought up the conundrum of God's silence. We know that God does speak, and we know that we have listened, or tried to, and we know that we have spoken. But what happens when God seems to be silent?

Mystical theology elaborates on the dark night of the senses and the dark night of the soul. Mother Teresa of Calcutta gave witness to that sense of abandonment through the publication of her diaries most recently. Extreme aridity, a moment, and sometimes a very protracted moment in the personal conversation with the Lord, the conversation that makes us saints. But God also seems to be absent in natural disasters. Voltaire made good use of the earthquake that shook Lisbon in his day to argue that God is obviously not Provident because so many innocent people died. We raise that doubt in the face of the tsunami of a few years ago. How is it that God does not protect us from the nature that He himself created, even though it's fallen because we are fallen? Even more problematic than the silence of God is spiritual aridity and His silence in human-made tragedies: the Holocaust, and other historical tragedies where God seems not to protect us, seems to have abandoned us. God is silent. How do we listen to a silent God? How do we speak to a silent God or about a silent God? This is the problem of evil, but expressed in a way that was quite experiential.

All of those topics will appear in some fashion in the post-synodal apostolic exhortation. Some of the topics will probably come up in your conversation in these days together. The topics help us to understand how the Word of God enters into the life and mission of the Church.

After the three-week meeting ends, the work of the synod continues through a permanent council of the synod that is elected at the synod. It is composed of ten bishops from around the world and five more appointed by the pope. It is served by the permanent secretariat and the permanent secretary, Archbishop Nikola Eterović. The council of the synod gathers up the propositions and puts them together in a way that will help the Holy Father write the apostolic exhortation. The council then begins to prepare the next synod. After the consultation, which has happened already, the Holy Father will choose a topic; then the synod council will begin to prepare for the next synod, which will take place in about two years. All of this work and the papers enter into the ecclesial dialogue that develops the conversation that is divine revelation.

What I'd like to close with is a reflection by Pope Benedict XVI, the homily that he himself gave at the first meeting of the synod. Recall that the synod began when some major economic institutions and even some of the governments were collapsing. Banks were defaulting, Bear Stearns had just disappeared in this country; some of the major German banks were beginning to look as if they were failing. The economic structures that we all took for granted were suddenly exposed for what they are: impermanent facades. The Holy Father spoke of the permanent substance that is God's Word. Contemplating the great paeon of praise to God for the Word that comes in the form of the law, the pope quoted Psalm 118, which we had just read and prayed together. It states, "In the beginning, O Lord, your Word is constituted, is created in the heavens. It gives firmness to the earth and it remains." The Holy Father explained that God's Word is the true reality on which one must base one's life. He reminded us of what Jesus said: "Heaven and earth will pass away, but my words will never pass away." Then Pope Benedict said that, naturally and humanly speaking, a word is just a little bit of breath. As soon as it's pronounced, it seems to disappear. "Nonetheless, words create history," the pope continued. "Words form thoughts, the thoughts that create the world. It is the word that forms reality. Furthermore, the Word of God is the foundation of everything. It is the true reality and, to be realistic, we must rely upon this reality. We must change our idea that matter, solid things, things we can touch, are the more solid, the more certain reality." Most of all, Pope Benedict insisted that the marks of visible success—career, money—will pass away and were passing away as he spoke. Money disappears. It's nothing. And thus all the things that would seem to be the true realities that we can count on, are only realities of a secondary order. The one who builds his life on these realities, on success, on matter, on appearances, builds upon sand. It's only the Word of God that is the foundation for our life here and our life that extends unto the heavens and eternity; that is our calling.

"So we must change our concept of realism," the pope said. It was extremely dramatic, because we were all coming from dioceses worried about their financial futures, and from parishes where the jobless rate was continuing to escalate. Pope Benedict wanted to reassure us: Don't worry that you're wasting time here because, in the end, this is the only thing that counts. Don't worry that you're abandoning your pastoral solicitude for your people, because here is where reality is at work. Here is where we have what lasts forever.

You can continue that study and that conversation here. Religion is not a hobby. The Word of God is not just a matter of occasional interest. It is the foundation for everything else and the sure vehicle to what lasts forever. Jesus's last command was spoken to the disciples at the end of the Gospel according to St. Matthew, chapter 28: "Go preach, make disciples, baptize." These were his last words to those who had listened to him: Go now and talk, speak. He gave that command to the eleven, after Judas's betrayal; and I like to think that all of us now are the twelfth apostle. The eleven were there, but now it's up to us to continue their apostolic mission, to receive the Synod on the Word of God in the Life and Mission of the Church and make it actual for us and for those we love today.

2

A Covenant Dialogue

U.S. Latino/a Catholics Reading the Bible

Renata Furst

⌒

Two disciples walk side by side, remembering, discussing, debating. A
stranger walks up, joins them, and asks: "What are you discussing with
each other while you walk along?" (Lk 24:17). They encounter a stranger
who reinterprets the events they are debating through the lens of Scripture. No one is holding a scroll, no one is quoting a written document, yet
all participants in the conversation are familiar with the "Scriptures." The
disciples recognize the stranger in the "breaking of the bread." The experience is transformative, and they are able to identify its location: "Were not
our hearts burning while he spoke to us on the way and opened Scripture
to us?" In the process of "opening Scripture" Jesus connects tradition with
daily life. How does this connection take place more than two millennia
later for Latinos in the United States? What are the implications for the use
of the Bible by Latinos for the U.S. Catholic Church as a whole?

Recent research on the U.S. Church points to the emergence of Latino
Catholics as a "leading indicator" pointing to the shape of the Catholic
Church in the near future.[1] Between July 2006 and 2010, the U.S. Census
Bureau estimates that the number of Hispanics will rise from 39 to 43 million, of which approximately 70 percent will be Catholic.[2] Latino population increases are due to high immigration and birth rates. Such a critical
mass of readers of the biblical text is bound to have an important impact
on the way the Bible is read in the Church in general, as well as on religious
practices and services provided to the Latino population. In light of the
issues raised by the synod on "The Word of God in the Life and Mission of
the Church," we will explore two important questions relating to the reading of the Bible among Latinos in the U.S. Church: (1) Is there a particular

way in which Latino/a Catholics interpret the Bible? (2) What opportunities do Latinos/as have for Scripture study from a Catholic perspective?

Latino/a Catholics and the Interpretation of the Bible

The story about the encounter between Jesus and the disciples on the road to Emmaus is a universal heritage that belongs to all Christians and all cultures. However, it is also an accurate representation of the Latino experience of interpreting Scripture. U.S. Latino theologians have identified the important qualities of *comunidad* and *acompañamiento*—the relational dimension that characterizes theological reflection in the Latino community. As C. Gilbert Romero explains, "the Hispanic Catholic in particular has a special relationship with the Bible. . . . [He or she] feels a strong attraction to the Word of God as expression of ongoing dialogue."[3] Dialogue is a relational-communal activity that is strongly present in Latino culture. According to Romero:

> In the Hispanic culture of the Southwest, there is a strong sense of family and community values (based on family, ethnic, historical and religious concerns) that provides the individual Hispanic a stronger bond of both belief and behavior to the community's value system than to the dominant set of values that are from outside the culture. This gives the Hispanic a sense of belonging and a strong sense of identity.[4]

This relational dimension is also a characteristic of the Word of God defined in the *Instrumentum Laboris*, the working document of the synod. Under the heading of "Pastoral Implications" it states that "the Word of God displays all the qualities of true communication between persons. . . . God communicates his truth . . . makes plain his manner of thinking, loving and acting; and . . . it is an appeal addressed by God to a person to be heard and given a response in faith."[5] The Bible uses the word *covenant* to name this interpersonal exchange in which God and a human person converse.[6] This collaborative approach also characterizes Latino/a theological reflection.

The disciples on the way to Emmaus accompany one another, yet it is only as they "walk with Jesus" that they reach back into their tradition and reinterpret Scripture. In doing so, they participate in the construction of an interpretative tradition for the entire Church. The *Lineamenta* describes this:

> the Word of God (which is Jesus) has also to be understood, as he himself said, "according to the Scriptures" (Luke 24:44–49). Christ-the-Word is in the history of the People of God in the Old Testament, which bears witness to him as Messiah; he is present at this historical moment in the Church, who proclaims Christ-the-Word through preaching, meditates on him through the Bible and experiences him through divine friendship.[7]

The construction of this tradition in dialogue is, for the disciples on the road to Emmaus, a transformative experience—a shift from a downcast to a burning heart, from dejection to passion.

Does this experience of walking with Jesus to interpret Scripture and construct a tradition exist among Latinos in the United States? If so, what are its characteristics? Gary Riebe-Estrella describes the process of handing on tradition in the Latino community as a conversation. It is the *process* of transmission, rather than the content, which constitutes the Latino perspective. "The Latino/a dimension of what is handed on does not come from the *what* in the revelation they are reflecting on, but rather on the lived context they use within which to understand the *what*."[8] When the content of revelation is found in Scripture, Latinos contribute to the process of creating an interpretative tradition. Riebe-Estrella identifies three dimensions that comprise the conversation in the transmission of tradition among Latinos: (1) the content of what is being handed down; (2) the experience of the individual Christian whose life is shaped by the revelation of Jesus Christ, as well as the experience of the community of faith in which what is handed down is reflected on and lived; and (3) the culture viewed as *the* convictions, values and biases that form a person's social setting and therefore point to the *formative* symbols and ongoing interpretations that shape that person's worldview.[9]

Each dimension of the conversation presents a *pastoral* challenge for Latino/a Catholics and their practice of reading the Bible. *Content*, the first dimension Riebe-Estrella identifies, raises the issue of accessibility. Do Latino Catholics have access to the biblical text in Spanish or English? Accessibility can be limited by the presence or absence of Bibles in the community, a person's economic capacity to purchase a copy of the biblical text, and the more subtle limitation—an individual's level of literacy in either Spanish or English.[10] Furthermore, for most Latino Catholics, contact with the biblical text takes place in an oral, rather than a written context—the proclamation of the Scriptures in the liturgy. This in turn affects the way in which Scripture is perceived and interpreted.

Experience is the second dimension of creating a tradition of biblical interpretation, and it too raises the issue of accessibility. Are there venues for Latino Catholics to share individual experiences of the biblical text? Are there opportunities for Latino Catholics to come into contact with the way the community interprets Scripture—especially with the exegesis of Scripture that underpins the Church's catechesis? Once again, the Sunday liturgy is the primary venue, but increasingly Latino Catholics encounter the Bible through their experience of renewal movements. Rite of Christian Initiation of Adults (RCIA) programs, a primary venue for English-speaking Catholics to encounter the Bible, are also available in Spanish, although finding qualified instructors to teach in Spanish can be a challenge.[11]

Finally, Riebe-Estrella defines *culture*—the third dimension of biblical interpretation—as a strategy for human survival that influences people's perceptions of themselves in the world. He notes that "culture acts both to broaden and to limit the common-sense parameters of a person's insights and in that way both links the person profoundly with those who share this horizon of meaning and separates him or her from those whose horizon has been differently formed."[12] This dimension of creating a tradition for interpreting the Bible with an awareness of one's culture is a work of faith in which culture is not a marginal or secondary component. In the letter by which he founded the Pontifical Council for Culture, Pope John Paul II made the following statement: "The synthesis between faith and culture is not only necessary for culture, but also for faith. A faith which does not become culture is a faith not fully received, not fully examined, not faithfully lived."[13]

Hispanic Catholics approach Scripture through the unique experience of their culture—a reality that needs to be acknowledged in programs that foster faith formation, and more specifically, biblical studies. According to the U.S. bishops' National Pastoral Plan for Hispanic Ministry,

> Hispanic spirituality has as one of its sources the "seeds of the Word" in the pre-Hispanic cultures, which considered their relationships with the gods and nature to be an integral part of life. In some cases, the

missionaries adopted these customs and attitudes; they enriched and illuminated them so as to incarnate the Divine Word of Sacred Scripture and the Christian faith to make them come alive in religious art and drama.[14]

Culture is an important component of interpretation, tradition, and faith, but one of the great pastoral challenges of an immigrant population, such as the Latinos/as in the United States, is to preserve a living memory of their culture of origin, while at the same time embrace aspects of the dominant U.S. culture.[15] As Jeanette Rodriguez explains, "Cultural memory transmits an experience rooted in history that has reached a culturally definitive transformative status. The myth/story of Guadalupe is a cultural memory because it 'enshrines the major hopes and aspirations of an entire society.'"[16] Access to an educational system that is knowledgeable and affirms both Hispanic and U.S. mainstream cultural memory is a key part of this process.

Latino/a experience of immigration has an impact on their culture. In fact, it puts into motion the construction of the new bilingual/bicultural identity. A new cultural memory is formed. According to Rodriguez,

> Cultural memory does not necessarily originate from a calamity, but most often it does arise out of events that are transformative, that bring about recognizable shifts in the world of meaning of people. Cultural memory fulfills the need to transcend certain events or circumstances . . . and/or to maintain a corporate identity. . . . Cultural memory is evoked around image, symbol, affect, or event precisely because it keeps alive and transforms those events of the past which continue to give meaning to the present.[17]

In some cases, it may take several generations for a bilingual/bicultural person or community to emerge. However, this process brings with it challenges. Reading Scripture through the lens of a shifting cultural memory challenges established traditions. As Jean-Pierre Ruiz explains:

> Poised on the permeable boundary between medium and message, reading can be a risky business because it does not merely transmit received *tradita* intact, bringing the contents of the past unchanged into the present. As performance—whether public or private—reading actively participates in the process of shaping tradition, re-presenting

it in the vernacular of the here and now of the reader and audience. . . .
This is no less true when the texts that are being read are invested with
special and normative authority as scripture.[18]

The process of reconstructing culture and identity can be greatly
enhanced through biblical training. The Bible maps the history of cultures
and languages and their transformation of the religious landscape of the
Ancient Near East. For many Latinos/as, Scripture study itself can develop
some of the skills needed to survive in the new educational system encountered by immigrants. In many Protestant denominations, "*institutos bíbli-
cos*" or Bible institutes provide noncredit learning opportunities for adults
that develop reading, writing, and studying skills that can then be transferred to other educational programs.[19] Bible programs are "feeder" programs for many Protestant-run universities in the United States.

Does the Hispanic/Latino church continually experience the creation
and renewal of its reading of Scripture? The synod document says:

> the Bible needs to be fully valued in pastoral programmes. Under the
> guidance of the Bishop, pastoral plans having the Bible as their foun-
> dation need to be formulated in each diocese. . . . Such a programme
> would assist the spread of biblical practise, foster a biblical movement
> among the laity, attend to the formation of leaders of listening groups
> or Bible groups with particular concern for youth, and provide courses
> in the faith, inspired by the Bible, to include even immigrants and the
> many who are searching.[20]

Faith formation programs addressing this unique need among Hispanic Catholics were rare or nonexistent in most dioceses—a situation
acknowledged in the United States Bishops' 1995 National Pastoral Plan for
Hispanic Ministry.[21] Sadly, this was also true of programs that train leadership—catechists and pastoral leaders for service among Hispanics. What is
the situation today? According to Allan Figueroa Deck:

> Despite the relentless growth of the Hispanic presence over the past
> fifty years there has not been anywhere near the appropriate develop-
> ment of what I would call a Hispanic ministry infrastructure. This is
> particularly true in my view at the regional and national levels. What
> I mean is that institutions of, for, and by Hispanics focused on the
> education, formation, and leadership development in ministry as well

as on visioning for the future have been inadequate. To say this is not to diminish the significant efforts that have been made over many decades by the Bishops Conference itself in sponsoring, for example, the three *encuentro* processes and *Encuentro 2000*. But the point is that most Hispanic leaders and the communities themselves have unfortunately not been touched by that process.[22]

As we shall see, development and visioning for the future for Latino/a Catholics in the area of biblical training has barely begun.

What Opportunities Do Latinos Have for Scripture Study from a Catholic Perspective?

As we have seen, from a Catholic perspective access to both Scripture and tradition is important. How is access to *both* Scripture and tradition available to Latino Catholics in the United States?[23] Most research on Latino/a Catholics focuses on training for ministry in a generic sense, or on training for reception of the sacraments. Surveys targeting the use of the Bible among Latinos/as are difficult to locate. For this reason, a brief informal telephone survey was used to discover what biblical training programs are available for Hispanics. (The questionnaire is provided as an appendix below.) The data from this survey is not comprehensive but does permit us to get a glimpse of the different programs offered for Latino/a Catholics.

Three major types of programs are developed or being developed in dioceses throughout the United States. These types are based primarily on the criteria of access not only to the biblical text but to professional teaching from a Catholic perspective. The programs described here are those that have been specifically designed to meet the needs of adult Latino Catholics.[24]

Flagship Programs

Designed for adults, these programs provide a general introduction to Scripture that can take anywhere from two to eight semesters. Participants receive an in-depth survey of the contents of Scripture and are given an overview of Catholic teaching on the interpretation of Scripture through exposure to sections of *Dei Verbum* or the Pontifical Biblical Commission's 1993 instruction, "The Interpretation of the Bible in the Church." Most are sponsored as part of the catechetical office of a particular diocese—the exception to this being the University of Dallas's School of Ministry, which provides biblical training for both Dallas and Fort Worth.[25] Examples of these programs are those sponsored by the dioceses of Los Angeles and Chicago.

When taught in English, these types of biblical programs rely on the expertise of biblical scholars available in local universities. However, when the programs are taught in Spanish, the availability of trained instructors is a problem. Some have resolved this issue by recruiting visiting scholars from Spain or Latin America.[26] Others have made a concerted effort to search out and hire instructors with a master's degree or licentiate in theology to meet this need. These Scripture programs usually use materials that have been developed in English and then translated into Spanish, or they use resources in Spanish imported from Spain or Latin America, which can be costly.

Bible Studies

Bible studies are usually designed for communities with limited access to trained instructors or facilitators. The material is meant to serve as a guide for interpretation without necessarily requiring a trained expert in biblical studies. For the most part, although Bible studies do give some historical background, their primary focus is to facilitate the link between biblical content and personal experience. The Mexican American Catholic College in San Antonio was encouraged by national leaders in Hispanic ministry to develop such a program for publication and distribution. A portion of this Bible study has been written and tested.[27] The Archdiocese of Galveston-Houston offers a free Bible study of the Gospels in Spanish. This is a translation of a program developed in English.[28] Finally, the Little Rock Bible program has been translated and adapted into Spanish. It provides three levels of study—beginner, intermediate, advanced—which can be flexibly adapted to different situations and time constraints.[29] These three sample programs are an excellent beginning, and they are very accessible, which is another important characteristic.

Informal Biblical Reading

"Informal" biblical reading entails exposure to the biblical text as a secondary activity; in other words, the biblical text is read as an aid to ministry, social reflection, prayer, or community building, rather than as an end in itself. Most Latinos encounter the biblical text through these experiences, often in renewal movements such as Cursillo, ACTS retreats, Charismatic Renewal, or Christian base communities. Another major source of exposure to biblical content is through the practices of popular piety or religiosity.[30]

Other Programs

In this section we take a brief look at Scripture programs that do not exactly fit the criteria defined for previous categories.

Instituto Fe y Vida: Instituto Fe y Vida is a national ministry focusing on the needs of young Latinos/as. Their mission is to help diocesan leaders respond to the challenges of a very large and growing segment of the Latino/a population—youth from eighteen to thirty years old. "Fe y Vida enables Catholic leaders at the grassroots, professional, and institutional levels to respond to the human, spiritual, and sociocultural needs of Hispanic youth and young adults."[31] Their vision is to train young Hispanic leaders to minister to their peers, to help them mature as human beings, grow in their Christian faith, improve their education, foster the development of future generations, fulfill their evangelizing missions, exercise leadership in the Church and society, and build a society inspired by Gospel values.[32]

Within these broader program areas, Instituto Fe y Vida provides basic training in Scripture reading for young adults between the ages of sixteen and twenty-five. Taught in Spanish, its primary focus is to give a biblical foundation—by teaching the major events and themes relating to Catholic teaching found in the Bible. The program also provides training for future Bible study facilitators. The advantage to this program is that it is mobile. Fe y Vida has provided biblical training for young adults in dioceses across the country, and in Latin America as well. They are currently working on online resources to extend their program even further. The challenge—which they are actively working to fulfill, is the adaptation of their programs to second- and third-generation Hispanic young adults.[33]

The Biblical Catechetical Program: The Biblical Catechetical Program sponsored by the Missionary Catechists of Divine Providence is a program that combines biblical training with catechetical components tailored to the needs of Hispanic pastoral leaders and others desiring to deepen their faith formation.

The interpretations of Scripture and catechesis are closely intertwined. Scripture itself contains many of the catechetical formulas that express the foundational truths of the Christian faith. Thus learning to *read* Scripture is the first and most basic step in catechesis. As the Pontifical Biblical Commission explains:

> Explained in the context of the tradition, Scripture provides the starting point, foundation and norm of catechetical teaching. One of the goals of catechesis should be to initiate a person in a correct understanding and fruitful reading of the Bible. This will bring about the discovery of the divine truth it contains and evoke as generous a response as possible to the message God addresses through his word to the whole human race.[34]

Catechesis is also grounded in the spirituality of the individual and the community, as well as their capacity to reflect biblically and theologically.

Skills that are traditionally involved in exegesis—consideration of the historical background, formation, genre, and narrative structure of the text—are the starting points for the program, because each participant needs to be aware that "the biblical word comes from a real past . . . but at the same time from the eternity of God, and it leads us to God's eternity."[35] In the process of actualization, or reading for the present moment, the reader of Scripture allows its message to echo in his or her personal and communal experience. Both sides come together by transmitting the "saving acts of God" reaching into the past, but taking into account the culture in which it is being interpreted. For Hispanic Catholics, this involves acknowledging the importance of popular religion and "the merging of a theology of beauty, spirituality and catechesis."[36] This engages the "cultural memory" described in the previous section in the process of reading the biblical text.

To conclude, the purpose of this program is to find ways for the stories, images, and meaning found in Scripture to echo in the faith experience and formation of Hispanic people. The Biblical Catechetical Program is a first step toward a pedagogy that would integrate Scripture, tradition, and Hispanic culture, but it still needs refinement, reworking, and reflection.

Conclusion

The success of any biblical teaching program can be measured by the degree to which it helps people connect with God and deepen their understanding of their faith. It is the process described by John Paul II: "The synthesis between faith and culture is not only necessary for culture, but also for faith. A faith which does not become culture is a faith not fully received, not fully examined, not faithfully lived."[37] The place where this type of reflection "touches the ground" and becomes a reality is in the pedagogy or teaching method of each program. The *Synod Instrumentum Laboris* calls for this, alluding once again to the importance of culture:

> Because of the Word of God's particular effect on culture, greater appreciation needs to be given to the Bible . . . by presenting a complete course in learning the most significant Bible texts and the methods of interpretation adopted by the Church. . . . Working towards an overall solution [to explaining the difficult texts in the Bible] needs to take into account what is provided by not only exegesis and theology, but also anthropology and pedagogy.[38]

The challenge is vast, interdisciplinary, and exciting. Like the disciples who returned to Jerusalem energized and challenged by their encounter with the risen Lord, reading the Bible through our Latino/a Catholic cultural memory is an important contribution to the Church in North America.

⌢

Notes

1. Allan Figueroa Deck, "Hispanic Ministry: New Realities and Choices" (lecture, Symposium on Hispanic/Latino/a Catholics in the United States, Center for Applied Research in the Apostolate, Georgetown University, Washington, DC, October 5–6, 2008), 2.
2. See Paul Perl, Jennifer Z. Greely, and Mark M. Gray, "How Many Hispanics Are Catholic? A Review of Survey Data and Methodology" (paper, Center for Applied Research in the Apostolate, Georgetown University, 2004), for a summary of the difficulties involved in determining who is Hispanic in the United States.
3. C. Gilbert Romero, "Tradition and Symbol as Biblical Keys for a United States Hispanic Theology," in *Frontiers of Hispanic Theology in the United States*, ed. Allan Figueroa Deck (Maryknoll, NY: Orbis Books, 1992), 44.
4. C. Gilbert Romero, *Hispanic Devotional Piety: Tracing the Biblical Roots,*

Faith and Cultures (Maryknoll, NY: Orbis Books, 1991), 24.

5. *Lineamenta*, "The Word of God in the Life and Mission of the Church," paragraph 9 (Vatican City: The General Secretariat of the Synod of Bishops, 2007), http://www.vatican.va/roman_curia/synod/documents/rc_synod _doc_20070427_lineamenta-xii-assembly_en.html.

6. From the preface to the Synod of Bishops, Twelfth Ordinary General Assembly, "The Word of God in the Life and Mission of the Church: *Instrumentum Laboris*," Vatican City, 2008.

7. *Lineamenta*, § 8.

8. Gary Riebe-Estrella, "Tradition as Conversation," in *Futuring Our Past: Explorations in the Theology of Tradition*, ed. Orlando Espín and Gary Macy (Maryknoll, NY: Orbis Books, 2006), 142.

9. Riebe-Estrella, "Tradition as Conversation," 147–48.

10. I could not find information about access to and use of electronic forms of the biblical text by Latinos/as (including podcasts).

11. A catechetical resource for RICA (*Rito de iniciación cristiana de adultos*) is published by the Mexican American Catholic College and by Liturgy Training Publications.

12. Riebe-Estrella, "Tradition as Conversation," 148.

13. John Paul II, in "Comisión pontificia de la cultura, Carta autógrafa de fundación" (1982, 7) wrote: "La síntesis entre cultura y fe no es sólo una exigencia de la cultura, sino también de la fe. Una fe que no se hace cultura, es una fe non plenamente acogida, no totalmente pensada, no fielmente vivida" (translation by Renata Furst). Available at http://www.vatican.va /holy_father/john_paul_ii/letters/documents/hf_jp-ii_let_20051982 _foundation-letter_sp.html. The "archival" edition of the letter is the Letter to Cardinal Agostino Casaroli, Secretary of State, May 20, 1982; Insegnamenti, vol. V/2, 1982, 1777ff.

14. National Conference of Catholic Bishops (NCCB), "National Pastoral Plan for Hispanic Ministry," in *Hispanic Ministry: Three Major Documents* (Washington, DC: United States Catholic Conference, 1995), 88.

15. This process is not completely foreign to Latino culture in the United States. Gary Macy states that the theology arising from Latino experience is "inherently intercultural," because of its Spanish roots. "Iberian Christian theology emerged from a continuous dialogue with other peoples

and faiths. . . . Hispanic theology, and hence U.S. Latino/a theology, is intercultural by heritage, history, and almost by instinct." Gary Macy, "The Iberian Heritage of U.S. Latino/a Theology," in *Futuring Our Past*, 55.

16. Jeanette Rodriguez, *Stories We Live / Cuentos que Vivimos: Hispanic Women's Spirituality* (New York: Paulist Press, 1996), 11.

17. Ibid., 11–12.

18. Jean-Pierre Ruiz, "Reading between the Lines: Toward a Latino/a (Re) configuration of Scripture and Tradition," in *Futuring Our Past*, 102.

19. I wish to acknowledge the contribution of Dr. Nora Lozano of the Baptist University of the Americas and Dr. Efraín Agosto of Hartford Seminary in Hartford, Connecticut, for this insight.

20. *Lineamenta*, § 26.

21. NCCB, "National Pastoral Plan for Hispanic Ministry," §§ 85–88.

22. Deck, "Hispanic Ministry," 5. How has the downturn in the economy affected Hispanic ministry? As I conducted an informal telephone survey, I kept hearing about how dioceses had closed their Hispanic ministry offices.

23. The data quoted in this section comes from an informal telephone survey. Scientifically collected data on Bible programs for Latinos in the Catholic Church is not readily available.

24. The synod document speaks of the encounter with Scripture in the liturgy as a primary locus of exposure. While this is true, it is not included in these categories, because it is an experience of listening and hearing, rather than *study* of the biblical text.

25. I would like to thank Pia Septien and Juan Rendon of the University of Dallas School of Ministry for the time they took to respond to the survey.

26. I would like to thank Maruja Sedano of the Archdiocese of Chicago for sharing her insights (in 2006) about organizing biblical training for Hispanics.

27. I would like to thank Dr. Arturo Chávez of the Mexican American Catholic College for the time he took to respond to the survey on biblical training, especially for his insights on biblical training and Hispanic ministry formation.

28. They offer a variety of resources, which can be viewed at http://www.archgh .org/wog/spanish/scripturestudies.htm.

29. The Little Rock Program in Spanish can be viewed at http://www .littlerockscripture.org/sp/Studies.aspx?ID=122.

30. For a critique of different forms of biblical interpretation from a Hispanic perspective, see Francisco Lozada, "Reinventing the Biblical Tradition: An Exploration of Social Location Hermeneutics," in *Futuring Our Past*, 113–40.

31. Instituto Fe y Vida, "Mission and Vision," http://www.feyvida.org/mission.html.

32. Ibid.

33. I would like to express my deep appreciation for the time Carmen Maria Cervantes, the Executive Director of Instituto Fe y Vida, spent responding to the telephone survey.

34. Pontifical Biblical Commission, "The Interpretation of the Bible in the Church," *Origins* 23, no. 29 (January 6, 1994): 497–524; also available at http://www.ewtn.com/library/CURIA/PBCINTER.htm.

35. Joseph Ratzinger, preface to "The Interpretation of the Bible in the Church," § 2.

36. Anita de Luna, *Faith Formation and Popular Religion: Lessons from Tejano Experience* (Lanham, MD: Rowman & Littlefield, 2002), 171.

37. John Paul II, "Carta autógrafa de fundación," 7. (See note 13 for the original Spanish.)

38. *Instrumentum Laboris*, § 45.

3.

"In the Breaking of the Bread"

The Bible and Liturgy

Raúl Gómez-Ruiz, S.D.S.

∼

Introduction

The Word is alive when people encounter it in the ordinary circumstances of their lives, whether at the breaking of the bread in the Eucharist or at an everyday meal. For Eugene LaVerdiere in his analysis of Luke's Gospel in which the Emmaus account occurs, "Every Christian meal reveals aspects of the kingdom of God, where guests are welcomed, people share with one another, broken covenants are renewed and all are reconciled."[1] When I was about seven years old I recall that the Mass was still in Latin, but because of the changes approved at Vatican II the Gospel was read in Latin and then in English. The passage was of the paralytic who had been lowered from the roof into the midst of the crowd around Jesus. The image of people going to such effort to lower a guy on his bed fascinated me. For me as a child it stayed at the level of marvel, but as an adult, feeling the need of Christ's healing and reconciliation in my own life and experiencing through others, I began to understand this passage in terms of my own spiritual well-being. I had been the paralytic and through the efforts of others I had been lowered into the circle around Jesus.

The liturgical reform of Vatican II has helped Hispanic Catholics be more aware of the importance of the Bible not only at worship but to their religious practices. It is well known that the Bible has always been a part of the Catholic liturgy in all of its forms. However, since the liturgy prior to Vatican II was celebrated in Latin, perhaps the faithful in general had less direct access to the Scriptures and less consciousness of their incorporation in various ways in liturgical celebrations. The XII Ordinary General Assembly of

31

the Synod of Bishops, held in October 2008, focused on the Word of God in the life and mission of the Church and has invited all Catholics to consider anew the role the Bible plays in Catholic worship.

In this essay I examine the use of the Word of God by Hispanics in the liturgy. Or better, I look at how the liturgical use of the Bible provides a pattern for Hispanics to interpret and apply its themes in their daily lives, particularly by means of popular religious practices. In order to show this I focus on how the Word is interpreted and applied in the liturgy, how the Scriptures function and are interpreted by means of a "liturgical herme-neutic" using the tool of typology. This is what Thomas O'Loughlin calls the "operative theology" of the liturgy.[2] In order to get at this I examine and employ the notions of "cultural memory," "mnemonic energy," and "figures of memory" as these apply to the liturgical and biblical foundations of His-panic popular religious practices as well. I will avoid rehearsing what we all know about the liturgy of the Word; rather, I only give a brief overview. Instead I want to show how Hispanics have taken the Scriptures proclaimed in liturgical events and applied them to their everyday lives by means of popular religious practices in imitation of what happens at Eucharist pri-marily; in this way these practices bear what Jan Assmann calls "cultural memory."[3] I end with recommendations on how the Word can become a greater force for Hispanic liturgical and devotional spirituality following the patterns given by the liturgy through the use of symbol and ritual.

The Bible in the Liturgy

The liturgical reform resulted in a more explicit use of Scripture reading as part of the Liturgy of the Word. Thus *Sacrosanctum Concilium* (SC) calls for "the treasures of the Bible . . . to be opened up more lavishly, so that a richer share in God's Word may be provided for the faithful" (SC, para-graph 51).[4] Specifically, "there is to be more reading from holy Scripture and it is to be more varied and apposite" (SC, paragraph 35.1). Consequently, a new Lectionary for Mass appeared in 1969, a second edition appeared in 1981, and in 1992, the United States Bishops approved another revision. More recently, in 1998 the United States Conference of Catholic Bishops (USCCB) approved a two-volume lectionary incorporating revised trans-lations from the *New American Bible*.[5] At the same time, for the liturgy in Spanish, the former Bishops Committee on the Liturgy (BCL) considered a recommendation by the then Subcommittee for Hispanic Liturgy that the lectionary of Mexico be used for the readings in the United States. This was due to a survey that had been taken of Spanish-speaking bishops and leaders in Hispanic ministry. The Scriptures therein were expressly translated into Spanish for liturgy. The subcommittee, of which I was a member, was to continue working on an adaptation for a U.S. edition. In the meantime, the use of the Mexican lectionary was approved by the USCCB in 2000.[6] This year the USCCB is set to approve the new Spanish-language lectionary in four volumes, which is an adaptation of the Mexican lectionary plus the Psalms from the lectionary of Spain.[7]

The Liturgy of the Word is the most obvious place where the Word is encountered at Eucharist. The General Instruction on the Roman Missal (GIRM, 2002) no. 55 explains that:

> In the readings, as explained by the homily, God speaks to his people, opening up to them the mystery of redemption and salvation and offering them spiritual nourishment; and Christ himself is present in the midst of the faithful through his word. By their silence and singing the people make God's word their own, and they also affirm their adherence to it by means of the Profession of Faith. Finally, having been nourished by it, they pour out their petitions in the Prayer of the Faithful for the needs of the entire Church and for the salvation of the whole world.[8]

The GIRM goes on to state that "In the readings, the table of God's word is prepared for the faithful, and the riches of the Bible are opened to them" (no. 57, n. 61 cites SC paragraph 51).

Some might attribute a greater hunger for the Bible by Catholics, and particularly by Hispanics, to this new emphasis and the more obvious preaching on the Word in homilies that has occurred since. Indeed, about twenty-five years ago when I was assigned to a parish for a pastoral year during my preparation for ordination, I was approached by a group of Hispanic women who asked me to start a Bible study for them. They wanted to know more about the Bible for several reasons: one was they noticed it being read more at Eucharist and second, they were being challenged by Evangelicals who claimed Catholics did not use or know the Bible.

Yet the liturgy in all of its aspects—Eucharist, the celebration of the Sacraments, and the Hours—has always been imbued with Scripture. During the efforts that led to the reform of the liturgy, scholars had identified a link between the use of Scripture by Christians in East and West at worship and the pattern established in synagogue morning worship. In particular, a tripartite pattern is discernible in the different rites consisting of reading from Scripture, followed by a song, usually a psalm, and ending with prayer in which the priest or leader gathers the prayers of the assembly and directs them to God.[9] The distribution and selection of readings in the diverse rites varied prior to the reform and continues to do so now, but in all of them the proclamation of the Gospel is the culmination of the Liturgy of the Word.

In the Roman rite Sunday Mass we went from a system that had one set of readings repeated year after year, that included one reading from either the New Testament (usually Paul) or the Old Testament (especially during Lent) and a Gospel passage according to the liturgical season, to a system of a three-year cycle of readings with two readings from Scripture prior to the reading of the Gospel, including more extensive use of the Psalms. This allows the participants to hear and hopefully reflect on the Word of God more. However, as Nathan Mitchell points out, "the liturgy treats the Bible quite freely as 'its own.'"[10] So much so that "in effect, [the liturgy] rewrites Scripture, suggesting meanings and interpretations that may lie beyond the scope of the text's writer and his or her intended audience."[11]

Consequently, the Lectionary becomes another "Bible," a "liturgical Bible" that is selective of which texts are used/read/reflected upon so as to communicate what the Church believes about what is essential in the revelation of God's salvific work in creation and to foster its application into daily life by the faithful. Pierre Jounel notes that the Church's use of Scripture, both by means of *lectio continua* and pericopes for certain occasions, reveals a certain theology of Scripture which says that all of Scripture is meant for our teaching and that it has meaning which functions at various levels of revelation. The Church especially favors a typological approach to the understanding of the particular biblical passage read.[12] This use is most marked in the celebrations of Christmas and Easter, Lent and Advent, where the biblical characters are presented as types of Christ and of ourselves in response to God's revelation in Christ.

The Bible constitutes the totality of the readings at Eucharist and most of the readings at the other liturgical celebrations. Yet the use of Scripture was not and is not confined to the Liturgy of the Word. As Jounel noted in 1958 on the eve of the liturgical reform, the liturgy is completely impregnated by the Bible.[13] It also serves as the fount for the texts of the hymns and songs that respond in some way to the Word of God and are interspersed throughout the celebration. Particularly the Psalms, scriptural in and of themselves, have been the favored source for the hymns sung in Catholic worship, although other parts of the Scriptures have also contributed themes and texts. In addition, the collects, the prayers over the gifts, the eucharistic prayers themselves, all also incorporate biblical themes and are inspired by them. These prayers, free creations of the religious genius of a certain people or era and often inspired by non-biblical sources, are nonetheless good examples of how biblical typology is applied so that they become meditations on a biblical occurrence or its fulfillment in Christ or in the gathering of the assembly. Perhaps this is so taken for granted that people do not think about these as scriptural.

Louis-Marie Chauvet[14] has written on the linguistic and communicative aspects of the Liturgy of the Word and on how the Sacred Scriptures inspire various elements of the liturgy, respectively. He agrees that the liturgy is at its root biblical.[15] Take the greetings by the priest at the beginning of Mass, which are based on St. Paul's letters; for example, "The grace of our Lord Jesus Christ . . ." is based on 2 Corinthians 13:13. Nonetheless, the majority of the biblical references are simple allusions. In Chauvet's view, the liturgy interprets the Bible, not by means of the tools of exegesis but by means of the tools of typology. For him, the liturgical use of the Bible is a special way to interpret it (or hermeneutic) saying:

> It is always an object of a new treatment by the simple fact of having been separated from the Book and from its historical and literary context and by having been transferred into the liturgical action. . . . This raises the question of the normative standing of the "liturgical Bible" in relation to the biblical canon. An important question since—"*lex orandi, lex credendi*"—the expression of the Church's faith, on the one hand, depends on the "liturgical Bible."[16]

Chauvet in fact does not completely address the issue of how the Scriptures contained in the Lectionary affect the *lex orandi, lex credendi*, but as Mitchell noted, the lectionary or "liturgical Bible" rewrites the Scriptures in order to convey meanings and interpretations beyond the writers' intended audience.[17] Mitchell calls the combination of readings in the Lectionary and their juxtaposition in the liturgy "intertextuality," saying this is biblical in and of itself: "In sum, intertextuality (in the sense of a juxtaposition of diverse texts from different sources and periods so that they 'comment' on one another) is a principle pursued not only in liturgical lectionaries, but also by the biblical writers themselves."[18] In my judgment, the effect of the liturgical Bible is that it stresses what it is the Church believes in terms of the economy of salvation over time and how God's saving actions continue to take place in this place and at this time. Thus, if we pray what we believe as the maxim *lex orandi, lex credendi* implies, the use of typology as a way to interpret the Bible liturgically is meant to help place the hearers of the Word in the midst of what is being read. They are to make the Word their own. This is "liturgical hermeneutics."

The liturgy is in fact knit together by biblical allusions, thereby giving it the power to evoke biblical images and values, and inspire responses by the participants. Thus it becomes the bearer of the "Catholic imagination." This term, popularized by Andrew Greeley,[19] refers to the Catholic worldview that God is radically present in the whole of creation and in human beings. Thus objects and other material things, as well as human beings, can be channels and sources of God's grace. This is what is meant by *sacramentality* or what can be called the "sacramental imagination," that is, the ability to see and/or experience God's hand at work in one's life which inspires one to "sacramentalize" it, to mark that experience by means of symbol and ritual so that one can access it again. Doing this also makes one alert to see and experience God's hand in other situations as well.

Scripture in the Lives of Hispanics

I believe hunger for and the extensive integration of Scripture in liturgy by Hispanics precedes the reform of the Roman rite at Vatican II. In fact, we see that in the ancient liturgical rite of Spain, now called the Hispano-Mozarabic rite, centered and still celebrated at Toledo, Scripture was stressed so that during Ordinary Time, there were always three scriptural readings and a psalm leading to the homily in what today we call the Liturgy of the Word. During Lent the number of readings was increased to four and an Old Testament canticle was added in addition to the Psalm. The structure followed during Ordinary Time includes a reading from the Prophets, followed by a reading from the Apostle (usually Paul but any of the New Testament according to the season), and then the Gospel. Jounel believed this structure, also followed in the disappeared Gallican and the still celebrated Milanese or Ambrosian rites, to have been followed in Rome prior to Gregory the Great's reform of the late sixth century. Thus, in his estimation the Milanese and Toledan rites became the guardians of the universal practice in the west.[20] The Roman rite returns to this structure after Vatican II. Much as the Roman rite has done, the Hispano-Mozarabic rite "rewrote" the Scriptures. It did this by *centonization*, or the combining and rearranging of scriptural texts to convey a particular message about salvation.[21] The themes appearing in the particular Gospel passage read on a certain day were then also incorporated into and elaborated upon in the *Illatio*, the equivalent to the preface of the Roman rite. This could have provided a pattern for people to take themes from Scripture and apply them to other things, such as blessings, sacramental rites, and devotional practices that flowed from the liturgy, imbuing them with a scriptural basis. When the Hispano-Mozarabic rite was superseded by the Roman rite in Spain, and lived on only through devotional practices, perhaps these scriptural connections became so diffuse and oblique in the minds of the clergy and people that the scriptural foundation was hardly discernible.

Nonetheless, the importance of the Bible for Hispanics in terms of the liturgy and devotional practices has not disappeared. That is because of the "operative theology" at work in liturgy. O'Loughlin explains that this is the theology communicated by "the actions, gestures, objects, buildings, décor, furniture, community atmosphere, and indeed the non-verbal aspects of public worship."[22] He notes, moreover, "it is a commonplace to observe that 'the people in the pews are not concerned about theology'; whether or not this is true, it is certain that they—as sentient symbol-using beings—pick up 'cues' in their ritual activity as in all their other human interactions and these cues form their imagination and understanding of what surrounds them. Rituals create our worlds."[23] So Hispanics in the pews may not recognize or quote clearly the Scriptures they listen to at Eucharist and other liturgical settings, but they apply and reflect on them in a variety of ways both at Eucharist and in devotional practices. These latter give an important glimpse of the operative theology at work distilled from the integration of the biblical and liturgical messages transmitted and received by participation in worship.

Gilbert Romero has shown how important the Bible is to Hispanic devotional piety in his groundbreaking book *Hispanic Devotional Piety: Tracing the Biblical Roots*.[24] Romero declares that "we must recognize an already existing bond between the two, in that Hispanics feel a strong attraction to the word of God as an expression of ongoing dialogue."[25] Possibly because they were aware of the difficulty in understanding the Scriptures in Latin,

Franciscans, Dominicans, Augustinians, and others in the thirteenth century began to translate the Word of God into beautiful but simple devotional practices, the "vernacular of the people." Thus *nacimientos* (crèche
scenes) alluding to Matthew 1, *posadas* (a novena reenacting Joseph and
Mary's search for lodging) alluding to Luke 1, and *visitas a las siete casas*
(visits to seven churches) alluding to the Passion in the Gospels, among
many other devotions, became a way to bring home the Sacred Scriptures
proclaimed at liturgy. This gave them life. Although it seems people forgot
or considered it unnecessary to look for the scriptural connections for these
practices, the Word was transmitted anyway.

Cultural Memory

One way Hispanic popular religious practices transmit the Word is through
the "cultural memory" they contain and hand on through "figures of memory." Cultural memory, a notion developed by Assmann, is contained in
objectivized culture such as rites, texts, images, buildings, monuments,
cities, and even landscapes, and in everyday exchanges such as jokes and
comments. These hold the identity of a group and make it accessible to the
members of the group to appropriate.[26] An important element in Assmann's
theory is the notion of "communicative memory," which involves everyday
communications that form part of the collective memory of a group.[27] He
says that train rides, waiting rooms, and the common table, among other
things, foster and to a certain extent predetermine such communications.
These follow certain rules. Thus, "through this manner of communication,
each individual composes a memory which . . . is (a) socially mediated and
(b) relates to a group."[28] These groups include families, neighborhood and
professional associations, political parties, nations, and churches.

In Assmann's view, memory and objectivized culture are coupled: "We
can refer to the structure of knowledge in this case as the 'concretion of
identity.' With this we mean that a group bases its consciousness of unity
and specificity upon this knowledge and derives formative and normative
impulses from it, which allows the group to reproduce its identity. In this
sense, objectivized culture has the structure of memory."[29] In other words,
rites, texts, and images are the cues that hold memory, not only history, and
link the everyday to the past. This cultural memory is maintained "through
cultural formation (texts, rites, monuments) and institutional communica-

tion (recitation, observance, practice). We call these 'figures of memory.'"[30] Assmann attributes the power of cultural memory to "mnemonic energy," saying that "in cultural formation, a collective experience crystallizes, whose meaning, when touched upon, may suddenly become accessible again across millennia."[31] Mnemonic energy is the source of power for the cues O'Loughlin talks about.

I see a link between Assmann's theory and one of the categories used by Latino/a theologians, that is, *lo cotidiano* (the quotidian). The activities of daily, ordinary life and communication involving exchanges among people such as jokes, a memory, gossip, a shared experience, or collective activity are filled with mnemonic energy. That is, *lo cotidiano* bears identity and culture and has a wealth of religious meaning that makes it a *locus theologicus* from which to discern God's action and presence in life. Thus, Hispanic religious activities have a cultural memory and a mnemonic energy relating them to a certain worldview and developing their identity as a unique part of God's people. This includes the liturgy and popular devotions.

One of the characteristics of cultural memory is that it preserves accumulated knowledge from which a group derives an awareness of its unity and uniqueness. Another characteristic is its "capacity to reconstruct" or relate knowledge to an actual, contemporary situation. Assmann declares that "cultural memory exists in two modes: first in the mode of potentiality of the archive whose accumulated texts, images, and rules of conduct act as a total horizon, and second, in the mode of actuality, whereby each contemporary context puts the objectivized meaning into its own perspective, giving it its own relevance."[32] Another key trait for him is that of "obligation" explaining that "the relation to a normative self-image of the group engenders a clear *system of values* and *differentiations in importance* which structure the cultural supply of knowledge and the symbols [employed]."[33] In sum, cultural memory contains the values and self-knowledge of a group and holds its memory of these by means of figures of memory such as rites, texts, and customs, which help the group access the values and identity contained therein. With this in mind, it seems that as a bearer of cultural memory, the use of typology as a liturgical hermeneutic of the Bible has the mnemonic energy to provide people with an encounter with the Word in their lives. This helps them generate certain figures of memory that give them access to that encounter periodically as occurs at worship and in Hispanic popular religious practices.

Examples of Cultural Memory

A good example of how cultural memory works is the story of the woman who always cut off the ends of the roast before cooking it. One day her daughter, who followed this practice, was asked why she did it. Not knowing why, other than to imitate her mother, she asked her about it; her mother answered she did it because that's how *her* mother did it. They asked Grandmother why she cut off the ends. She answered, "Because I didn't have a pot big enough." This figure of memory had been handed on for three generations. For the grandmother it was a question of practicality, but for the daughter and granddaughter it was a link to the grandmother as well as a way to identify how this family makes roast. This might be seen as a "negative" handing on of a custom through misinterpretation, but I suspect that it was meaningful to them and may even make the roast taste better to them because it is how this family cooks roast.

Another example comes from my own family. My twin brother Rubén and I discovered that my mother's great-grandparents on her mother's side were Sephardic Jews who had settled in northern Mexico. We got this knowledge because of certain things my mother would or would not do. For example, she never made tamales with pork, always with roast beef; the more common is to use pork. Also, usually the only time of year we ever ate pork was the ham at Easter. Her reason was because pork was dirty (that is, *treif*, unclean, forbidden). Perhaps eating ham at Easter signaled we were Christians and allayed any suspicions. There were other customs that after inquiry we discovered had been handed on from my great-grandmother to my grandmother to my mother.[34] As we dug into these we found other family secrets about our ancestry—certainly not always pleasant. By my grandmother's generation they had embraced Catholicism somewhat and its religious practices also became part of the mix. Nonetheless, cooking customs and certain expressions that had been handed on orally or through rituals had become identifiers for us of who we were, at least in part. Through these cues we were able to access their mnemonic energy, their meaning, and see our link to the past.[35]

I discern in Hispanic religious practices something similar at work. Though some Hispanics engage in building *altarcitos* (home altars), for example, or making their distinctive *persignación* (sign of the cross), they are not consciously aware of the link to the Church's liturgy, particularly the Eucharist. The *altarcito* of course has its parallel in the altar of Eucharist— the place of worship and offering of sacrifice and prayer. In the *persignación* with its concomitant prayer ("*Que por la señal de la Santa Cruz, de nuestros enemigos, líbranos Señor Dios nuestro, en el nombre del Padre y del Hijo y del Espíritu Santo, amén*"),[36] we see not only the ritual of signing one's forehead, lips, and breast, imitating the signing of oneself at the reading of the Gospel, but also an echo of the Liturgy of the Hours when the first hour of the day begins with "*Señor abre mis labios / y mi boca proclamará tu alabanza*" (cf. Ps 51:17) with the participants making the sign of the cross over their lips.[37] It also echoes the second stanza of the *Benedictus,* which says: "*Es la salvación que nos libra de nuestros enemigos y de la mano de todos los que nos odian*" (cf. Lk 1:70–71).[38]

Perhaps unknowingly those who do these things are partaking of the cultural memory that links Hispanic popular religious practices to the liturgy through these distinctive figures of memory. If that is the case, then those of us who have access to the cultural knowledge and mnemonic energy these figures of memory contain can draw on them and help people make further links to the Church's liturgy and prayer. In this way the theological stance of *Sacrosanctum Concilium* 10 is fulfilled, in that Christian life and activity flow to and from the liturgy so that people find their lives celebrated in the liturgy and the liturgy celebrated in *lo cotidiano* of their own lives. In my judgment, this is how Scripture has functioned in liturgy and in Hispanic religious practices. The Word has inspired their response to the invitation to be disciples by means of participation in liturgy and religious devotional practices. Yet the inspiration of the Word has been vaguely recognized as well.

Enhancing the Word's Inspiration among Hispanics

I have three recommendations for enhancing the role of the Word in Hispanic worship both liturgically and devotionally. First, draw out the scriptural foundations for what they are doing in these activities. For example, the events of Holy Week, particularly the Good Friday liturgies, processions, and related devotions, are clearly based on the Scriptures. They are the basis for the Veneration of the Cross Liturgy and for the *Via Crucis* following Jesus's path to Calvary. In places where *pasos* (a type of float) containing images of the Passion are carried in procession, often the different aspects of the Passion as described in Scripture are arranged in the processions so as to form a living tableau of the Scriptures, thus connecting word and image.[39] A related example is that of *las siete palabras*. Though not an official liturgy, many places hold services on Good Friday at 3:00 p.m. where Jesus's last seven words on the cross are the basis for a lengthy sermon on these words found in the Gospels. The service consists of the sermon interrupted by the related Scripture passage, prayers, and penitential songs in response to the passages. On Good Friday morning people make what is called the *Visita a las siete casas*. This devotion consists in visiting the Blessed Sacrament in seven different churches recalling the seven places where Jesus was forced to go after the agony in the garden: (1) before Caiaphas, (2) before Annas, (3) at the Sanhedrin, (4) before Pilate, (5) before Herod, (6) back before Pilate, (7) to Calvary.[40] They become a way to accompany Jesus in his moments of suffering, pain, and loneliness. Organizing Bible study may be a way to help participants make these connections.

An example not related to Holy Week but just as meaningful is the Rosary. It is well known that Domingo de Guzmán, founder of the Order of Preachers (Dominicans), popularized the recitation of the Rosary in the thirteenth century through his preaching. After that, the recitation of the Rosary consisted of praying fifteen decades until 2002 when John Paul II added another five to stress even more Christ's saving action.[41] Although the use of prayer beads may have been influenced by Islamic practice in medieval Spain, already in the ninth century, Christians had begun to recite 150 Our Fathers in lieu of the 150 psalms prayed during Morning and Evening Prayer, which were ultimately replaced by daily Mass. The praying of psalms twice a day, begun in the fourth century, came to be substituted first by the recitation of 150 *Paters* by the people and then by 150 *Aves,* thereby simplifying their prayer. Clearly the first half of the Hail Mary is almost a direct quote of Luke 1:28. Eventually the fifteen decades were spaced out by inserting Scripture passages, other prayers, and meditations on the Mysteries of Jesus and Mary and assigning them to various days of the week. In this way the cultural memory of the importance of praying and meditating on the 150 psalms was reconstructed to include the parallel praying of 150 Hail Mary's, thereby creating an unconscious link to the liturgy through this figure of memory, while also providing a means to extend scriptural themes into popular religious practices. In a sense this evinces a "hermeneutic of ritualization," in which ordinary people applied the Scriptures to their daily lives and interpreted them by means of this devotional practice.

A second recommendation concerns preaching. Its importance as the means for explaining the Scriptures and applying them to daily life has been noted already above in the citations of the SC and the GIRM. However, preaching to a predominately English-speaking congregation is not the same as preaching to a predominately Spanish-speaking one. In another article I explain three principles that are important when preaching.[42] First, connect the listeners to their religious experience. Second, know your audience and what they want to hear. Third, name God's action in their lives and in the events of their lives. Of course this presumes that one is preaching from the Word proclaimed. Rosa María Icaza advises that "homilists must listen to and publicly relate the scriptural readings, the social and political events of the world and of the community, and the cultural traditions of the members of the assembly. Yes, homilists need to be aware also of the cultural spirituality of the members of the assembly. What are their ideas of God, of Jesus, of Mary, of the saints?"[43] To know the audience is to know their cultural values, since the Scripture message is heard differently by English speakers and Spanish ones. Icaza suggests "perhaps Hispanics would need to hear not about our dependence on God, since we know in theory and practice that everything comes from God, but that, trusting in God, we need to do our part. A similar case would be preaching in a poor community."[44] An aspect of knowing your audience is to know how the members of the congregation ritualize and symbolize their religious experience.

The third recommendation is to pay attention to ritual and symbol. One of the main ritual postures we engage in at liturgy is that of listening, especially to the proclamation of the Scriptures, but also the homily and the prayers offered in the assembly's name. In this regard Antonio Donghi writes: "listening is the fundamental posture of the disciple of the Lord, whose faith is born in the announcing-personalization of the word."[45] Also, since listening is the basic ritual posture of those at worship, it points to the importance of being able to understand by means of the vernacular spoken by the members of the congregation. Even so, as Donghi notes, listening is not a simple auditory event but a placing oneself in the gaze of the Master so as to "be a living 'Here I am' before God and sing of his life-giving fidelity in the word proclaimed in the liturgy and lived in daily life."[46]

The posture of listening helps one make connections between the readings and the actions that take place later in the Eucharist. Unfortunately, too often the liturgy is marked by a flood of words washing over the participants. What remains are only the *huellas*, the water tracks left behind. Somehow the Scriptures and the words of the liturgy have to be enlivened. Attention to the preparation of readers, presiders, and other ministers is an important element, but more attention must also be paid to symbol and ritual, since actions speak louder than words (as the saying goes). In this way words and actions together can enliven the Word for the participants at liturgy and inspire them to integrate it into their daily lives. This is the beauty of Hispanic devotional practices: they too serve as a hermeneutic of the Word proclaimed at liturgy and an application of the values inspired by the Word of God.

Images play important roles in bringing to mind the personages and events of the Scriptures. In Hispanic devotional practice they are often meant to be three-dimensional, dressed, and taken out on the streets, not hidden in some niche in a darkened church. Jaime Lara gets at what underlies this, noting "Word and image go hand in hand, and for those of us who stand in the Christian tradition, Scripture and picture are necessarily complementary. The 'Word became flesh' implies not only that it became audible, but that it also became visible. The Word became image . . . this has been especially the case in Latino/Hispanic heritage."[47] Hispanic popular religious practices are a synthesis of Word and faith experience in three ways, according to Juan Sosa: "First, popular religion . . . actively [proclaims] the paschal mystery outside the liturgy and in small communities. Second, popular religion [embodies] the church through living out the gospel by church people. Third, the blessings of the church [are] the ongoing affirmation of God's continuing assistance and company to God's people."[48] Sosa adds that "popular religion can become a preaching tool to the degree that it proclaims, more than in words, in signs, gestures, movements and attitudes . . . the saving act of God who sent his only son to redeem the world and not to condemn it (John 3:16–17)."[49]

Image and symbol are part of ritual. The need to ritualize is seen in a very common practice nowadays at the Our Father. Here I refer to the holding of hands. Johnson notes that "whatever might be said in favor of or against this practice, what we are encountering here is a felt need on the part of the faithful, a striking reminder that true ritual springs from the hearts of people rather than from church committees or offices."[50] This same need can be seen in the prolonged sign of peace among Hispanics; it seems to ritualize Matthew 5:23–24: "If you bring your gift to the altar and there recall that your brother has anything against you, go first to be reconciled with your brother, and then come and offer your gift" and Matthew 5:47: "If you greet your brothers only, what is so praiseworthy about that?" (New American Bible).[51] This could be seen as a "hermeneutic of ritualization" by means of which the faithful ritualize a certain interpretation of the sign of peace.

The instructions of the Roman Missal give many options and directions that can help make the words come alive. A good example is the simple honoring of the Word by carrying the Book of the Gospels, in a beautiful cover, in procession and executing well the gestures surrounding the proclamation of the Gospel. Tad Guzie declares "symbols are tangible, and when we touch them we touch a mystery that is at once familiar and elusive."[52] They are visible and even audible at times. He adds, "symbols, not discourses or discussions, do the most effective job of bringing into our awareness the realities of loving and being alive, living and struggling and dying together."[53] O'Loughlin says "in any ritual situation—from a simple shake of hands at a meeting to the celebration of the Eucharist—we have to recall that words say one thing, gestures another, while the props and setting may perhaps convey something different again."[54] Again, rituals and symbols help form and bear cultural memory, making an encounter with the Word accessible. The liturgical use of Scripture provides a pattern.

Conclusion

The clear proclamation of the Word and its application to everyday life are key factors in all this, for it has to be alive in order for people to find its power in the ordinary circumstances of their lives. Remember, we believe in the Word made flesh, in a human being, and not in the word written as a dead letter on a piece of paper. Jesus asks the two disciples on the way to Emmaus: "Why do you seek the living one among the dead?" (Lk 24:5). LaVerdiere notes this question brings up another: "If the body of the Lord, the living one, is not to be found in the tomb among the dead, where is he to be found?"[55] The answer is in the story of Emmaus. For LaVerdiere, Luke's Gospel is the story of the Eucharist told in a story of meals and journeys with Jesus, Son of God and Son of Man. Presenting Jesus's life as a journey in which meals and hospitality play a critical part means that all of his disciples, including us, are a people on a journey, a people who offer and receive hospitality. Applying a liturgical hermeneutic, we see that in the Emmaus story the Eucharist is "the supreme expression of that hospitality, sustaining them on their journey to the kingdom of God."[56]

In order for the Eucharist and the rest of the liturgy to be the center and fount of Catholic worship, those who participate in it must recognize the presence of the Lord. This is the operative theology of the liturgy. The Last Supper is not the last meal Jesus shares with his followers; rather he continues to share a meal with us at every eucharistic celebration.[57] Our everyday meals as a part of our daily lives can also be an anticipation and a prolongation of that encounter at Eucharist, depending on how well we integrate the Word into our lives.

Moreover, LaVerdiere declares that the Emmaus story reveals that Jesus's presence is a sacramental one.[58] Through gathering to worship with symbol and ritual, through image and word, the bearers of our Catholic Christian cultural memory, Christ makes himself present. Therefore, from LaVerdiere's perspective, "Eucharistic hospitality requires that those who minister recognize the Lord's presence, that they respond to the Lord's presence by being present to him in return. They do this by listening and attending to his word."[59] Likewise, popular religious practices have no Christian value if they are not a response to the Word and if that Word does not lead to the Kingdom of God celebrated in the liturgy. For in the liturgy Christians claim the story of salvation as their own and pass it on to others.

The liturgy in general and the Eucharist in particular proclaim the gospel in symbol and deed as well as in sign and word, so that the participants may become what they receive, the Body of Christ. By joining Christ in his sacrifice, doing what he did in memory of him, we make his sacrifice an active force in our lives and in the world. Thus we must offer our own lives that all might live, *haciendo el bien sin mirar a quien* ("doing good to others without distinction"). Consequently, to hear the Word of God and to put it into practice means that we have to *be* Eucharist, which is knowing, living, and being the gospel of Jesus Christ, Lord and Savior of all. Hispanics have over the centuries engaged in a hermeneutic of ritualization by taking their experience of Christ and his grace found in the liturgy and applying it to their lives by means of popular religious practices. As they come to know better how these practices are informed by the Word, I trust they will come to appreciate more the bond that exists between those practices and the liturgy so that in the breaking of the bread, whether at Eucharist or a common meal at home, they will come to recognize Christ in their midst.

⌣

Notes

1.　Eugene LaVerdiere, preface to *Dining in the Kingdom of God: The Origins of the Eucharist in the Gospel of Luke* (Chicago: Liturgy Training Publications, 1994), vii.

2. Thomas O'Loughlin, "The Liturgical Vessels of the Latin Eucharistic Liturgy: A Case of an Embedded Theology," *Worship* 82, no. 6 (2008): 482–504.

3. Jan Assmann, "Collective Memory and Cultural Identity," *New German Critique* 95 (Spring/Summer 1995): 125–133 (translated by John Czaplicka; originally published in *Kultur und Gedächtnis*, ed. Jan Assmann and Tonio Hölscher [Frankfurt am Main: Suhrkamp, 1988, 9–19]).

4. See Second Vatican Council, Constitution on the Sacred Liturgy (*Sacrosanctum Concilium*), www.vatican.va/archive/hist_councils /ii_vatican_council/documents/vat-ii_const_19631204 _sacrosanctum-concilium_en.html.

5. Lawrence J. Johnson, *The Word and Eucharist Handbook*, 3rd ed. (San Jose, CA: Resource Pubs., 1998), 36.

6. See Bishops' Committee on the Liturgy newsletter, November 2000, available at www.usccb.org/liturgy/innews/112000.shtml.

7. See "Adoption of the *Leccionario* for the United States," *Amén* 21, no. 1 (Spring 2009): 3.

8. Available at www.usccb.org/liturgy/current/revmissalisromanien.shmtl. Cites SC § 33 in n. 58 and SC § 7 in n. 59.

9. See Pierre Jounel, "La Biblia en la liturgia," in *La inspiración bíblica de la liturgia*, Cuadernos Phase 176, ed. Josep Urdeix (Barcelona: Centre de Pastoral Litúrgica, 2008), 5–34; originally published as "La Bible dans la liturgie," in *Parole de Dieu et liturgie* (Paris, 1958), 17–49. It is important to note here that the New Testament emerged for liturgical purposes, whereas in synagogue worship parts of the Bible, particularly the Torah and Psalms, were already written and incorporated into the worship, providing the model for Christian worship.

10. Nathan D. Mitchell, "The Amen Corner," *Worship* 83, no. 1 (2009): 73.

11. Ibid.

12. Jounel, "La Biblia en la liturgia," 11. Even so, other approaches can be discerned as well, such as historical, spiritual, moral, anagogical, sociological, anthropological, a hermeneutic of faith, and even a hermeneutic of suspicion, especially in terms of how the homily functions.

13. Ibid., 7.

14. Louis-Marie Chauvet, "La dimensión bíblica de los textos litúrgicos," in *La inspiración bíblica de la liturgia*, Cuadernos Phase 176, ed. Josep Urdeix (Barcelona: Centre de Pastoral Litúrgica, 2008), 55–70; originally published as "La dimension biblique des texts liturgiques," *La Maison-Dieu*, 189 (1992): 131–47.

15.   Ibid., 57.

16.   Ibid.; *"siempre es objeto de un nuevo tratamiento por el simple hecho de haber sido separado del Libro y de su propio contexto histórico y literario y de haber sido trasladado al interior de la acción litúrgica. . . . Esto plantea la cuestión del estatuto de la 'Biblia litúrgica' en su relación con el Canon bíblico. Cuestión importante, puesto que—'lex orandi, lex credendi'—la expresión misma de la fe de la Iglesia, por una parte, depende de la 'Biblia litúrgica'"* (translation by Raúl Gómez-Ruiz).

17.   Mitchell, "The Amen Corner," 73.

18.   Ibid., 75; the Bible is to be seen as a whole, not as a collection of separate pieces.

19.   Andrew Greeley, *The Catholic Imagination* (Berkeley: University of California Press, 2000).

20.   Jounel, "La Biblia en la liturgia," 8.

21.   Raúl Gómez-Ruiz, *Mozarabs, Hispanics, and the Cross*, Studies in Latino/a Catholicism (Maryknoll, NY: Orbis Books, 2007), 56, 57. On the other hand, the Roman rite has opted in general for the *lectio continua* of the Scriptures.

22.   O'Loughlin, "The Liturgical Vessels," 486.

23.   Ibid., 504.

24.   C. Gilbert Romero, *Hispanic Devotional Piety: Tracing the Biblical Roots* (Maryknoll, NY: Orbis Books, 1991).

25.   Ibid., 20.

26.   Assmann attributes his work to the foundation set in the 1930s by the sociologist Maurice Halbwachs and art historian Aby Warburg, who independently developed two theories of a "collective" or "social" memory (see Assmann, "Collective Memory," 125).

27.   Ibid., 126, building on Halbwachs.

28.   Ibid., 127; he calls the rules "laws of the market," which he attributes to Pierre Bourdieu, *Esquisse d'une théorie de la pratique: Précédé de trois études d'ethnologie kabyle* (Geneva: Droz, 1972), in note 8.

29.   Ibid.

30.   Ibid., 128–29.

31.   Ibid., 129.

32.   Ibid., 130.

33.   Ibid., 131, italics in original.

34.   One of these was to call our great-grandmother *yaya* (the Greek word for "grandmother," used by Sephardim who had settled in Greece and the Balkans).

35. Interestingly enough, years later our suspicions were corroborated by our cousin Luis, who had been shown some jewelry and other things of Jewish origin that our grandmother had been keeping. She told him that this was our family origin that he should know about as her closest grandson.

36. "Through the sign of the holy cross, free us from our enemies, Lord our God, in the name of the Father, of the Son, and of the Holy Spirit, amen."

37. In English: "Lord, open my lips / and my mouth will proclaim your praise." See General Instruction of the Liturgy of the Hours (1971), no. 34, available at www.fdlc.org/Liturgy_Resources/Liturgy_of_the_Hours-General _Instruction.pdf.

38. That is, "Through his holy prophets he promised of old that he would save us from our enemies, from the hands of all who hate us" (from Gospel Canticle for Morning Prayer, Lk 1:68–79).

39. See, for instance, my description and analysis of the Good Friday Processions in Toledo: Gómez-Ruiz, *Mozarabs, Hispanics,* 108–21.

40. See *Faith Expressions of Hispanics in the Southwest,* rev. ed. (San Antonio, TX: Mexican American Cultural Center, 1990), 18.

41. See John Paul II, "Apostolic Letter *Rosarium Virginis Mariae*" (2002), 3, available at: www.vatican.va/holy_father/john_paul_ii/apost_letters /documents/hf_jp-ii_apl_20021016_rosarium-virginis-mariae_en.html.

42. Raúl Gómez, S.D.S., "Preaching the Ritual Masses among Latinos," in *Preaching and Culture in Latino Congregations,* ed. Kenneth G. Davis and Jorge L. Presmanes (Chicago: Liturgy Training Publications, 2000), 103–19; see especially 104–8.

43. Rosa María Icaza, CCVI, "Living and Sharing the Word among Hispanics," in *Preaching and Culture,* 31.

44. Ibid., 39.

45. Antonio Donghi, *Actions and Words: Symbolic Language and the Liturgy,* trans. from Italian by William McDonough and Dominic Serra. English text edited by Mark Twomey and Elizabeth L. Montgomery (Collegeville, MN: Liturgical Press, 1997), 31.

46. Ibid., 34.

47. Jaime Lara, "Visual Preaching: The Witness of Our Latin Eyes," in *Preaching and Culture,* 75.

48. Juan J. Sosa, "Preaching and Popular Religion," in *Preaching and Culture,* 99.

49. Ibid., 101.

50. Johnson, *The Word,* 112.

51. In fact, in the Hispanic liturgical heritage found in the Hispano-Mozarabic rite, the Sign of Peace takes place in a protracted intermediary rite between

the Liturgy of the Word and of the Eucharist; see Gómez-Ruiz, *Mozarabs, Hispanics,* 59.

52. Tad Guzie, *The Book of Sacramental Basics* (New York: Paulist Press, 1981), 47.

53. Ibid., 48.

54. O'Loughlin, "The Liturgical Vessels," 484.

55. LaVerdiere, preface, 155.

56. Ibid., 9.

57. Ibid., 122.

58. Ibid., 171; cf. Lk 24:13–35.

59. Ibid., 76.

4.

The Bible and Catechesis

Hosffman Ospino

~

They were conversing about all the things that had occurred.
—Luke 24:14

From the early moments of Christianity until today, Sacred Scripture and catechesis have shared an intimate relationship. In the New Testament, we see Jesus with a crowd at the mountain, teaching them about the new law and the new covenant (cf. Mt 5–7). In his teaching he built on the meaning and centrality of the Hebrew Scriptures and affirmed that he did not come "to abolish the law or the prophets. I have come not to abolish but to fulfill" (Mt 5:17). His teaching ministry was firmly rooted in the love and knowledge of the Scriptures: "He came to Nazareth, where he had grown up, and went according to his custom into the synagogue on the Sabbath day. He stood up to read and was handed a scroll of the prophet Isaiah . . . Rolling up the scroll, he handed it back to the attendant and sat down, and the eyes of all in the synagogue looked intently at him. He said to them, 'Today this Scripture passage is fulfilled in your hearing'" (Lk 4:16–17; 20–21). After the resurrection, he appears to two disciples on the road to Emmaus (Lk 24:13–35). Once again, we witness a masterful catechetical moment when Jesus clarifies the Scriptures to these disciples and explains the fullness of meaning of the Jerusalem events. The disciples "were conversing about all the things that have occurred" (Lk 24:14), they wanted to see how the latest events affected their lives and their hopes, how God's plan was being fulfilled, and wondered what exactly was going to happen next. The conversation with a stranger, who in the end happened to be the risen Lord himself, made the difference: "Were not our hearts burning within us while he spoke to us on the way and opened the scriptures to us?" (Lk 24:32).

Many other passages in the New Testament affirm the intimate relationship between catechesis and Sacred Scripture, among them: Philip explaining the prophets to the Ethiopian eunuch (Acts 8:26–39), Paul's letters and their abundant references to the Hebrew Scriptures, and the beautiful discourse on faith in the letter to the Hebrews (Heb 11:1–40). Likewise, early Christian writings affirmed that essential relationship. The Didache or "Teaching of the Twelve Apostles"[1] contains plenty of references to the Scriptures available at the moment of its composition; the Apostolic Fathers and the works of most Christian writers in the first centuries of the Christian era exhibited a profound knowledge of the Scriptures and did not separate teaching from devoted meditation on the sacred writings.[2] Unique are the contributions of St. Augustine. In many of his remarkable works he dealt with the intimate relationship between catechesis and Sacred Scripture.[3]

Religious educators participate in a tradition that dates back to the earliest Christian communities, became greatly articulated in the works of many Christian educators throughout history, and continues to give life as we share our faith with one another in the Church. It is important to note that as the centuries passed, catechists have been confronted with different questions, have needed to take seriously the multiple contexts where they educated in the faith, and have adapted this ministry in light of the signs of their own time. The variety of responses to the changing circumstances in the life of the Church has simultaneously shaped the engagement of Sacred Scripture in the catechetical world. From a historical perspective, this has truly been an enriching experience.

Contemporary reflections continue to affirm the centrality of Sacred Scripture in the Church's catechetical ministry, but we do this remaining attentive to the particular context in which these reflections take place. We are privileged to enjoy a unique awareness about new methodologies, interpretations, theological developments, and conversations with various fields of knowledge that makes our work as religious educators very exciting. Such awareness informs how we read Sacred Scripture and how we educate in the faith. While Christian educators share common convictions about the basic content of catechesis and its goals, the role of the Scripture in sharing faith, and the impact of catechetical ministry in the life of the Church, we also remain aware about the unique circumstances that shape the lives of people whom we encounter in our ministry. Contemporary reflection on catechesis is more attentive to the complexity of the human experience and to the challenges posed by the social and cultural location(s) of those who participate in this ecclesial activity.

In this essay we explore how the relationship between Sacred Scripture and catechesis becomes alive among Latino/a Catholics in the United States. The essay has three major sections. First, we look at some ecclesial documents that describe the present understanding of the relationship between Sacred Scripture and catechesis. Second, we examine how U.S. Latinos/as can and do insightfully engage Sacred Scripture through catechesis in the context of everyday moments of encounter with the sacred. Third, we look at some major pathways and challenges that U.S. Latino/a Catholics encounter as we read Sacred Scripture in the Church and catechetical contexts.

The Word of God and Catechesis: Catholic Perspectives

The second part of the twentieth century witnessed a powerful renewal in the study of Sacred Scripture among Catholics around the world. Much of such renewal was the result of the new air that the Second Vatican Council (1962–65) gave to the Church. We must observe, nevertheless, that Vatican II brought together many insights of a number of renewal movements that were maturing in the Church in different parts of the world during many years before the Council, as well as the impulse given through some ecclesial statements on the interpretation of the Bible.[4]

At Vatican II, the Dogmatic Constitution on Divine Revelation, *Dei Verbum,* affirmed that the Church holds fast to the Word of God as a source of the "divine treasures" revealed by God to humanity in history.[5] God's Word comes to us in history mediated through Sacred Scripture and Sacred Tradition together; both "form one sacred deposit of the word of God."[6] Catechesis, a central moment in the Church's evangelizing mission,[7] would thus emerge as one of the key contexts where this relationship is uniquely fostered. Scripture and Tradition remain inseparable in the Church's catechetical experience. Though at some moments of the process of handing on the Word of God catechists, teachers, and ministers can emphasize an element of Scripture or one of Tradition to clarify a certain point, such separation is rather artificial because Scripture implicitly leads to Tradition and Tradition to Scripture.[8]

Scripture and Tradition together are the source of catechesis: "catechesis must be impregnated and penetrated by the thought, the spirit and the outlook of the Bible and the Gospels through assiduous contact with the texts themselves; . . . catechesis will be all the richer and more effective for reading the texts with the intelligence and the heart of the Church."[9]

This essential relationship of catechesis to the Word of God, transmitted in the Scriptures and Tradition, requires that catechetical processes introduce those who are part of them to a profound yet dynamic and transforming encounter with the particularity of each dimension of God's Word without sacrificing its unity. On the one hand, catechesis is a unique moment in the Church's evangelizing process to familiarize the faithful with the Bible, its origins and structure, its messages, and the various ways in which the Church reads the sacred text. On the other, catechesis is a privileged space to enter in close dialogue with the Magisterium, to learn in detail about how Christians have lived and reflected about their faith throughout the centuries, and to discern what God says to us here and now as a community of faith in the context of our daily lives.

One important element that Catholics engaging God's Word in the context of catechesis must continuously keep in mind is the role of the Magisterium vis-à-vis the revealed Word. The Church exercises its teaching office regularly through the interpretation, guarding, and communication of God's Word, placing itself not above the Word but at is service.[10] Catholic tradition recognizes that the Magisterium has been charged with the responsibility of handing on the faith received from Jesus and the Apostles through the centuries. Yet, the Magisterium does not do this alone: "In a harmonious collaboration with the Magisterium in the Church's mission of Evangelization, all the members of the People of God, priests, deacons, men and women religious, and the lay faithful, hand on the faith by proclaiming the Good News in Jesus Christ and communicating God's gift of his own divine life in the sacraments."[11] Handing on the faith in the Church through catechesis actualizes one of the most powerful exercises of ecclesial collaboration: catechists and teachers of the faith acknowledge the central role of a Magisterium placed at the service of the Word, participate in the teaching ministry of the Church in communion with the Magisterium,[12] and are empowered/authorized by the same members of the Magisterium to share the faith in the name of the Church.[13]

Having affirmed that Scripture and Tradition are inseparable because they are one source, we can say some words about the *specific* relationship that exists between Sacred Scripture and catechesis. Catechesis in this essay is understood as *the pedagogical process of handing on the faith of the Church to women and men who have heard the message of the Gospel, a process that leads to a transformative and salvific encounter with Jesus Christ and to living authentically as Christian disciples in concrete socio-historical-cultural contexts.*[14] When the Church hands on the faith through catechesis, it engages

Sacred Scripture with special care and devotion following the example of Christians for many centuries: "Through the ages of the Church, study of Sacred Scripture has been the cornerstone of catechesis."[15] This is truly evident in the commentaries on the Scriptures by Christians in the patristic era, the works of many reflective women and men who engage Scripture as the soul of theology,[16] and the thousands of Bible study groups that meet to meditate upon God's written Word throughout the world. The National Directory for Catechesis reminds us that catechesis "takes Sacred Scripture as its inspiration, its fundamental curriculum, and its end because it strengthens faith, nourishes the soul, and nurtures the spiritual life. 'Scripture provides the starting point, foundation, and norm of catechetical teaching.'"[17]

God's Word in Sacred Scripture nourishes the community within which it is proclaimed, especially in the context of the liturgy. The Church "unceasingly receives and offers to the faithful the bread of life from the table both of God's Word and of Christ's body."[18] Something similar though not necessarily exactly occurs every time Sacred Scripture is shared in catechetical moments. Catechetical processes continuously bring to life the message of Sacred Scripture into the lives of women and men who hear it and strive to make it part of their everyday lives. This encounter with the Scriptures leads to growth in the knowledge of the faith, one of the central tasks of catechesis.[19] The encounter of God's Word in its written form through catechesis is not exclusively reserved to adults with some knowledge of theology or biblical theory. All Christians are invited to read Sacred Scripture, study it, pray with it, and integrate its message into their lives. All forms of catechesis (e.g., children,[20] youth,[21] adults,[22] catechumens[23]) must affirm and safeguard the centrality of Sacred Scripture in their pedagogical processes.

The *Catechism of the Catholic Church* plays a very important role in the catechetical ministry of the Church. The *Catechism* ought to be understood, given its intimate relationship with Sacred Scripture, as a normative instrument of catechesis.[24] The *Catechism* is a compendium of truths and convictions that Catholics hold as part of our faith that should never be understood apart from or in competition with Sacred Scripture. Quite the opposite, the *Catechism* is at the service of the Word of God and is intended to complement the Scripture;[25] the foundation of the *Catechism* is Sacred Scripture.[26]

These reflections situate the ministry of catechesis in the larger context of the Church's evangelizing mission and provide an overview of the ecclesial dimension of such an important task. The Word of God comes to us as one source of divine revelation mediated through the gifts of Sacred Scripture and Sacred Tradition. Catechetical ministry, thus, is firmly rooted in these gifts and aims at preserving the unity of God's Word in all its expressions. Catechesis aims at nurturing the knowledge of the faith, particularly in a way that leads those involved to a transformative encounter with Christ and to live such faith in the concreteness of their lives. Sacred Scripture inspires the Church's catechetical activity, remains at its heart, and ultimately serves at its end. In the words of St. Jerome, "to ignore the Scriptures is to ignore Christ."

If catechesis, as stated above, leads to a transformative and salvific encounter with Jesus Christ and to living authentically as Christian disciples in concrete socio-historical-cultural contexts, then we must pay attention to the various ways in which we read Sacred Scripture in our catechetical contexts. One look around our faith communities confirms that reading the Scriptures in the Church is far from homogeneous and monotonous. There are different lenses through which this is done, different motivations, approaches, and methodologies that we can avail of when we read the sacred text. In the following section of this essay we venture into some explorations of what reading the Scriptures as Latino/a Catholics in the United States entails. When Latinos/as engage in the process of educating in the faith, we read the Scriptures with the Church, yet we read them in light of the situatedness of our own Latino/a experience.

The Bible and Catechesis
in the U.S. Latino/a Catholic Experience

To speak of a catechesis that is essentially unique to the U.S. Latino/a experience with characteristics that are relevant mostly because of the U.S. Latino/a reality poses a twofold challenge: one, it can send religious educators in search of something that may not exist as specifically defined or creatively imagined; two, it may lead to the temptation of isolating, perhaps caricaturizing, catechesis with Latinos/as—the effects of which would be very detrimental. Nonetheless, there are experiences that U.S. Latino/a Catholics share in common that shape our identity and allow us to ask specific questions about our relationship with God and others in society and the Church. These experiences serve as lenses through which U.S. Latinos/as see reality, interpret it, and respond to it. This does not happen outside the larger ecclesial community but is firmly rooted in it. U.S. Latino/a Catholicism must neither be construed as a separate or alternative experience of Church, nor as something that possesses lesser value when compared to other experiences of being Catholic. The uniqueness of Latino/a Catholicism—and thus of the way catechesis takes place in our communities as well as how we read Sacred Scripture—rests in its profound ecclesiality. When we catechize, we do it as Latinos/as and not only for Latinos/as. When we read Sacred Scripture, we read it as Latinos/as and not only for Latino/as.

Instead of pursuing the idea of a "Latino/a catechesis" and how the Bible would be used within such reality, I propose that we look at what can be named "everyday moments of encounter with the sacred"[27] in the experience of Latino/a Catholics in the United States and explore the engagement of the Scriptures within these moments. Catechesis for many Latinos/as, as well as for many non-Hispanic Catholics, oftentimes happens in classrooms and in the context of formal catechetical encounters. However, catechesis is not limited to these moments. The more aware we are about the everyday moments of encounter with the sacred that characterize the religious experience of U.S. Latino/a Catholics and the more we stress their catechetical value, the better we will be able to appreciate their potential to mediate people's experience of God. These moments simultaneously reveal an initial appropriation of Sacred Scripture and yearn for a more profound engagement of the sacred text and its message.

Liturgical and Prayer Moments

Perhaps the most regular encounter with the Scriptures for many Latino/a Catholics is the Word proclaimed in the various liturgical celebrations of the Church, more particularly in the Eucharist. There, the faithful are nourished from "the table both of God's word and of Christ's body."[28] The liturgy within the Catholic tradition is highly regarded as "the primary place of encounter with the Word of God, because the Risen Lord is really present in sacramental signs."[29] By participating in the liturgical celebrations around the sacraments, the faithful have the opportunity to experience Sacred Scripture become life not only in the proclamation but also in the ritual celebration of God's Word. Thus, participation in the liturgy has a double catechetical effect: we encounter Sacred Scripture through words (proclamation) and actions (ritual).

Along with the encounter with Sacred Scripture in the liturgy, the Church encourages Catholics to read the Bible as part of our daily spiritual exercises.

Indeed, this is a significant development in the recent history of Catholicism, considering that only a century ago those who read the Scripture on their own, when they had a copy, were considered somewhat suspect. *Dei Verbum* insisted that "easy access to Sacred Scripture should be provided for all the Christian faithful."[30] This proximity to Sacred Scripture becomes truly palpable in the centuries-long practice of *Lectio Divina*, a simple yet profound approach to the sacred text in prayer that is well known among many Latino/a Catholics in the United States, particularly *los jóvenes*, and continues to be practiced in homes, Bible study groups, and small Christian communities. Through *Lectio Divina* we listen to God's own words addressing our lives, we become familiar with the biblical texts, and we engage Sacred Scripture as a compass that guides our existence in today's world.[31]

Formal Study of the Scriptures

One of the many blessings of the Catholic experience in the United States is the existence of a large number of educational centers where people can engage in the formal study of Sacred Scripture. Universities, seminaries, schools, diocesan programs, pastoral institutes, parishes, among others, offer various programs of study at different levels that ultimately lead Christians to a more educated understanding of the sacred text. In these centers it is encouraging to see that numerous educators and scholars combine efforts to share their best insights to read Sacred Scripture with the ecclesial community and thus equip women and men interested in the Bible to better read the text in light of current scholarship and creative methodologies.

Other essays in this collection address how Sacred Scripture is read and studied in these centers. I would like to highlight the amazing role of the various *institutos pastorales* serving Hispanic Catholics throughout the United States. These pastoral institutes are true schools of leadership formation rooted in the study of Sacred Scripture for Latinos/as. I have been invited to teach in some of them and am familiar with the curriculum of others. Nearly all of them provide solid introductory programs to Sacred Scripture. The number of Hispanic Catholics who attend these pastoral institutes is significantly much larger than those who attend universities and seminaries. Thus, all recognition, support, and accompaniment ought to be given to these institutes committed to faith formation of Latino/a Catholics. They are indeed unique centers of encounter with the Bible.

In some sense, these first two everyday moments of encounter with the sacred are very familiar to Latino/a Catholics and religious educators. We could say that they are more regular, formal, and even "official." Let us now turn to three other moments of encounter with the sacred where Latinos/as engage Sacred Scripture in profound and transformative ways. These perhaps do not enjoy the formality or the recognition of the first two, yet they significantly shape the religious experience of millions of Latino/a Catholics in the United States.

Lived Experience

Lived experience is the unfolding of human life in the context of *lo cotidiano*, the everyday.[32] Latino/a theologians and faith educators would concur with the observation that lived experience is perhaps the most powerful catechetical school that we possess. U.S. Latino/a Catholics struggle to fully affirm our identity as Latinos/as, as Catholics, and as citizens in the everydayness of our lives. It is in *lo cotidiano* where we discover what it means to be in relationship with God and others. In the everyday we learn that faith makes sense when it provides meaning to our experience as women and men whose lives are uniquely shaped by the particularity of our ethnicity and our sociocultural location. *Lo cotidiano* is the school where we hand the faith on to our children, to the new generations of Catholics, and to anyone who is open to perceiving the loving presence of God in the here and now of our daily lives. The complexity of our lived experience continually invites us to name—and rename—our reality through expressions, practices, and symbols that point to the sacred. This constitutes what I call our Hispanic Catholic imagination, or what Virgilio Elizondo calls "the treasure of Hispanic faith."[33] Such naming indicates that Latinos/as are continuously reading the presence of God in our lives and in our reality with the conviction that we live in a world that is sacred.[34] Lived experience is catechesis at its best because it simultaneously grounds our human experience in the greatness of the Christian revelation while bringing such revelation to fully relate to who we are here and now: human beings created in God's image who search for meaning within the confines of history and whose dignity is inalienable.

Reading Sacred Scripture in *lo cotidiano* is an exercise of transformative dialogue in which we read the text in light of our own experience while allowing the text to read us. Justo González has insightfully articulated the relationship: "To read the Bible is to enter into dialogue with it. In that dialogue, there is a sense in which the text is normative. . . . At the same time, the other pole of the dialogue is just as important. It is I, from my context and perspective, who read the text."[35] Our lived experience is the context in which we become who we are and witness others "become." Lived experience as a school of catechesis is personal and communal, formative and transformative; it affirms the present and anticipates the future. Consequently, when Latinos/as read Sacred Scripture in this school of catechesis, "we read the Bible, not primarily to find out what we are to do, but to find out who we are and who we are to be."[36]

Popular Catholicism

The experience of God among Latino/a Catholics is deeply shaped by a powerful sense of the sacred perceived in unique ways in the various practices of popular Catholicism. These practices (e.g. *posadas, altarcito, Via Crucis*) embody an understanding of the faith that is rooted in the particularity of people's lives and experiences. This is the sense in which such practices are to be deemed popular. Practices of popular Catholicism are articulations rooted in the people's reflection and interpretation of the sources of Christian revelation after significant periods of time—sometimes centuries. Such articulations embody understandings that bring together official convictions and formulations of the faith, along with the insights about God, reality, and the life of people of faith. Popular Catholicism is simultaneously a way of knowing[37] and the most available language for the majority of U.S. Latino/a Catholics, many of whom live in the margins of our society, to express our faith in a way that is accessible and familiar.

Popular Catholicism's intrinsic pedagogical character becomes manifest when it serves as a means to hand on the faith of the Church, the faith of the people, through practice and symbol. Latinos/as have in popular Catholicism a life-giving resource to learn about the faith of our mothers and fathers, to deepen into the mysteries of that faith, and to transmit what we believe and celebrate to others in the Church. As we saw in the previous section, the Word of God is the primary source of catechesis. Likewise, the Word of God, available to us in history through Scripture and Tradition, is the primary source of popular Catholicism, where it is largely mediated through the experiences of regular women and men living in diverse socio-historical-cultural contexts. Building on the fact that both catechesis and popular Catholicism share this common source, we can make three observations that have profound pedagogical implications.

First, popular Catholicism and Scripture share in common a similar matrix: the world of the people. Ecclesial documents on the Scriptures and the work of contemporary biblical scholars coincide with the conviction that the Bible emerged as part of long processes of reflection in various communities, Jewish and Christian. This process took place in the midst of experiences of women and men of faith who did not know that what they wrote or reflected upon would eventually be considered "sacred text." The Jews who wrote the Hebrew Scriptures and the early Christians who articulated the narratives and letters that later became the New Testament had a lot in common with many of the contemporary Christians whose faith is nourished through popular Catholicism: they perceived the world as a sacred place where God becomes present in incredible ways; they used language (e.g., parables), practices (e.g., annual feasts), and symbols (e.g., Passover) that were part of their everyday lives to speak and interpret their faith; they lived in times where life was constantly defined in terms of struggle. To become familiar with popular Catholicism can be considered as an approximation into the world of the Bible—both in terms of social location as well as in terms of interpretive frameworks.

Second, popular Catholicism teaches us about Sacred Scripture. Nearly all expressions of Latino/a popular Catholicism have a strong biblical background. Oftentimes they are reenactments of biblical scenes (e.g., Las Posadas, the Via Crucis) or are interpretations of biblical themes that become live in particular practices (e.g., *penitentes*).[38] Popular Catholicism serves a catechetical function in the life of the Church when it communicates various messages from Sacred Scripture in the form of ritual and symbol. The appeal of popular Catholicism to the senses and to our religious imagination helps us to see biblical moments come to life in the here and now of our experience as a community of faith. The actualization of those biblical moments through popular Catholicism may not be historically accurate, it may not be sophisticated enough to suit the critical eye of some theologians and other scholars, or it may be the result of a naive reading—for which there must always be room[39]—of the biblical text, yet it is the people's reading of the sacred text and as such it deserves some contemplation. Catechists and teachers who foster participation in practices of popular Catholicism have a great tool that does most of the pedagogical work by itself. The message carried by the practice or the symbol is self-explanatory: it points to a specific element of the treasure of our Christian faith, yet it remains open to other connections and distinct interpretations by the people. Rather than teaching only about Sacred Scripture, popular Catholicism catechizes with Scripture by making the text alive and relevant to people's present experience.

Third, popular Catholicism is renewed by a continuous reading of Sacred Scripture in light of the Church's experience here and now. Popular Catholicism should neither be considered as the ultimate interpretation of Sacred Scripture nor the only way to make the biblical message relevant in the life of the people. However, its role in fostering Christian spirituality among Latinos/as must be duly affirmed. Its pedagogical character is enhanced by renewed contact with the sacred text in the liturgy, catechesis, and theological reflection. Women and men involved in catechetical ministry have a responsibility to acquaint people and communities for whom popular Catholicism is a central element in their spiritual lives with the suggested guidelines for reading the Bible with the Church.

Sacred Scripture and popular Catholicism are intimately related in the various catechetical processes that nurture the life of faith of U.S. Latino/a Catholics. Popular Catholicism is in itself the people's way of making their faith a tradition, not unrelated or adversarial to official efforts of interpretation of God's Word, yet distinct and complementary: a true expression of the Church's *sensus fidelium*.

Reading Sacred Scripture in Small Communities

The experience of small ecclesial communities is not foreign to Latino/a Catholics. Reading the Bible, reflecting about faith in the everyday, and celebrating God's Word in small communities has been a hallmark of the Latino/a Catholic experience in Latin America and in the United States. Needless to say, this is how Christianity thrived in its beginnings, has done in missionary contexts, and continues to be sustained in many parts of the world.

Sacred Scripture has been and remains at the heart of Latino/a small ecclesial communities. Most of these small church cells (also called base communities in some parts of the world) gather around Sacred Scripture to hear the Word of God proclaimed, to pray with it, and to see how the sacred text sheds light into people's particular circumstances. The exercise of reading Sacred Scripture in small communities is powerful and transformative at least in four ways: (1) it empowers us to access Sacred Scripture as a text that speaks to us in the here and now of everyday life; (2) it introduces us to a transformative dialogue with God's Word in the Bible that invites to conversion; (3) it fosters a deeper understanding of God's divine revelation; and (4) it creates communion among those who read the text together with the Church. This experience is pedagogical in nature and, consequently, every catechetical effort among Latinos/as should look at small ecclesial communities as privileged spaces to hand on the faith of the Church.

Recent Church statements make reference to the great value of small ecclesial communities in the evangelization of Latinos/as. *Encuentro and Mission: A Renewed Pastoral Framework for Hispanic Ministry* (2002), a pastoral statement by the bishops of the United States refocusing the Church's commitment to Hispanic ministry in this country, looks favorably to small ecclesial communities. The statement affirms that these communities "have been and continue to be a valuable expression of the evangelization efforts of the Church";[40] they are effective for promoting leadership formation.[41] Citing an earlier document on the value of these communities, *Encuentro and Mission* corroborates that when "solidly rooted in Scripture, church tradition, and Hispanic religiosity, small church communities constitute a new moment in the Church's self-understanding, epitomizing the celebration and proclamation of the Church."[42] In 2007 the bishops of Latin America and the Caribbean met in Aparecida, Brazil, for their Fifth General Conference. Some bishops and leaders from the United States participated in the gathering. Their presence was very significant, considering that millions of Latino/a Catholics now living in the United States were formed within the structures of the Church in Latin America and bring that experience as a part of our gift to the Church in the United States. *Aparecida* speaks of small communities as "schools that have helped form Christians committed to their faith, disciples and missionaries of the Lord."[43] These communities are instrumental to "enable the people to have access to greater knowledge of the Word of God, social commitment in the name of the Gospel, the emergence of new lay services, and education of the faith of adults."[44]

Indeed, these are not the only everyday moments of encounter with the sacred where catechesis and Word of God meet as part of the experience of U.S. Latino/a Catholics. Our goal in this section has been to assert that there are unique moments within the Latino/a Catholic experience that have a significant catechetical value and that these must be seen as privileged opportunities to foster a forming and transforming encounter with God's Word. For catechists working with Latino/a Catholics, these are great resources to advance the ministry of sharing faith.

Pathways and Challenges:
An Agenda for Further Research

Without a doubt, God's Word mediated through Sacred Scripture is not foreign to the lives and experiences of Latinos/as. Our people are thirsty for God's Word and catechesis is a privileged context to satisfy such thirst. As I approach the end of this reflection on the relationship between Sacred Scripture and catechesis in the context of the Latino/a Catholic experience in the United States, I must briefly address a number of challenges that require our immediate attention. Given the limitations of space, I will simply outline five situations that for catechetical leaders emerge as signs of hope accompanied by some signs of concern. I see these as situations that are simultaneously pathways and challenges.

First, the number of Latino/a Catholics approaching Sacred Scripture through prayer groups is positively high. One major reason for this trend is the growing participation of Latinos/as in Charismatic Renewal groups and the central role that the Bible plays in them. It is estimated that the Charismatic Renewal is the single most influential form of ecclesial spirituality among Latino/a Catholics in the United States.[45] *Nevertheless*, empirical observation among scholars and church leaders indicates that many, perhaps most, leaders and catechists in these groups are poorly prepared in the study of Sacred Scripture. The immediate consequences of such lack of preparation are erroneous readings and interpretations of the Bible, as well as a tendency to read the sacred text in fundamentalistic ways.

Second, most Latino/a Catholics living in the United States are in continuous interaction with non-Catholic Christians, for whom Sacred Scripture is the only norm of faith. Such interaction often happens in ordinary life moments like work, school, or neighborhood events. Oftentimes the encounter happens in religious contexts. Such contact requires a better understanding of Sacred Scripture to enter into conversation with these Christian women and men. At the same time, it is important that Latino/a Catholics learn how to dialogue with other Christians and take advantage of the fact that we share the sacred text in common. Latino/a theologians, fortunately, have taken gigantic steps in this conversation and many have developed great resources illustrating this interaction. *Nevertheless*, ecumenical dialogue is rarely part of the catechetical agenda among most Latino/a Catholics, particularly in parishes and similar pastoral settings. Very seldom do the work and insights from Latino/a scholars on ecumenism make it to Latinos/as in catechetical programs. The majority of immigrants from Latin America (millions!) lack a culture of ecumenical dialogue; many still read the Bible and think of non-Catholic Christians in pre-Vatican II terms. To this we must add that most guidelines for ecumenical dialogue available to Catholics often address the relationship with so-called historical churches but say little about how to engage in conversation with groups such as Mormons, Jehovah's Witnesses, and Pentecostals, the groups most commonly present in Latino/a neighborhoods. Some of these groups are considered Christians, others pseudo-Christians. Yet all of them have some connection to Sacred Scripture.

Third, Catholicism in the second part of the twentieth century developed an increasing awareness about the correct readings of Sacred Scripture vis-à-vis the Jews.[46] This awareness is part of a commendable effort to better dialogue with non-Christian women and men in the world. Recent ecclesial documents call for a renewed catechesis that educates the faithful to value the contributions of the Jewish experience in salvation history and to preclude any forms of anti-Semitism.[47] This ecclesial consciousness about reading correctly the Jewish experience in the New Testament and today has led to great steps in the Jewish–Christian dialogue, and catechists have certainly been at the forefront of this dialogue. *Nevertheless*, catechesis among Latino/a Catholics overall has fallen short of building on these developments. Two main reasons can be adduced for such a situation: one, the number of Jews who are Hispanic is very small both in the United States and in Latin America. This has prevented Latinos/as from being more aware of the Jewish experience and participating in mutually enriching dialogue with Jews in their communities. Two, many Latinos/as still hold prejudiced views about Jewish people given their "cultural Catholicism" from Latin America[48]—even among Protestants. We are exposed to very few opportunities in Latino/a communities to participate in Jewish–Christian conversations, which require balanced readings of Sacred Scripture as well as solid theological training.

Fourth, the rapid development of technological resources has provided almost unlimited access to Sacred Scripture online, by means of portable devices, radio, television, sound recordings, and print. Along with this unrestrained access to Sacred Scripture, Latino/a Catholics read commentaries, interpretations, analyses, and studies, in English and Spanish (and sometimes other languages), that become available to us in the same way that the sacred text does. *Nevertheless*, it is important that catechesis provides Latino/a Catholics with the appropriate criteria to evaluate these resources. Not all translations of the Bible available online are accurate, not all commentaries and studies affirm the rich tradition of the Church, not all readings lead to a better understanding of Sacred Scripture as read in the ecclesial community. It is imperative that catechetical moments address this challenge by introducing, correcting, and guiding the reading of Sacred Scripture in light of contemporary scholarship and according to the wisdom of the Church.

Fifth, many materials for the study of Sacred Scripture used in U.S. Hispanic contexts usually become available as resources brought from Spanish-speaking countries or as translations from works in English. These are very helpful, as they serve to introduce Latinos/as to the sacred text and to formal study. *Nevertheless*, resources that are imported from outside the United States, or those that are literally translated from resources in English developed in cultural contexts that reflect little or nothing of the Latino/a experience, can be significantly limited. As we saw above, there is considerable value to "reading the Bible in Spanish" and to engaging Sacred Scripture in light of our own particular experience. The Bible is not merely a study text or a reference book where moral norms and doctrines are spelled out for us to extract without any interpretive effort. The Bible as God's Word in written form speaks to us as Latinos/as, reads us as Latinos/as, and interprets who we are as Latino/as. We must develop and use catechetical resources that engage Sacred Scripture in ways that do precisely that. For this we must foster increasing dialogue between Latino/a theologians and Scripture scholars with Latino/a catechists and anyone else who catechizes in Latino/a contexts; we must empower Latinos/as to develop materials that reflect the particularity of our experience; we must creatively envision pedagogies that bring this experience to life in the various ways in which we teach and learn.

These five pathways and their corresponding challenges have a direct impact on how Sacred Scripture and catechesis interrelate as we educate U.S. Latinos/as in the faith. Further research is needed in each area to better assess the status of these challenges and to determine the most appropriate responses to them. May this be an invitation to catechetical leaders, ministers, theologians, other scholars, and ecclesial and academic institutions to appropriate resources to advance this kind of research, as well as to support the women and men who are leading the way in this effort. Exploring the relationship between Bible and catechesis in the context of the Latino/a Catholic experience as we have done in this essay is one example of how such a project might evolve.

⁓

Notes

1. Cf. "The Didache or The Teaching of the Twelve Apostles," in *The Didache, The Epistle of Barnabas, The Epistle and the Martyrdom of St. Polycarp, The Fragments of Papias, and the Epistle to Diognetus*, trans. James A. Kleist, Ancient Christian Writers: The Works of the Fathers in Translation (New York: Newman Press, 1948), 1–25.
2. See, for instance, the collection of baptismal homilies from several fourth-century Fathers compiled by Edward Yarnold, *The Awe-Inspiring Rites of Initiation: The Origins of the RCIA*, 2nd ed. (Collegeville, MN: Liturgical Press, 1994), 67–250.
3. Cf. *De Doctrina Christiana* and *De Catechizandis Rudibus*.
4. Of particular interest for Catholic scholars and educators is Pius XII's encyclical *Divino Afflante Spiritu*, published in 1943, in which contemporary methods of biblical interpretation were recognized as valid resources to better read and interpret Sacred Scripture in today's context.
5. Cf. Dogmatic Constitution on Divine Revelation, *Dei Verbum*, § 6 and 10, http://www.vatican.va/archive/hist_councils/ii_vatican_council/documents/vat-ii_const_19651118_dei-verbum_en.html.
6. *Dei Verbum*, § 10.
7. Cf. Paul VI, *Evangelii Nuntiandi*, § 17, and John Paul II, *Catechesi Tradendae*, § 18.
8. For a very accessible guide and reflection on the place of Sacred Scripture in the Church, see Daniel J. Harrington, *How Do Catholics Read the Bible?* (Lanham, MD: Rowman & Littlefield, 2005).
9. *Catechesi Tradendae*, § 27; cf. United States Catholic Conference of Bishops (USCCB), *National Directory for Catechesis* (Washington, DC: United States Conference of Catholic Bishops, 2005), 53.

10. Cf. *Dei Verbum*, § 10.

11. *National Directory for Catechesis*, 16B.

12. Ibid., 18.

13. Cf. United States Conference of Catholic Bishops, *Co-Workers in the Vineyard of the Lord: A Resource for Guiding the Development of Lay Ecclesial Ministry* (Washington, DC: USCCB, 2005), 55.

14. A working definition.

15. *National Directory for Catechesis*, 24B.

16. Cf. *Dei Verbum*, § 24.

17. *National Directory for Catechesis*, 24B. This passage makes reference to the document "The Interpretation of the Bible in the Church," § 39, prepared by the Pontifical Biblical Commission in 1993.

18. *Dei Verbum*, § 21.

19. Cf. *National Directory for Catechesis*, 20.

20. Ibid., 48E.

21. Ibid., 48D.

22. Ibid., 48Λ.

23. Ibid., 35D.

24. Ibid., 24C; See also Congregation for the Clergy, *General Directory for Catechesis*, 120, available at http://www.vatican.va/roman_curia /congregations/cclergy/documents/rc_con_ccatheduc_doc_17041998 _directory-for-catechesis-en.html.

25. Cf. *National Directory for Catechesis*, 24C.

26. Ibid.

27. The sacred should not be reduced to something otherworldly or something radically transcendent or even something contrary to human experience. The sacred is the perceived presence of God in the realm of life, history, and nature. It is what enables women and men to see the world as sacramental. For Christians, the sacredness or sacramentality of life, history, and the world is mediated through the salvific mystery of Jesus Christ.

28. *Dei Verbum*, § 21.

29. Synod of Bishops, XII Ordinary General Assembly, "The Word of God in the Life and Mission of the Church," *Instrumentum Laboris*, Vatican City, 2008, § 13, http://www.vatican.va/roman_curia/synod/documents /rc_synod_doc_20080511_instrlabor-xii-assembly_en.html. At the time of the writing of this essay Catholics still await the Apostolic Exhortation that usually follows this type of ecclesiastical gathering. The *Instrumentum*

Laboris nonetheless is as a reliable resource that provides a good sense of what points the papal exhortation will highlight.

30. *Dei Verbum*, § 22.

31. Cf. "The Word of God in the Life and Mission of the Church," *Instrumentum Laboris*, § 38. For further reflection on the value of reading Sacred Scripture in prayer, see Demetrius R. Dumm, *Praying the Scriptures* (Collegeville, MN: Liturgical Press, 2003), particularly chapter 5, where he speaks of *Lectio Divina*.

32. Cf. Ada María Isasi-Díaz, *En la Lucha / In the Struggle: Elaborating a Mujerista Theology*, 10th anniversary ed. (Minneapolis: Fortress, 2003), 89–92.

33. Virgilio P. Elizondo, "The Treasure of Hispanic Faith," in *Mestizo Worship: A Pastoral Approach to Liturgical Ministry*, ed. Virgilio P. Elizondo and Timothy M. Matovina (Collegeville, MN: Liturgical Press, 1998), 75.

34. For an interesting analysis of how U.S. Latino/a Catholics see the sacraments in the Church in light of their cultural and religious experience, see James Empereur and Eduardo Fernández, *La Vida Sacra: Contemporary Hispanic Sacramental Theology* (Lanham, MD: Rowman & Littlefield, 2006).

35. Justo L. González, *Santa Biblia: The Bible through Hispanic Eyes* (Nashville: Abingdon, 1996), 14.

36. Ibid., 115.

37. Cf. Orlando O. Espín, "Traditioning: Culture, Daily Life and Popular Religion, and Their Impact on Christian Tradition," in *Futuring Our Past: Explorations in the Theology of Tradition*, ed. Orlando O. Espín and Gary Macy (Maryknoll, NY: Orbis Books, 2006), 8.

38. Of particular help in reflecting about the relationship between some expressions of popular Catholicism and Sacred Scripture is the work of C. Gilbert Romero, *Hispanic Devotional Piety: Tracing the Biblical Roots* (Maryknoll, NY: Orbis Books, 1991).

39. Cf. Justo L. González, *Mañana: Christian Theology from a Hispanic Perspective* (Nashville: Abingdon, 1996), 80.

40. United States Conference of Catholic Bishops (USCCB), *Encuentro and Mission: A Renewed Pastoral Framework for Hispanic Ministry* (Washington, DC: United States Conference of Catholic Bishops, 2002), 41, http://www .usccb.org/hispanicaffairs/encuentromission.shtml.

41. Ibid., 40.

42. Ibid., 42. The document refers to the following source: USCCB Committee on Hispanic Affairs, *Communion and Mission: A Guide for Bishops and Pastoral Leaders on Small Church Communities* (Washington, DC: USCCB, 1995), 25.

43. Consejo Episcopal Latinoamericano, Aparecida Concluding Document (Bogotá, Colombia: Conferencia Episcopal Latinoamericana, 2007), 178.

44. Ibid. Cf. Puebla Concluding Document, 629.

45. Pew Hispanic Center and Pew Forum on Religion & Public Life, *Changing Faiths: Latinos and the Transformation of American Religion* (Washington, DC: Pew Research Center, 2007), 27–38, http://pewhispanic.org/files/reports/75.pdf.

46. Cf. Second Vatican Council, "Declaration on the Relation of the Church to Non-Christian Religions," *Nostra Aetate* (1965).

47. Cf. *Nostra Aetate*, § 4; "The Interpretation of the Bible in the Church," chapter 4, A, 3.

48. Cf. Tom W. Smith, *Hispanic Attitudes toward Jews: Report* (New York: American Jewish Committee, 2007), https.//www.policyarchive.org/handle/10207/11858.

5

"He Walked Along with Them"

Las Posadas, the Via Crucis,
and Parish Biblical Proclamation

Arturo J. Pérez Rodríguez

~

Introduction

As the title of this article suggests, "He walked along with them," we have been personally invited to be the "them" of the title. Let me begin by sharing with you two personal memories and one confession of negligence which highlight my part of this "them."

For many people the *camino a Emaús* Scripture evokes the familiar image of two disciples leaving Jerusalem after Jesus's crucifixion and burial. On the road to Emmaus, a stranger, whose appearance is apparently unnoticed, interrupts their conversation and begins asking questions about what has happened. An emotional dialogue follows. Words like *sad*, *gloomy*, and *surprise* characterize the encounter. Jesus's identity is recognized at the end of the journey in the famous phrase "in the breaking of bread." My memory of this phrase is a painful one. It was the time when the Archdiocese of Chicago closed many parishes and schools. I was the pastor of a trilingual parish which was planning our centennial celebration when we entered into a discernment process with the surrounding parishes. The discernment process was long, arduous, and hurtful as neighboring communities had to decide which parishes would remain open and which would not. Our parish was canonically eliminated. It was a death experience for all of us who were involved. I remember the parishioners vocal disappointment and anger when we were not able to celebrate the hundredth anniversary of the parish's foundation.

Once the decision had been publicly announced as to who would close and who would remain open, a stranger, sent from the Archdiocese, came to talk to our staff. She began our meeting by reading the Emmaus narrative. After reading it she asked a simple question, "Can you share with me the story of these past months?" Her question took me by surprise. It was the first time during the discernment process of meetings and discussions that anyone had come to ask us how we felt, in other words to simply walk with us in a way that was personal, caring, and healing. She listened attentively to each of our stories. We vented our feelings with words like confusion, anger, frustration, doubt, and sorrow. When she left she was no longer a stranger. Now whenever I read this text the painful memory of that moment returns. The Word of God by its very nature evokes and provokes memories, yet it never rids those memories of the feelings that they contain.

We can all say that the proclamation of the Word of God has power, but it is not until we unite personal experiences of that Word, not until we are confronted and confounded with the Real Presence of the Lord in the Word that we come into contact and touch the life that the Word contains. Like a stranger, it waits for us to share our stories. This involves a risk of revealing ourselves.

In this essay we encounter God's Living Word, God's Real Presence, in two Hispanic religious traditions, Las Posadas and the Via Crucis. Let me take a risk by sharing a second memory. This one concerns the Via Crucis Viviente, the Living Stations of the Cross as I experienced it in San Antonio, Texas. I was invited to attend and reflect on the Holy Week services as they were annually celebrated at San Fernando Cathedral by Father Virgilio Elizondo, who was the rector of the cathedral at the time.

San Fernando Cathedral had a reputation for successfully integrating the religious practices of Hispanic popular Catholicism into the Roman Catholic official liturgy of the Church, thus serving as a working example of liturgical inculturation. It is what I call a mestizo liturgy. This is an experience of the official liturgy that is translated into the religious life experience of the people that celebrate it.

The Good Friday service typically called the Via Crucis, or the Stations of the Cross, reenacts the last hours of Christ's life. It begins with his trial before Pontius Pilate, moves on with the scourging, carrying his cross, his meeting his mother, and culminating with his crucifixion.

The Via Crucis reenactment is an all-day community religious ceremony. Although there are the regular holiday tourists, local new reporters, and curious bystanders, the majority of people who participate see this event as a public act of faith that proclaims the Gospel of Christ's Passion and death. The service begins in the early morning at the local *mercado* and ends after the sun has set at the cathedral. The procession walks down the street actually named Via Dolorosa, loosely translated as the Road of Sorrow. After Christ's crucifixion, the ceremony concludes with the Pésame a la Virgen, the customary wake service with Mary, Christ's mother, and finally the Santo Entierro, Christ's burial.

This was certainly not my first experience of celebrating the Via Crucis. As a parish priest I have actively helped plan and celebrate these services. This particular event was different for me because this time I was invited and privileged to take part and experience it not as a planner, implementer, or celebrant but rather as a participant observer. I was to simply be one of the crowd. Again I say "privileged" because I was free from any and all obligations other than to be present, to witness, and to live the experience.

I remember thinking that the sunny San Antonio weather was perfect for this kind of event. The man who took the role of Christ was condemned by Pilate. He was scourged and mocked by the Roman soldiers. Theatrical blood stained his clothes. The heavy rough wooden cross was placed on his shoulders. He began to walk down the street surrounded by Roman soldiers, the jeering Jerusalem townspeople, tourists, and his faithful followers. I took my place in the procession as part of the crowd that followed Jesus on his way to Calvary, which was located on the front steps of the cathedral. Everything seemed so commonplace to me. What was so ordinary for me changed dramatically in one spontaneous moment.

As I was walking behind Christ, being pushed and crowded by many people who surrounded me, I by chance looked down on the cobblestone street and noticed a vibrant red spatter of blood, shimmering and reflecting in the San Antonio sun. I tried to avoid stepping into it. My mind told me this was artificial stage blood. What my mind and I would dare to say my heart—did was to pause and instantly remember all the times that I had witnessed blood splatters on the streets of the parishes where I have served. Blood staining the streets came from traffic accidents and drive-by shootings. Memories of visiting bleeding, wounded teenagers moaning in hospital emergency rooms flashed before me. I remembered hearing the distraught mothers and families crying and asking "Why my son?" I recognized this fresh blood on this San Antonio street.

This was no longer a staged drama but a personal experience of my own anger at innocent suffering, of my frustration at what has become common street violence, of my own feeling of being unable to change anything, of being a voiceless spectator at a gross injustice. So much can happen in a moment of instant recognition. I looked up and I saw Christ walking before me. I felt I witnessed the living Word of God walking the street of the *Via Dolorosa*. Needless to say, I was not expecting to have this kind of experience. I grew hungry to live the rest of whatever might happen that day.

Religious experiences like Las Posadas and the Via Crucis are the links, the bridges that bring to life the Scriptures for our parish communities. What we share in common as ministers and community is the way these two events incarnate the Paschal Mystery; the life, death, and resurrection of Christ. We witness this Mystery coming to life in the lives of the people that we are privileged to serve. For many people *these practices* are the way that faith is lived, the way that the Word is proclaimed, the way that the Word is preached, and the way that we find hope as we together, ministers and community, confront the challenges that we face.

We have heard that confession is good for the soul. My confession of negligence is that I hardly ever thought about anyone who was in jail, nor about what impact incarceration would have on their families or upon the victims, prior to my first visit to a jail six years ago. I was sad for the families that were touched by the accused and sometimes wondered how they would live through their heartache. I was glad that it was not me or someone I knew. The victims and the accused were names printed in the newspapers or heard on the television. Now as the director of Kolbe House, the Archdiocese of Chicago's ministry to those in jail and prison, I filter all my experiences through the lives of those who are incarcerated in Cook County Jail, their families, and the victims of criminal behavior. This detention facility houses roughly ten thousand men and women. My primary ministerial role is to visit the men housed in the maximum-security or "super max" division of the jail.

I have become the stranger open to whatever those in front of me want to share. I simply walk with them and listen to the stories of their lives. I have learned from the men in the super max division of county jail to value the Word of God in new ways. I have put names on the biblical passages of Las Posadas as people wait to see if they will be deported once they have been released from jail. I have seen the face of the Via Crucis Christ both falsely accused and unjustly sentenced in the men with whom I pray. I witness the suffering of the innocent Christ who bears the burden from the criminal behavior of others. I confess that looking down at the streets is no longer an ordinary event. It has become a contemplative experience of the Word of God as it is lived in the lives of the people that I serve both in and out of jail. Las Posadas and the Via Crucis stir my memory.

All of us have memories that are stirred by the Word of God. My purpose here is to highlight the living word of God in two particular religious traditions, Las Posadas and the Via Crucis. These traditions mark the beginning and the ending of Christ's earthly existence, forming a living dialogue of faith between God and his people. I would like to first place Las Posadas and the Via Crucis into the context of Hispanic popular Catholicism and then reflect on how these traditions began. We can then see the pastoral meaning they hold for our parish communities. I will conclude with questions for us as ministers of the Word and a personal note of how these two celebrations reveal the presence of Christ the Criminal.

Hispanic Popular Catholicism

"*Soy creyente pero no practicante*" is a common response to the question of "why don't you come to Mass?" Roughly translated, this Hispanic saying means that "I am a believer but do not necessarily practice my faith." The popular understanding is that this person believes in the presence of God, prays and even defends the Catholic Church, but does not necessarily practice their faith according to the rules and rubrics of the Catholic Church, for example, by attending Mass every Sunday, confessing their sins at least once a year, being registered in their local parish, or even being married in Church. The various traditions that make up Hispanic popular Catholicism are practices and expressions of faith. It is the religion of the people rooted in the faith of the Catholic Church.

The Third General Conference of the Latin American Episcopate held in 1979 in Puebla, Mexico, defines popular Catholicism in its final document:

> By religion of the people, popular religiosity, or popular piety, we mean the whole complex of underlying beliefs rooted in God, the basic attitudes that flow from these beliefs, and the expressions that manifest them. It is the form of cultural life that religion takes on among the people. In its most characteristic cultural form, the religion of the Latin American people is an expression of the Catholic faith. It is a people's Catholicism. (no. 444)[1]

This document goes on to state that it is marked by worship of the suffering Christ, processions, novenas (no. 912),[2] with an openness to the Word of God, an attitude of prayer and sense of friendship, charity, and family unity (no. 913).[3] Popular Catholicism, this document states, is the cultural matrix (no. 445)[4] of this people. We can say that popular Catholicism is the religious expression of Hispanic spirituality.

From a pastoral perspective I would say that popular Catholicism is the way the majority of our Hispanic Catholic community belongs and identifies with the Church. These religious practices have no prerequisites. These practices do not rely on, nor are they necessarily governed by, ordained clergy to organize or implement them. They are guided and determined by the people who gather to celebrate them. They are inclusive rather than exclusive. Simply attending, being personally present, is the way that a person practices his or her belief in God. The larger than normal attendance at the annual Our Lady of Guadalupe masses, Ash Wednesday, Palm Sunday, and Good Friday services attests to this.

I limit myself here to Las Posadas and the Via Crucis as examples of biblical proclamations of the Word of God for the Hispanic community. I am indebted to Mark Francis for providing us with a framework in which to view these two particular religious dramas from the Hispanic perspective.[5] He notes that three of the most obvious characteristics of Hispanic worship can be summed up by four adjectives: visual, processional, personal, and sensual.

Visual

There is a Spanish proverb that explains the highly visual nature of Hispanic liturgical practice: "*Ojos que no ven, corazón que no siente*" (the heart cannot feel what the eyes do not see). Communal worship in the Hispanic context is intensely visual and dramatic: Seeing and walking with Mary and Joseph as they seek lodging in Bethlehem streets, watching Jesus and his disciples enter Jerusalem on Palm Sunday, observing the Lord washing the feet of his disciples, suffering in the garden, being condemned, being tortured and crucified, seeing the joyful reunion of mother and Resurrected Son on Easter morning in *el santo encuentro*, draw all who are present into this religious event in such a way that the community is able to *feel* what is proclaimed in the Scriptures. The Word lives.

The dramatically visual and popular side of the Hispanic popular religion in many ways reaches its climax during the year in the *Via Crucis Viviente*, the living Stations of the Cross, when parishioners reenact Jesus' final hours. No one can be left indifferent when confronted with this reenactment of Christ's condemnation and painful progress to Golgotha. The Gospel and its truths are proclaimed in ways that stir the emotions and not just the intellect.

Processional

Hispanic popular religion is also very processional and public.[6] The dramatic and visual presentations of Jesus' last days are evoked in the liturgies of Las Posadas and Holy Week. In fact "walking with" becomes a metaphor for the way in which God accompanies us in life. It is a spiritual experience for the believer. Physically walking—in procession, through the neighborhood, in the church—with other members of the faith community largely sums up the sociocentric nature of Hispanic popular religion. While these practices are intensely personal, their power and meaning derive from the fact that they are done with others who are our companions on the journey of life. We are never alone. Walking out into our neighborhood's streets sanctifies, makes them holy, and publicly proclaims our faith. The sacred and the secular are no longer two different realities but one unified place where the Word of God is lived.

Personal

At no other time in the liturgical year do the ultimate questions of human existence—in Christ's birth and death, in his crucifixion—present themselves so forcefully and with such unity. This unity is prayerfully considered through the intense identification with the people in these Gospel events, with Mary, Joseph, Jesus, his disciples, and the community members who walk with them. The dialogue of Las Posadas involves someone asking for a place to stay and being turned away. This dialogue stirs the memory and feelings of rejection of people who, after waiting in what seems to be endless lines, filling out numerous bureaucratic forms, are then summarily rejected and treated as nonpersons. The death of Jesus is a calamity for the whole Hispanic community that readily sees in the death of the Savior the death of so many who die before their time, due to gang violence, drunk driving, or spontaneous revenge. The identification with the Sorrowful Mary is for but one more mother among so many others who grieve for their children. It makes the *Pésame a la Virgen*, or wake service for Mary, all the more touching. As they would for any other mother who has tragically lost a child, the community goes to church to accompany her in grief.

The Spanish phrase most often heard at wakes in the Mexican community, "*Te acompaño en tus sentimientos*" (I accompany you in your sorrow), sums up the sense of Good Friday in the Hispanic community. *Acompañamiento* (accompaniment, companionship) is key to these events. It is an understanding, a remembering of each person's experience of suffering and death that forms a community's pain. Everyone comes together to share the grief and offer the healing gesture of his or her presence in the most terrible of life's passages. To these three important characteristics I would add one more: sensual.

Sensual

Sensuality implies a use of the five senses, yet the more popular understanding makes it a word loaded with sexual images, fantasies, and side issues. The standard definition of sensuality is "relating to or consisting in the gratification of the senses."[7] This simple phrase speaks volumes about the way the human body is viewed. This is a very limited understanding, especially when it is considered in reference to the liturgy and Hispanic popular Catholicism, which depends on sensuality to communicate its message and makes its connection with the lives of the people who gather to celebrate it. Liturgical symbols, including the Word of God, are to be felt. Sensuality speaks to the whole human experience in a given moment. We cannot deny that sexuality is part of sensuality. No liturgy or prayerful experience of God is asexual.

The Hispanic tradition is rooted in the indigenous perspective that sees harmony within all areas of nature and therefore within human nature itself. The four great elements—fire, earth, wind, and water—are connected through a fifth element, the Spirit of life. There is no separation in creation. The sensual nature of our body is the bridge that connects us with the Creator. To say that the Word became flesh (John 1:14) is to state that the proclamation of the Word of God is to be heard, seen, smelled, touched, and tasted for it to be understood. It needs to be felt, experienced openly and publicly.

These four characteristics—visual, processional, personal, and sensual—provide a framework, a cultural context, a living translation from which the Posadas and the Via Crucis become the living Word of God and proclamation of God's Real Presence within the lives of our people that celebrate them. This is not a dialogue confined by ecclesiastical rubric or theological opinion, but rather a personal encounter of faith that unites past memories and feelings with the Living Presence of God. The Word casts a light on this encounter and waits for a response.

The Vulnerability of God

Las Posadas and the Via Crucis are two of the most popular celebrations for the Hispanic community. One reason for this is that they center on a particular Scriptural image of Christ. They focus the community's attention on the vulnerability of God as found in the person of Jesus. This is a paradoxical image of a vulnerable human Jesus and omnipotent God, the Savior of the world. I say paradoxical because the image of the poverty of a child born to homeless parents and the figure of an innocent, powerless condemned man are different from images of the omnipotent titles used for God in the prayers of the Roman Missal. "Almighty God and Father of light . . . Father in heaven, creator of all . . . All powerful and unseen God . . . Almighty and eternal God" are examples of the titles directed to God in the prayers for the Christmas season and the Good Friday General Intercessions.

The paradox continues within the Hispanic community. The human and the divine are incarnated not only in the person of Christ but also in the life of the people who identify with him. We are vulnerable and limited when it comes to parish rules and requirements for receiving the sacraments or practicing our religious traditions. We seem to be so powerless while we confront the ecclesiastical and political worlds in which we live. Yet we are the Church, the Body of Christ that brings hope and healing, that continues to be faithful in spite of all the obstacles that we face. This relationship between Christ and people speaks of the mutual need we have for one another. In Las Posadas and Via Crucis Jesus needs us for protection, help, and defense. We need Jesus's help to sustain us in our vulnerable moments. We are *carnales* to the person of Jesus. This mutual vulnerability is what draws us to Christ and makes him believable. He speaks our language and knows our lives.

The Origin of Las Posadas

Danza is inaccurately translated into English as "dance." *Danza* is a religious movement, a physical, sensual expression of a person's connection with the divine. It is prayer in movement not necessarily confined to particular individuals but rather acted out by the entire community. *La danza* is an essential part of any indigenous religious ceremony. In 1528, barely seven years after the conquest, Fray Pedro de Gante noted that the religious practices of the people centered in song and dance in front of their gods. In 1541 Fray Toribio de Motolinia writes in his memoirs that in the city of Tlaxcala, during the Christmas celebrations, the people entered the church dancing, singing, and carrying flowers.

It is worth noting that the corral or atrium of the church was the locus of many liturgical processions. In addition, by the late fifteenth century *corral* also meant "theater," and this sense of the word should not be undervalued. "It has much to do with the catechesis and the theatricalized liturgy. . . . Its *posa* chapels, which acted as stational chapels for processions, show signs of having had an altar or a shelf that functioned as a temporary altar for resting objects."[8]

The word *posada* we know means "lodging," yet in the sense that it was used by the early missionaries it was also a sacred public outdoor space and place used during processions for prayer. A unity of prayer and faith existed inside and the outside of the church building. Both were linked through the activity of what was taking place.

Las Posadas were begun as a response from the Augustinian missionary priests to replace the annual indigenous Aztec spiritual practice in honor of the god Huitzilopochtli. This annual Aztec event took place in December. Fray Diego de Soria is attributed with beginning Las Posadas ceremony in an organized way after he obtained from Pope Sixtus V a document authorizing "*Misas de Aguinaldo,*" nine pre-Christmas masses, in 1586. The masses began in the parish church of Acolman, located forty kilometers northeast of Mexico City. They were basically a novena of masses commemorating the nine months of Mary's pregnancy, interspersed with Scripture passages and short dramatic scenes that were celebrated in the atrium of the church. We could say that this is an enacted catechesis that prepared the people for the birth of the Christian Savior. The masses eventually traveled from the church's atrium and proceeded each day to different surrounding chapels that came under the jurisdiction of the local parish church. These celebrations were seen as festive moments, with music adapted to the ceremony, fireworks, and piñatas.

What these particular early missionaries did was to take into account the natural ways and natural places that the indigenous people expressed their faith. They translated the Word of God into the language of the people. By language I do not mean the words but the more expansive, inclusive meaning of language where verbal and physical gestures and the emotional, intellectual, and spiritual all meet. These became the living translations of the pre-Christmas and Christmas Scriptures. Scripture was experienced in ways that people felt its connection to their lives. The effect was immediate insofar as Las Posadas became popular in other parts of Mexico.

The Origins of the Via Crucis

We know that the earliest Christian communities were more interested in staying alive in the midst of persecution than cultivating devotion to any sacred place. Their identity with the Paschal Mystery came in the form of martyrdom. When the Church gained its freedom after 313 CE, pilgrims began visiting the places where Christ suffered his Passion and death. The faithful could come and touch these holy places. To walk the *Via Sacra,* the Holy Road, was the new way to share in the Lord's last moments. Stations were constructed at these sacred places and appropriate liturgies were designed so that pilgrims would stop and pray at the very site where Christ suffered and died. These stations became the popular way of connecting with the pivotal moments of Christ's life on a personal level.

The saying "Preach always. If necessary use words" is attributed to St. Francis of Assisi (1182–1226 CE) the founder of the Franciscan order. His was a time when the official liturgy was celebrated by the professional prayer persons, namely, the clergy. Its rubrics and ritual were handled by the clergy with the community as passive observers. I would venture to say it was outside of the life experience of the ordinary people who came to witness it. It was in this reality that Francis grew up.

Francis is noted as the innovator of the Christmas manger scene and the Stations of the Cross, which visualized and dramatized the Scriptural account of Christ's humble birth and his Passion and death. It was a creative way of having the people pray and feel a connection to the liturgy of the church that was being celebrated by the clergy. Francis centered his own spirituality on the suffering of Christ.

In 1342 the guardianship of the *Via Sacra* was given over to the Franciscan order. The exact number of Stations would vary, as would the actual incidents that were portrayed down through the centuries. The practice of the Stations became popular and was brought to different areas of the world by the Franciscans. I am indebted to the pivotal work of Jaime Lara, who cites the work of the Franciscans in Mexico:

> The Way of the Cross—an imitation of the Via Dolorosa of Jerusalem—was one such invention transported from the Holy Land to Iberia in the fifteenth century and thence to the new world. In Spain the stational practice was first introduced in cities and towns that, not by chance, possessed Franciscan convents. The individual stations, *calavarios*, evolved from the *humilladero* chapels, which were the ubiquitous large crosses placed on the outskirts of towns, usually on a promontory. . . . The *Alto* of Puebla became the stage set for one such Way of the Cross.[9]

Lara goes on to state:

> Indeed erecting calvaries was one of the first tasks of the friars in Mexico. In that way, the friars relocated the hill of Golgotha in its topographically correct location: outside the (imaginary) walls of the American Jerusalem. The processional line from the town plaza to Golgotha stills acts as a *via sacra* within the cityscape [of Puebla].[10]

The Franciscan missionaries who came to Mexico in the sixteenth century were steeped in the spirituality of the Passion of Christ. The enactment of their evangelical and catechetical efforts was an expression of this spirituality.

What some missionaries did was to translate the Word of God into the life experience of the people they served. Our goal here is not to delineate the methodology of evangelization that many used but to recognize an underlying structure that already exists within the Hispanic community as it hears the Word of God proclaimed. Lara summarizes this well when he writes:

All the verbal activities, such as preaching, moral exhortations, catechesis, were aimed at bringing the Indians into liturgical action and reception of the sacraments. The Nahua converts were desperate for a cosmic order and for new rituals, and they had a passion to perform them. . . . Thus one way to appreciate the success of the evangelization of Mexico is to recognize that it provided the native peoples with a new set of metaphors, narratives, protectors, advocates, heroes and heroines, patrons and patronesses, and ritual patterns and activities—all of which allowed them to cope and coexist with the changed and changing situation.[11]

Parish Biblical Proclamation:
The Pastoral Meaning of Las Posadas
and the Via Crucis for Our Parish Communities

I return to the San Antonio experience of the Via Crucis as a way of bridging Hispanic popular Catholicism with the blood that I saw on the streets of the *Via Dolorosa*. I confess that I was awed by that moment. It is still a live memory that continues to inspire and yet haunt me each Good Friday. It was not until I read Nathan Mitchell's words that I came to grasp more fully, appreciate more deeply what our people have long experienced: "Awe is not about us, or our preferences, or our reactions. It is the wholly unexpected irruption of God into human life—excessively, incomprehensively. Those who expect to be awed never are."[12]

The parish biblical proclamation of Las Posadas and Via Crucis is an unexpected irruption of the Presence of God into the lives of our communities. The Word is a dialogue. These two celebrations publicly act out the will and power of people to confront together the obstacles that they face in the journey of life. We are awed to be in God's Presence.

We meet the Lord face-to-face as we walk with him seeking shelter. There is little doubt that Las Posadas, the dramatization of the journey of a pregnant Mary and her husband Joseph being guided by an angel, have taken on a political overlay. This outdoor procession is linked with the exile experience of the Holy Family when they are forced to flee into Egypt to avoid persecution. It is a fact that Las Posadas have greater meaning today in the climate of the current immigration debate. Words like *Minutemen*, *factory raids*, *deportation*, *border patrols*, and *sanctuary* form the text for the Posadas script of today. Seeking shelter is a metaphor for safety and security among the most vulnerable of our society. It connects itself with anyone who is homeless. This is not just a Hispanic experience but a human one that is incarnated in lives of all peoples. Borders, be they geographical, racial, economic, or legal, only exist on paper. The people behind the words have families and personal histories.

The Via Crucis dramatized on the streets where our people live highlights the injustices that our communities face. Themes such as domestic violence, physical or sexual abuse of any person, excessive police force, gang warfare, and drive-by shootings are the modern equivalents of the Passion of Christ as he suffers among us. I see blood on the streets and know that there are faces, names, individuals who are angry, frustrated, frightened, bewildered, worried, and grieving over what has happened. The Word of God is incarnated in the lives of the people who look down at the streets and see real blood. The Via Crucis is a communal proclamation of God's irruption into the life of a city. For me, this draws me to the present-day justice system and the needs of those who are incarcerated as well as the victims of crimes.

At the beginning of this essay I stated that the proclamation of the Word of God has power, yet it is not until we unite our personal experiences of that Word, not until we are confronted and confounded with the Living Presence of the Lord in the Word, that we come into contact and touch the life that the Word contains.

Christ in the Emmaus story is a stranger who invites the two disciples that he encounters on the road to tell him their stories, to share with him what is going on in their lives, to trust him with their memories of days just past. They open up to him and let out all the raw emotions that they have experienced. I believe that we can say that these two particular Hispanic religious traditions serve as examples of Christ the stranger who continues to walk with us. He continues to invite us to reveal ourselves in trust through the ways we as Latino Catholics meet him in our devotions and practices of popular Catholicism. Two examples of these devotions are the *adoración nocturna* and the devotion to the Sacred Heart.

La adoración nocturna is a men's devotion to the Blessed Sacrament. They spend the night in vigil before the Blessed Sacrament where they pray, socialize, share Scripture, and dedicate themselves to service. Devotion to the Sacred Heart is not so much an image of the suffering Christ but rather an experience of the passionate love of Christ for those who open their hearts to him. This image calls to mind the Last Supper Scripture passage where John the apostle physically leaned upon the chest of Christ. Christ is personally met.

Popular devotions are alive. They are constantly developing and touching the realities of the people that they serve. The statue of the *Santo Niño de Atocha* is found in Plateros, Mexico. This image of a standing Child Christ dressed in medieval clothing is a popular pilgrimage destination. A similar image is found in Mexico City's cathedral. It is almost the same depiction of the Christ Child but with one difference: his left hand holds a pair of handcuffs. This Christ is called the *Santo Niño Cautivo*. He draws those who have family members, friends, or associates who have been kidnapped and are being held for ransom. This devotion is rapidly gaining popularity as kidnappings increase in Mexico.

The Emmaus narrative also reveals the stranger's frustration and surprise when he says, "How foolish you are! How slow of heart to believe all that the prophets spoke" (Lk 24:25). He goes on to reveal the meaning of the past events and relate them to the plan of God for them. Is this not what is still missing for us as pastoral agents to do for and with our parish communities today? The biblical proclamation of these religious traditions still needs reflection so as to let the Light of the Word of God illuminate the experiences that we are living today. An encounter with the Living Word of God is a dialogue of faith that is always a new encounter. I have met this stranger in a new way.

Christ the Criminal

I confessed to you that before I began my present ministry I did not think very often about jail, and even less about those who were housed there. It was the initiative of a mother, a sorrowful mother who asked me visit her son in jail, that started my journey. That visit opened me up to a new way life. Since I began visiting the detainees of Cook County Jail I filter all of my experiences through this lens. The stories of the lives of these men, both guilty and innocent by their own words or proclaimed by jury or judge, have become my central focus.

When I look at Las Posadas and the Via Crucis I am looking at the image of Christ the Criminal. The scriptural proclamation that is proclaimed in Las Posadas casts this image onto a particular and integral part of our Hispanic community. The undocumented are illegally here in the United States. According to many people in the United States, sadly even some of our fellow Catholics, they are by definition criminals. The pregnant Mary represents for some all of the free prenatal and childbirth care that is being unnecessarily provided to those who have crossed the borders. Joseph is the man who tries to provide for his family through his carpentry and construction job skills, his service jobs in restaurants and lawn care, his farm and field underpaid labor, his walking and grooming of horses at racetracks. All of this work is done in the shadows of the law, since he is illegally here in this country. He and his wife, according to the laws of this land, are criminals. The child that Mary carries is also a criminal about to be born.

The Via Crucis is the dramatization and identification with an innocent man unjustly condemned and sentenced to death. The two criminals at his side also remind us of those who are judged as being guilty of criminal behavior. Some are repentant, some are not. Christ is also found in every person who has been convicted and sentenced to serve time in prison.

The Via Crucis is a living biblical narrative that highlights the Passion of Christ the Criminal. We see in this Christ the men and women who are found in the criminal justice system under which we all live and perhaps take for granted until we are personally touched by the proverbial strong arm of the law. The improper defense provided, the subjective and political interpretation of the law, the treatment of those who are not yet found guilty yet treated as already convicted, the limited rights of families to visit those in jail and detention facilities, the inhumane punishment of long-term isolation are all incarnations of Christ present in our jails and prisons. The Via Crucis is not an annual event for the juveniles, men, and women found in our jails and prisons, but the daily life that they lead hidden away from the consciousness and sight of the greater society and in many respects from the Church community. All of our parishes have juveniles, men, and women who are incarcerated.

We must remember that the Via Crucis is also an expression of the suffering of those who are the innocent victims of crimes. Their sentence has no time limit. We suffer with them as we struggle to speak words of healing, reconciliation, and forgiveness. They are another face of the vulnerable Christ alive in our parishes. I confess that I have learned from those that I visit in jail, their families, and those who are victims of crimes not to look down at the street but rather into the eyes of those who are willing to tell me their story.

I began this essay by sharing uneasy personal memories. The prayerful expressions of Las Posadas and the Via Crucis are examples of the way the Word of God comes alive and touches me personally and the people we are all privileged to serve. I ended with the image of the Criminal Christ who also is among us, and the need for us to recognize his presence.

Conclusion: He Walked with Them

Let me conclude by stating the obvious. The biblical proclamation of Las Posadas and the Via Crucis is an encounter with the Lord who walks with us. These popular religious expressions form the dialogue between God and those who are willing to listen. We can ask: Who are Las Posadas and the Via Crucis for? They are for the people who recognize the unexpected irruption of God, the real presence of Jesus walking our streets, identifying with our vulnerabilities, and consecrating the ground on which we live.

The image of Christ the Criminal raises more questions: Who will open their doors and provide the safety and security that is being sought by both immigrants and those recently released from prison? Where do I stand as an individual and where do we stand as a parish community on the legal issues of today? Are we interested observers, curious, religious-minded tourists? Are we nonjudgmental companions with those persons most recently incarcerated?

The most poignant question for ministers of the Word to consider is: Who is the stranger who walks alongside of us and invites us to share the stories of our vulnerabilities? Like the Emmaus disciples, we are emotionally involved with events that we have lived through. We feel the burn of the Word in our hearts speaking to us. As ministers of the Word, we cannot give to others what we do not have. We cannot ask those we serve to do what we have not first done ourselves. We take the risk to spill out our hopes and disappointments, frustrations and anger, desires and dreams.

The proclamation of the Word of God is always a familiar conversation, a straightforward dialogue that pushes and pulls us in directions that we may not want to go. It provokes and evokes memories, many of them painful.

The Word never lets up. It raises issues that we have to face every day. It asks for our response.

There is a proverb that says *"Entre dicho y hecho hay mucho trecho"*—between what is said and what is done there exists a great division. Las Posadas and the Via Crucis offer ways to heal the divisions that exists between what is lived on the streets and what is proclaimed in our churches. Las Posadas and the Via Crucis teach us to read the Word of God not with our eyes but with our hearts *para que no hay trecho*, so that we are never divided.

~

Notes

1. Quoted in *Puebla and Beyond*, ed. John Eagleson and Philip Scharper (Maryknoll, NY: Orbis Books, 1979), 184.
2. Ibid., 241.
3. Ibid.
4. Ibid., 184.
5. Mark Francis, introduction for the unpublished book *Semana Santa*, 2001.
6. For a historical discussion of this characteristic, see Jaime Lara, *Christian Texts for Aztecs* (Notre Dame, IN: University of Notre Dame Press, 2008), chapter 6, "Processional Liturgy: The Witness of Feet."
7. *Merriam-Webster's Collegiate Dictionary*, 11th ed. (Springfield, MA: Merriam-Webster, 2003).
8. Lara, *Christian Texts for Aztecs*, 175–76.
9. Jaime Lara, *City, Temple, Stage: Eschatological Architecture and Liturgical Theatrics in New Spain* (Notre Dame, IN: University of Notre Dame Press, 2004), 107.
10. Ibid., 109.
11. Lara, *Christian Texts for Aztecs*, 260.
12. Nathan D. Mitchell, "The Amen Corner," *Worship* 81, no. 6 (2007): 562.

6.

"Beginning with Moses and All the Prophets"

Latino Biblical Scholarship and the Word of God in the Church

Jean-Pierre Ruiz

~

That very day two of them were going to a village seven miles from Jerusalem called Emmaus, and they were conversing about all the things that had occurred. And it happened that while they were conversing and debating, Jesus himself drew near and walked with them, but their eyes were prevented from recognizing him. He asked them, "What are you discussing as you walk along?"

—Luke 24:13–17

> *Todo pasa y todo queda,*
> *pero lo nuestro es pasar,*
> *pasar haciendo caminos,*
> *caminos sobre el mar . . .*
> *Caminante, son tus huellas*
> *el camino, y nada más;*
> *caminante, no hay camino,*
> *se hace camino al andar.*
> *Al andar se hace camino,*
> *y al volver la vista atrás*
> *se ve la senda que nunca*
> *se ha de volver a pisar.*
> *Caminante, no hay camino,*
> *sino estelas en la mar.*
> —Antonio Machado, "Proverbios y Cantares"

Introduction: Reading along the Road

Let me invite you to imagine with me, for just a moment or two, how these words might resonate had they not been written in the early years of the twentieth century. Let us together imagine instead that they were written toward the end of the first century:

> *Caminante, son tus huellas*
> *el camino, y nada más;*
> *caminante, no hay camino,*
> *se hace camino al andar.*

Imagine with me, for just a moment or two, that these poetic lines were written not in the resonant Spanish verse of Antonio Machado, but in the polished Greek prose of an author who may have been too modest to claim his own work by name, a writer to whom venerable Christian tradition assigns the name of Luke and the title of evangelist:

> *Todo pasa y todo queda,*
> *pero lo nuestro es pasar,*
> *pasar haciendo caminos*

Imagine with me, for just a moment or two, that these words were born not in Spain and not in writing, but instead as words softly spoken out loud on the road from Jerusalem to Emmaus, spoken by the crucified and risen Word-made-flesh to two downcast travelers as he walks with them, not yet unrecognized as he shares their journey:

> *Al andar se hace camino,*
> *y al volver la vista atrás*
> *se ve la senda que nunca*
> *se ha de volver a pisar.*

If you have allowed your imagination to journey with me at least this far, then we have learned a little something about just how important roads are for Luke, and about just how important journeys and wayfarers are for this evangelist. It is Luke's narrative of the encounter between the risen Jesus and two of his disciples along the road to Jerusalem (Lk 24:13–35) that provides the theme for our gathering here at Notre Dame, and that provides a framework for my reflections this afternoon as I speak with you about Latino/a biblical scholarship and the Word of God in the Church. Because that narrative weaves its way through the chapters of this book, I hope you will allow me to dwell on this text a bit more, and I ask this because I hope that our time together will be *less* a matter of my *telling* you *about* Latino/a biblical scholarship, and more a matter of our engaging in biblical scholarship together *latinamente*. To tell you the truth, if we have allowed ourselves to reimagine Luke's narrative through the words of Antonio Machado's poem, we have already begun to do that together.

Luke does not tell us very much about the two disciples themselves. We don't know what they looked like, we don't know where they came from, we only know one of them—Cleopas—by name. Some biblical scholars have wondered whether the unnamed disciple is a woman, even Cleopas's own wife, and why not, because Luke's Gospel tells us that women too were part of the circle of Jesus's disciples? It is for that reason that Filippo Piccone's beautiful image, "Camino a Emaús," portrays one of the two disciples as a woman. As we read the story of their journey from confusion to confidence, from despair to hope, from fear to faith, perhaps the very reason Luke tells us so little about the two disciples is because the story isn't about them. In the end, the story is about how they come to recognize Jesus. We meet them on the road, and in the midst of their conversing about the things that had just occurred in Jerusalem (Lk 24:14) Jesus draws near and begins to walk with them. To borrow a line from Matthew's Jesus, "Where two or three are gathered together in my name, there am I in the midst of them" (Mt 18:20). As they continue along together with their unrecognized companion, the disciples on the road to Emmaus share their story—or at least as much of it as makes sense to them. It is up to Jesus to put the pieces together: "'Was it not necessary that the Messiah should suffer these things and enter into his glory?' Then beginning with Moses and all the prophets, he interpreted what referred to him in all the scriptures" (Lk 24:26–27). Not until their guest became their host, not until Jesus sat at table with them, "took bread, said the blessing, broke it, and gave it to them" (Lk 24:30), were their eyes opened, and only then did what transpired on the road in his company make sense: "Were not our hearts burning within us while he spoke to us on the way and opened the scriptures to us?" (Lk 24:32). For the wayfarers along the road to Emmaus, the encounter with Jesus—in word and sacrament—changed absolutely everything. Walking with Jesus, the road to

Emmaus became the road away from despair, and the Scriptures become their road map to faith in the resurrection.

> *Al andar se hace camino,*
> *y al volver la vista atrás*
> *se ve la senda que nunca*
> *se ha de volver a pisar.*

The evangelist Luke's fascination with roads and with journeys extends to the Acts of the Apostles. It is, after all, along the road from Jerusalem to Damascus that Saul sees the light—so to speak—and is addressed by the risen Jesus (Acts 9:1–21; also see Acts 22:1–16). For our purposes, though, I would like to call our attention to another encounter on another road, the encounter on the road from Jerusalem to Gaza between Philip and the Ethiopian court official in Acts 8:26–40.[1]

Philip is instructed by an angel to head south to what is described as a "wilderness road" (Acts 8:26), and when he arrives there Philip crosses paths with an Ethiopian court official as that official, seated in his chariot, reads—presumably out loud—from the prophet Isaiah: "Then the Spirit said to Philip, 'Go over to this chariot and join it.' So Philip ran up to it and heard him reading the prophet Isaiah. He asked, 'Do you understand what you are reading?' He replied, 'How can I, unless someone guides me?' And he invited Philip to get in and sit beside him" (Acts 8:29–31). Together, they read the words of Isaiah 53:7–8: "Like a sheep he was led to the slaughter, and as a lamb before its shearer is silent, so he opened not his mouth. In [his] humiliation justice was denied him. Who will tell of his posterity? For his life is taken from the earth" (Acts 8:32–33). The Ethiopian asks Philip, "I beg you, about whom is the prophet saying this? About himself, or about someone else?" and Philip "opened his mouth and, beginning with this scripture passage, he proclaimed Jesus to him" (Acts 8:34–35). Evangelized by Philip, and convinced of the truth of the Good News he has just received, the Ethiopian receives baptism at the hands of Philip (in what is probably the fastest RCIA process on record in the history of the Church). On the road to Gaza with the Ethiopian, as with the two disciples on the road to Emmaus, Machado's verses find new resonances:

> *Al andar se hace camino,*
> *y al volver la vista atrás*

se ve la senda que nunca
se ha de volver a pisar.

I would like to suggest that some key features of this story have important implications. First of all, Acts identifies both characters according to their ethnicity. The Philip of Acts 8:26–39 is the very same Philip who launches the proclamation of the Gospel beyond Jerusalem in Acts 8:5–12. He is one of the seven men who are chosen by the twelve in Acts 6:1–6 to address the first reported case of ethnic tension in the post-Pentecost church: "when the disciples were increasing in number, the Hellenists complained against the Hebrews because their widows were being neglected in the daily distribution of food" (Acts 6:1). The decision to appoint Philip, along with Stephen and five others (Prochorus, Nicanor, Timon, Parmenas, and Nicolaus [who is himself described as "a proselyte of Antioch"]), is made because the apostles concluded that "It is not right that we should neglect the word of God in order to wait on tables" (Acts 6:2). Despite the division of labor according to which the higher calling of the apostles involves the proclamation of the Word of God, Acts never does tell us anything about the work that these seven undertook in the first-century Jerusalem church's food pantry or soup kitchen. We hear only about the ministry of the Word exercised by Stephen and Philip, and nothing more at all about the other five. Oh, how often do we in Hispanic ministry find ourselves doing the sorts of things we never expected to do! The more things change (even in the Church), the more things stay the same! Immediately after his appointment to attend to the material needs of the Greek-speaking widows, we find Stephen stirring up opposition by the forcefulness of his preaching (Acts 6:8–7:60), and we find Philip proclaiming the Good News about Christ to good effect in Samaria (Acts 8:5–12).

The Ethiopian court official remains anonymous, but he is identified in Acts 8:27 according to his ethnicity, according to his condition, according to his position in the court of the Ethiopian queen, and according to the magnitude of his responsibilities in her service (he is "in charge of her entire treasury").[2] We don't know anything about the Ethiopian's business in Jerusalem (and neither does Philip), nor do we know what prompted the Ethiopian to read from Isaiah as he traveled on the Gaza road (and neither does Philip). What we do know is that the Ethiopian is riding in some sort of chariot, that he is sitting in the chariot, and that it is comfortable enough for him to be reading while he makes his way headed south along the Gaza road. We also know that it is no accident that he meets up with Philip along the road. It's part of God's plan for Philip and for the Ethiopian. Running up to meet the dignitary's "motorcade," Philip asks—without even introducing himself—"Do you understand what you are reading?" and the Ethiopian replies, "How can I, unless someone guides me?" (Acts 8:30–31).

Reflections on Reading the Bible *Latinamente*

I have invited you to read two texts along with me, suggesting at the outset that it might be more effective for us to read together *latinamente* than it would have been for me to take the theoretical high ground to *tell* you what Latino biblical scholarship is all about and what difference it makes. As a matter of showing and not just telling, I have chosen to lead us down a different road, one that takes the experience of reading seriously. That decision, I would suggest, is one of a number of intersecting characteristics of reading the Bible *latinamente*. What, then, does it mean to read any text *latinamente*, and, more specifically, what does it mean to read the Bible *latinamente*? What is it about the ways we have just considered Luke 24 and Acts 8 that characterizes what we have done together as a matter of reading these texts *latinamente*? Does one have to be a Latino to read the Bible *latinamente*, and if not, do Latinos read the Bible *latinamente* any "better" or any more *latinamente* than non-Latinos read it *latinamente* or otherwise?

Given the events that transpired during the first summer of the Obama administration in Washington, it is hard to ask that set of questions without hearing echoes of certain pundits who took issue with one line that was lifted out of context from Judge Sonia Sotomayor's 2001 lecture, "A Latina Judge's Voice." In that Judge Mario G. Olmos Memorial Lecture, delivered at the University of California, Berkeley, School of Law, Judge Sotomayor said, "I would hope that a wise Latina woman with the richness of her experiences would more often than not reach a better conclusion than a white male who hasn't lived that life."[3] If you have not yet read the speech in its entirety, I highly recommend it. Reflecting autobiographically on what it means for her to be a Latina, here is what she shared:

> If I had pursued my career in my undergraduate history major, I would
> likely provide you with a very academic description of what being a

Latino or Latina means. For example, I could define Latinos as those peoples and cultures populated or colonized by Spain who maintained or adopted Spanish or Spanish Creole as their language of communication. You can tell that I have been very well educated. That antiseptic description however, does not really explain the appeal of *morcilla* . . . to an American born child. It does not provide an adequate explanation of why individuals like us, many of whom are born in this completely different American culture, still identify so strongly with those communities in which our parents were born and raised.

America has a deeply confused image of itself that is in perpetual tension. We are a nation that takes pride in our ethnic diversity, recognizing its importance in shaping our society and in adding richness to its existence. Yet, we simultaneously insist that we can and must function and live in a race and color-blind way that ignore[s] these very differences that in other contexts we laud. That tension between "the melting pot and the salad bowl"—a recently popular metaphor used to described New York's diversity—is being hotly debated today in national discussions about affirmative action. Many of us struggle with this tension and attempt to maintain and promote our cultural and ethnic identities in a society that is often ambivalent about how to deal with its differences. In this time of great debate we must remember that it is not political struggles that create a Latino or Latina identity. I became a Latina by the way I love and the way I live my life.[4]

With all due respect to my fellow Nuyorican, let it be known that at least for this Queens-born Nuyorican, *morcilla* has not the slightest appeal whatsoever, and I hope that this confession does not make you think that I am any less Latino than Sonia Sotomayor! So, then, what does it mean to read the Bible *latinamente*? Does it mean reading the Bible in Spanish? Things get complicated here too, and Judge Sotomayor's insights help to clarify matters. She explained, "Being a Latina in America also does not mean speaking Spanish. I happen to speak it fairly well. But my brother, only three years younger, like too many of us educated here, barely speaks it. Most of us born and bred here, speak it very poorly."[5] In my own family, my older brother (the only one of us born in Puerto Rico) and I both speak Spanish quite well, while my younger brother—just a year younger than I—barely understands it at all. This means that using Antonio Machado's poem alongside Luke 24 and Acts 8 isn't enough to qualify that reading as a Latino interpretation. After all, Latinos and Latinas read lots of poets—even the German poetry of Johann Wolfgang von Goethe.[6]

I would also suggest that reading the Bible *latinamente* does not simply mean reading the Bible just as Latin Americans do. The betwixt-and-betweenness of the U.S. Latino context makes a difference in what it means to read from *this* place, and crossing borders makes a difference in the view.[7] To be sure, the rich heritage and enormous vitality of Latin American biblical scholarship provides currents that nourish U.S. Latino/a biblical and theological scholarship. These insights include, among others, a serious and critical rethinking of the value of biblical scholarship and of the deference given to interpretations proposed by professionally trained biblical scholars over those that emerge from communities of ordinary readers of the Bible. As Pablo Richard writes:

> The exegesis of the last one hundred years has produced works of enormous importance and relevance; many exegetes, both women and men, have emerged as authentic teachers of the faith and prophets. However, the dominant *spirit* of this exegesis has been, without a doubt, the spirit of modernity—marked by positivism, rationalism, liberalism, individualism, and existentialism. Exegesis normally takes place in closed academies, where the search for power and prestige has been informed by the spirit of competition and the economy of the marketplace.[8]

Consider the crucial question of whose understandings of the Bible are to be taken seriously, of whose understandings of the biblical text are normative. Nigerian Catholic biblical scholar, Justin Ukpong, borrows a page from the insights of Latin American biblical scholarship to underline ways in which academic approaches to understanding the Bible have unfortunately asserted their exclusive—and exclusionary—authority: "In classical Western readings, the epistemological privilege is given to the academy, for it is only the interpretations of trained experts that are regarded as valid within the academy. Non-expert interpretations of ordinary people are regarded as uninformed and therefore inconsequential for ascertaining the true meaning of the biblical text."[9] The rehabilitation and retrieval of reading strategies that had often been dismissed as naive and disparaged as "precritical" called for professional biblical scholars in Latin America—most of whom were trained in European and North American academic

settings—to remap their relationships with communities of ordinary readers of the Bible, to understand themselves not as teachers or as mediators
but as fellow listeners and as fellow learners. While U.S. Latino biblical
scholars and theologians have taken this insight very much to heart, it has
not made much headway in other quarters.

So then, if it is not to be understood simply as the northward migration
of Latin American practices of biblical interpretation, what does it mean to
read the Bible *latinamente* in the United States? Allow me to suggest just
two characteristic features of this approach to the Bible:

- Reading *as*: Interpretation and Context
- Reading *with*: Interpretation and Community

By identifying these two features as characteristics of reading the Bible
latinamente, I am not implying by any means that either of them is exclusive
to Latino reading practices. Nor am I proposing that anyone who embraces
either or both of them qualifies as an authentically Latino interpreter of
the Bible. I am suggesting that these features characterize an approach to
biblical interpretation that resonates in significant ways with the experience
of Latino Catholic Christians in the United States, an approach to biblical
interpretation that has much to offer to the Church at large—Catholic *and*
Protestant—in the United States and beyond.

Reading *As*: Interpretation and Context

By suggesting that reading the Bible *latinamente* is a matter of reading *as*, I am
recognizing that Latino biblical interpretation, like African American biblical interpretation and Asian American biblical interpretation, is an intentionally contextual approach to understanding the Bible. Such approaches
build on the insight that, as James Earl Massey puts it, "Interpretation of the
Bible depends largely on the social perspective of the interpreter." He suggests that "The quest to be able interpreters and effective sharers of biblical
meanings needs to be allied with an understanding of how our thinking and
world view have been shaped. We need to recognize and appreciate how the
differing social communities within the larger society have given us not only
our identities but also our different perspectives on Scripture."[10] In the words
of Fernando Segovia and Mary Ann Tolbert, biblical studies have begun "to
take seriously the role of the reader in interpretation and hence the relationship between interpretation and the social location of the interpreter." From

a number of different directions, biblical scholarship has "begun to call into question older, established exegetical and theological methods, which had often claimed for themselves universality and objectivity under the construct of an objective and scientific reader, a universal and informed reader." In the service of that reconfiguration of the discipline of biblical studies, "factors traditionally left out of consideration were now becoming areas of exploration—for example, gender, race, ethnic origins, class . . . with a focus on real flesh-and-blood readers who were always and inescapably situated both historically and culturally and whose reading and interpretation of the texts were seen as affected by their social location."[11]

The turn to the real flesh-and-blood reader in contextual biblical interpretation represents a significant shift from what had for many decades been the predominant paradigm in academic biblical studies (even in Roman Catholic circles); namely, the historical-critical approach, with its focus on the world behind the text. As Segovia explains, "The historical-critical model approached the biblical text primarily as a means, as historical evidence from and for the time of composition. As such, the text was to be read and analyzed within its own historical context and regarded as a direct means for reconstructing the historical situation that it presupposed, reflected, and addressed."[12] According to the peculiar asceticism that the historical-critical paradigm imposed on its practitioners, exegetes were required to become aware of the presuppositions with which they approached the biblical text so that, with appropriate neutrality and complete impartiality, the original meaning of the text could be retrieved.[13] Approaching the task of interpretation without fully setting aside any and all assumptions and presuppositions (whether theological, sociocultural, or otherwise) was understood to put the scholar at risk of contaminating the objectivity of biblical scholarship and substituting *eis*egesis (reading meaning *into* the text) for exegesis—understood naively as a matter of allowing the text to speak for itself to any suitably trained and well-disposed interpreter. This led to a strange division of labor according to which it fell to the exegete to arrive at a determination of what the biblical text *meant*, while it was the task of the theologian to explain what the text *means*.[14] Understood as exegesis pure and simple, biblical interpretation according to the historical-critical paradigm was rightly criticized as elitist and as a discipline isolated from the life of the Church. The Pontifical Biblical Commission's 1993 Instruction, "The Interpretation of the Bible in the Church," frames the critique in these terms:

Instead of making for easier and more secure access to the living sources of God's word, it makes of the Bible a closed book. Interpretation may always have been something of a problem, but now it requires such technical refinements as to render it a domain reserved for a few specialists alone. To the latter some apply the phrase of the Gospel: "You have taken away the key of knowledge; you have not entered in yourselves and you have hindered those who sought to enter" (Lk 11:52; cf. Mt 23:13).[15]

In his intervention during the Fourteenth General Congregation of the Synod of Bishops on October 14 of last year, Pope Benedict XVI emphasized the need to overcome the dualism between exegesis and theology that is an unfortunate by-product of a deficient understanding of biblical interpretation as exegesis pure and simple. The pope insisted, "When exegesis is not theological, Scripture cannot be the soul of theology, and vice versa; when theology is not essentially Scriptural interpretation within the Church, then this theology no longer has a foundation."[16]

As a deliberately contextual approach to biblical interpretation, Latino biblical scholarship insists not only that it is impossible to check one's assumptions and presuppositions at the door prior to engaging in biblical interpretation, but that such assumptions and presuppositions (theological, sociocultural, and otherwise) are no less important for biblical interpretation than the grammatical, linguistic, and historical tools that are the standard equipment of academic biblical interpretation. Reading the Bible *as* Latinos and Latinas means reflecting on the questions that our history, our experiences, our beliefs and practices bring to the text. Reading the Bible *latinamente* honors the relationship between Scripture and tradition by rejecting the disparaging characterization of biblical interpretation prior to the nineteenth-century birth of the historical-critical approach as "pre-critical." To pretend that serious biblical interpretation only began with the development of historical-critical exegesis ignores more than five centuries of biblical interpretation in the Americas, and many more centuries of biblical interpretation among our Jewish and Christian forebears. Reading the Bible *latinamente* rejects the privileging of academic biblical interpretation and invites readers in various settings—pastoral, popular, and academic—to learn with and from each other.

Reading *With*: Interpretation and Community

By suggesting that reading the Bible *latinamente* is a matter of reading *with*, I want to foreground an ethical principle that has significant traction among Latino/a biblical scholars and theologians alike, namely, the notion of *teología de conjunto*. Inspired by the notion of *pastoral de conjunto* that first took shape during the *Encuentro* process as the Catholic Church in the United States was beginning to come to terms with the reality of the Hispanic presence, the notion of *teología de conjunto* recognizes that the primary subject of theological reflection is not the isolated individual pastoral minister or scholar. The work of theology takes place not in the first-person singular, but in the first-person plural, for the primary subject of the theological endeavor is the community—the Church. Because biblical interpretation is a theological discipline, the same must be said of reading the Bible *latinamente*, which is to be undertaken in and for the sake of the community, and not *just* the Latino community, but for the sake of the whole Church.

To speak about "the Latino community" pure and simple is not especially helpful. After all, there are lots of very different Latino communities. What does it mean to be Latino in the first place? In the wake of the Sotomayor nomination to the Supreme Court, the Pew Hispanic Center directed its attention to that question. The report explains that "In 1976, the U.S. Congress passed the only law in this country's history that mandated the collection and analysis of data for a specific ethnic group: 'Americans of Spanish origin or descent.' The language of that legislation described this group as 'Americans who identify themselves as being of Spanish-speaking background and trace their origin or descent from Mexico, Puerto Rico, Cuba, Central and South America and other Spanish-speaking countries.'"[17] Yet side by side with this approach, the U.S. Census Bureau has adopted a more open-ended approach according to which you *are* "Hispanic" if you say you are, and you are *not* Hispanic if you do not claim to be Hispanic. The authors of the Pew study scripted the following Q & A to illustrate the point:

Q. *I immigrated to Phoenix from Mexico. Am I Hispanic?*
A. You are if you say so.
Q. *My parents moved to New York from Puerto Rico. Am I Hispanic?*
A. You are if you say so.

Q. *My grandparents were born in Spain but I grew up in California.*
Am I Hispanic?

A. You are if you say so.

Q. *I was born in Maryland and married an immigrant from*
El Salvador. Am I Hispanic?

A. You are if you say so.

Q. *My mom is from Chile and my dad is from Iowa. I was born in*
Des Moines. Am I Hispanic?

A. You are if you say so.

Q. *I was born in Argentina but grew up in Texas. I don't consider*
myself Hispanic. Does the Census count me as an Hispanic?

A. Not if you say you aren't.[18]

Following this line of reasoning, being Hispanic isn't just a matter of being *born* that way. To borrow a line from John's Gospel, it is a matter of being born *and* of being born *again*, of deliberately embracing that identity. Even so, claiming my own individual identity does not automatically make me a member of a community, whether Latino or otherwise: there is much more at stake in belonging to a community. Let me take this right to the next level: what forms us into a community of Latino Catholics is the Eucharist. In parishes across the United States, in every diocese and in every neighborhood, immigrants from every nation in Latin America and their children, their grandchildren, and so on and so on, are brought together by the Spirit of God into the community that is the body of Christ, the community without borders, sustained by the Word of Truth and nourished by the Bread of Life that makes us who and what we are. Reading the Bible *in* and *with* that community—the communion that is the whole Church—makes all the difference in the world. Perhaps that is why the testimony of the disciples who encountered Jesus along the road to Emmaus rings so true for us as Latinos, why it comes as no surprise to us that they came to recognize Jesus in the breaking of the bread.

What of those Latinos with whom we share Christian faith but with whom we do not share full communion? What about the common ground between Latino Catholics and Latino *evangélicos*? Can we and should we read the Bible with these Christian brothers and sisters of ours despite our differences? Let me provide an example of the productive ways in which that can happen, of ways in which it is happening, by acknowledging my own friendship with my colleague, Rev. Dr. Efraín Agosto, a Pentecostal Christian who has served as professor of New Testament and academic dean at Hartford Theological Seminary.[19] Dr. Agosto and I have been friends and colleagues for a long time, working together on many projects in a friendship that has been nourished by our common passion to be led by God's Word and to be at the service of that Word in our service to Latino Christian communities. Dr. Agosto and I co-contributed chapters to a book called *Building Bridges, Doing Justice: Constructing a Latino/a Ecumenical Theology*, a project that brought together Latino Catholics and Protestants not to gloss over our differences or to build walls of suspicion between us, but to work together to see what steps we might take to do serious theology together *latinamente* for the sake of the Church.[20] It fell to Dr. Agosto and me to work out an ecumenical Latino theology of revelation, and it did not come as much of a surprise to either of us that in the end we have come very close to working out a theology of revelation that is genuinely Latino *and* genuinely ecumenical. I am confident that Dr. Agosto would agree with me that Latino Catholic Christians and Latino Protestant Christians have nothing to fear and everything to gain from patient, generous, and open-minded dialogue with each other. Only such dialogue will lessen the fear and suspicion that keeps Latino/a Catholic Christians and Latino/a *evangélicos* from recognizing each other as brothers and sisters in Christ.

I must also add that it is not enough for us as Latinos to keep our reading-with *entre nosotros*. After all, Philip was called by God to journey along the Gaza road with an Ethiopian, with someone very different from himself, and it was in the pages of the Scriptures that they found common ground. As Latino *Catholics* in the United States, we have much to learn, and much to offer, in reading the Bible together with African Americans and Asian Americans, with Native Americans and with all the descendants of those who came to these shores. Reading *latinamente* must open us to reading *as* Catholic Christians who read the Bible in *catholic* ways, aware that the Word of God is addressed to peoples of every tongue and nation in an idiom that is their own.

Conclusion: *Somos un Pueblo que Camina*

caminante, no hay camino,
se hace camino al andar.

Al andar se hace camino,
y al volver la vista atrás
se ve la senda que nunca
se ha de volver a pisar.

As Latino and Latina Catholic Christians, like the disciples along the road to Emmaus, and like the Ethiopian on the Gaza road, *somos un pueblo que camina.* For us, the road is challenging but we can walk with confidence and without fear, for we know that Jesus himself walks with us, accompanying us and guiding us, opening our eyes to recognize him in the Scriptures and in the breaking of the bread. We know also that God's Holy Spirit sends us people like Philip to help us make sense of the Scriptures and, even more importantly, to help us make sense of our lives with the guidance of the Scriptures, and some of those whom God sends our way might even be biblical scholars who read *with* us along life's journey.

Todo pasa y todo queda,
pero lo nuestro es pasar,
pasar haciendo caminos

⌒

Notes

1. The *Instrumentum Laboris* for the Twelfth Ordinary Assembly of the Synod of Bishops, focused on "The Word of God in the Life and Mission of the Church," makes explicit reference to this text: "Familiarity with the Sacred Scriptures is not an easy task. Like the minister of the Queen of Ethiopia, understanding the contents of a biblical text requires a pedagogy which begins in Scripture itself and leads to an understanding and acceptance of the Good News of Jesus (cf. Acts 8:26–40)," *Instrumentum Laboris* § 47, http://www.vatican.va/roman_curia/synod/documents/rc_synod_doc_20080511_instrlabor-xii-assembly_en.html.
2. With respect to the ethnographic and geographical significance of this character, see Clarice J. Martin, "A Chamberlain's Journey and the Challenge of Interpretation for Liberation," *Semeia* 47 (1989): 105–35. With respect to the identification of the Ethiopian as a eunuch, see F. Scott Spencer,

"The Ethiopian Eunuch and His Bible: A Social-Science Analysis," *Biblical Theology Bulletin* 22 (1992): 155–65.

3.   Sonia Sotomayor, "A Latina Judge's Voice," *New York Times*, May 14, 2009. Available at http://www.nytimes.com/2009/05/15/us/politics/15judge.text.html.

4.   Ibid.

5.   Ibid.

6.   See, for example, Jean-Pierre Ruiz, "The Word Became Flesh and the Flesh Becomes Word: Notes toward a U.S. Latino/a Theology of Revelation," in *Building Bridges, Doing Justice: Constructing a Latino/a Ecumenical Theology*, ed. Orlando O. Espín (Maryknoll, NY: Orbis Books, 2009), 47–68.

7.   See Fernando F. Segovia, "Two Places and No Place on Which to Stand: Mixture and Otherness in Hispanic American Theology," *Listening: A Journal of Religion and Culture* 27 (1992): 26–40.

8.   Pablo Richard, "The Hermeneutics of Liberation: A Hermeneutics of the Spirit," in *Reading from This Place*, vol. 2: *Social Location and Biblical Interpretation in Global Perspective*, ed. Fernando F. Segovia and Mary Ann Tolbert (Minneapolis: Fortress, 1995), 275.

9.   Justin S. Ukpong, "Reading the Bible in a Global Village: Issues and Challenges from African Readings," in *Reading the Bible in the Global Village: Cape Town*, ed. Justin S. Ukpong et al. (Atlanta: Society of Biblical Literature, 2002), 22.

10.   James Earl Massey, "Reading the Bible from Particular Social Locations: An Introduction," in *The New Interpreter's Bible: A Commentary in Twelve Volumes*, ed. Leander E. Keck et al. (Nashville: Abingdon, 1994), 1:150. Also see Massey, "Reading the Bible as African Americans," in *The New Interpreter's Bible*, 1:154–60; Chan-Hie Kim, "Reading the Bible as Asian Americans," in *The New Interpreter's Bible*, 1:161–66; Fernando F. Segovia, "Reading the Bible as Hispanic Americans," in *The New Interpreter's Bible*, 1:167–73; George E. Tinker, "Reading the Bible as Native Americans," in *The New Interpreter's Bible*, 1:174–80; Carolyn Osiek, "Reading the Bible as Women," in *The New Interpreter's Bible*, 1:181–87; as well as *Voices from the Margin: Interpreting the Bible in the Third World*, ed. R. S. Sugirtharajah (Maryknoll, NY: Orbis Books, 1991).

11.   Fernando F. Segovia and Mary Ann Tolbert, preface to *Reading from This Place*, vol. 1: *Social Location and Biblical Interpretation in the United States*, ed. Fernando F. Segovia and Mary Ann Tolbert (Minneapolis: Fortress, 1995), 1:ix.

12. Fernando F. Segovia, "'And They Began to Speak in Other Tongues': Competing Modes of Discourse in Contemporary Biblical Criticism," in *Reading from This Place*, 1:10; reprinted in Fernando F. Segovia, *Decolonizing Biblical Studies: A View from the Margins* (Maryknoll, NY: Orbis Books, 2000), 10.

13. Segovia, "'And They Began to Speak in Other Tongues,'" 1:12; reprinted in Segovia, *Decolonizing Biblical Studies*, 14.

14. On this "division of labor," see Krister Stendahl, "Biblical Theology, Contemporary," in *The Interpreter's Dictionary of the Bible*, ed. George Arthur Buttrick et al. (Nashville: Abingdon, 1962), 1:418–32.

15. Pontifical Biblical Commission, "The Interpretation of the Bible in the Church," April 23, 1993, http://catholic-resources.org/ChurchDocs/PBC _Interp0.htm#Intro.

16. Pope Benedict XVI, "Address during the 14th General Congregation of the Synod of Bishops," October 14, 2008, http://www.vatican.va/holy_father /benedict_xvi/speeches/2008/october/documents/hf_ben-xvi_spe _20081014_sinodo_en.html.

17. Jeffrey Passel and Paul Taylor, "Who's Hispanic?" Pew Hispanic Center, May 28, 2009, http://pewhispanic.org/reports/report.php?ReportID=111.

18. Ibid., 2.

19. Agosto is the author of *Servant Leadership in Jesus and Paul* (St. Louis: Chalice Press, 2005).

20. See Efraín Agosto, "*Sola Scriptura* and Latino/a Protestant Hermeneutics: An Exploration," in *Building Bridges, Doing Justice*, 69–87; also Ruiz, "The Word Became Flesh."

7.

The Way of Justice

A Latino Protestant Reading of Luke 24:13–35

Efraín Agosto

~

Introduction

What does it mean to analyze Luke 24:13–35 from a Latino Protestant perspective? First, a confession is in order. While Protestant, I am not exclusively of the "mainline Protestant" variety. I belong to a Latino congregation
that is part of a mainline denomination, the United Church of Christ. However, I still consider myself Pentecostal in some shape or form since that
was the tradition in which I was reared and which has affected my faith and
life forever. For example, I am more Wesleyan than Reformed, but more
importantly I am convinced of the important role of religious experience in
the Pentecostal believer's self-understanding, sometimes over against his or
her grounding in the Bible or doctrinal expressions of the Bible taught by
his or her specific Pentecostal denominational group.

In many ways, I study the New Testament from the perspective of a
Latino raised in the urban Hispanic Pentecostal church, where both mainline Protestants and Roman Catholics were suspect in terms of their faith
and practices. Yet years of ecumenical experience, participation in Latino
Baptist and Congregational churches, and scholarly training in biblical
studies in both evangelical and mainline Protestant schools have helped
me overcome prejudices ingrained in me against fellow believers in Christ,
including Latinos and Latinas. I see myself as part and parcel of that great
Latino/a reality that populates our country from all parts of Latin America,
with all kinds of religious traditions, including Protestant, Catholic, and
Pentecostal.

Toward a Latino/a Protestant Pentecostal Hermeneutic

The question remains: what does it mean to have a Pentecostal hermeneutic and how does that influence my reading of the New Testament? Moreover, how does a Protestant Pentecostal—this Latino Protestant Pentecostal— read Luke 24:13–35, the postresurrection encounter between two traveling disciples and Jesus? To be a Pentecostal reader of the Scriptures means a variety of things.[1] Certainly, Latino/a Pentecostals have always had a high view of Scripture, although they have not always practiced it quite like our Anglo Protestant, especially Evangelical, cohorts have. Pentecostal theologian Eldin Villafañe affirms that Pentecostals have tended to believe in "the four basic principles of the Reformation: *sola gracia, solo Cristo, sola Escritura,* and *sola fe.*" Yet Pentecostalism, Villafañe asserts, has its roots in what he calls the "left-wing of the Reformation," which had as its main constituency the poor and the oppressed.[2] In addition, Pentecostalism also focused on the Reformation teaching about the internal witness of the Holy Spirit. Given a constituency in need of social justice and a belief in the ongoing presence of God's Spirit, Villafañe writes that "implicitly Hispanic Pentecostals subscribe to a view of revelation that is dynamic and continuous in nature," reading the Bible in an "existential-spiritual manner."[3] Thus the role of experience is essential to a Latino Pentecostal reading of the Bible, and I daresay that marks many of us in Latino Protestantism and Catholicism, as well.

Second, given the constituents historically served by Latino Pentecostalism, there is a critical role for justice in the Latino/a Pentecostal hermeneutic. For example, Villafañe himself explores the leadership of the prophet Amos in the Hebrew scriptures.[4] He discusses the nature of biblical justice that Amos calls for from his fellow Israelites. According to Villafañe in his reading of Amos, justice is about commitment to one's community:

> The picture that Scripture paints is that of the human person created in and for communion—created to live in community. In the Old Testament, above all, one sees the importance of living in relationship with God and with each other. Individuals were in relationship with God through the covenant that existed between God and [God's] people.[5]

Relationships in human life must be guided by the search for justice, because justice lies at the heart of divine nature. Thus, whether among nations outside Israel or inside Israel itself, the practice of justice, especially to the poor and oppressed, is a mark of closeness to God. Amos denounces injustice everywhere and calls for Israel in particular to practice justice as the people of God.

For Villafañe, these are fundamental teachings of the Bible. Liberation and justice, in community, lie at the heart of the gospel message. Villafañe decries the tendency in Protestant Evangelical scholarship, for example, to divide the personal aspects of the gospel from its social aspects. He writes, "If our nation—for that matter, our world—is to hear the whole Word of God, we must do away with those false dichotomies that would limit the Word of God and define the gospel as either evangelism or social justice. . . ." Such a division between personal salvation and social justice divides the gospel in two, and therefore undermines the biblical teaching of one gospel that promotes God's "passionate concern for justice for all—especially the poor, the weak, and the oppressed members of society."[6] A dichotomized gospel limits the creation of community. Thus, for this Pentecostal scholar, Scripture promotes justice and community, and any biblical interpretation that undermines these values is not scriptural.

Another Latino Pentecostal scholar, Samuel Solivan, focuses on a Latino theology of suffering from the perspective of U.S. Hispanic Pentecostals. His theological construction of "orthopathos," redemptive suffering, is "informed fundamentally but not exclusively by the Scriptures of the Hebrew Bible, the New Testament and the person of Jesus Christ as Savior." Besides the Christological focus that must inform all understanding of scriptural revelation, Solivan argues that "alongside these we must place tradition, reason and critical reflection on our present situation." We must include "modern critical scholarship which appropriates the text and the sociopolitical situation" from which one reads the text. Such an eclectic approach "demonstrates a high regard for the authority of Scripture, a keen insight into the sociopolitical issues of the day, a great sensitivity to the needs of lay people and a wise use of critical biblical scholarship."[7]

In this way, Solivan offers a Pentecostal hermeneutic that incorporates reflection on the person and work of Christ, tradition, reason, critical scholarship, and reflection on the present situation, all standing together with Scripture, "both informing the issues and the present task." Otherwise, without such juxtaposition of the variety of social and theological issues, "the critical historical method tends to divest the Scripture of its power to speak anew to us today" when it stands alone. Solivan asserts that we must "shift" from a reliance on a so-called objective historical process by itself "to the witness of the Spirit both in the tradition of the church and in the reflecting community." In this way, the community "retains the power of the Word."[8]

Solivan also addresses the question of authority in scriptural interpretation as viewed by Latino/a Pentecostals. He argues that rather than resting authority in the internal witness of Scripture itself, Latino/a Pentecostals tend to seek out order or direction from those in authority related to family and community, including their religious community. The "need for order, direction and harmony is expressed in the church through the matrix of biblical and spiritual authority in both ordained and lay leadership."[9] This points again to the importance of being in a community in order for authentic biblical interpretation to take place.

Solivan points out that Pentecostal biblical interpretation owes its roots to one of its ancestors, Methodism, and to the "quadrilateral principle of Scripture, experience, reason and tradition." However, Solivan also affirms that "of these four, Scripture as illuminated by the Holy Spirit and experience as guided by the Holy Spirit in practice possess the greatest weight in authority."[10] In this sense, Pentecostalism goes back to Calvin and his assertion that "what lends authority to the Scriptures is not its authors or preciseness of its claims but the internal witness of the Holy Spirit in our hearts and minds which bears fruit in our transformation."[11] However, Solivan argues that much of North American Pentecostalism got away from such a "pneumatological" understanding of scriptural authority and interpretation in its desire to move from the "side streets" to "main streets" in terms of acceptance among North American Fundamentalists and Evangelicals with their faith statements about the inerrancy of Scripture and the words of Scripture. Latino Pentecostals have tended to hang on to "the clue given by Calvin in recognizing the internal witness of the Spirit in the Word and its transforming power in one's life (*Institutes* 7.5)."[12]

In addition, there is a socioeconomic dimension to views about biblical authority among Latino Pentecostals. Pentecostalism as a whole "was and continues to be rooted in the life of the poor" and thus "the literary medium," not always accessible to the poor, "was regarded with suspicion." They employed a "hermeneutic of suspicion" if the "letter of the law" were the only means of authority in their lives. After all, some books, such as law books, had often been employed to control the poor.

Solivan also cites the reality of transformed lives as a criterion for determining scriptural authority:

Transformation, both personal and collective, [was] the canon against
which questions of authority were to be determined. The verification
of Scripture's claims was not to be found in the internal claims made
by Scriptures themselves, but in the external power of the Holy Spirit
transforming people's lives in light of those claims.[13]

Experiencing God through healing and transformation made Scripture
come alive and gave it its authority.

Nonetheless, personal healing and transformation were not the only
signposts for biblical authority, argues Solivan, but also liberation from
destructive patterns that alienate neighbor from neighbor. These too "point
to Scripture's authority."[14] Thus, once again justice and community come to
the fore as the critical aspects of authentic biblical interpretation as understood by Latino Pentecostals. Scriptural authority relates to the power of
such Scripture, as experienced through God's Spirit, to bring about transformation, not just in the life of individuals, but also in the life of communities. To be a community that affirms the authority of the Bible as a guide
for faith and life means that Scripture comes alive in each person's life as he
or she lives out his or her faith in community. For Solivan, we cannot make
claims about faith without experiencing the results of faith and Scripture in
our lives. Moreover, without the experience of faith, propositional truths
around the authority of Scripture become static and decontextualized. We
need statements about Scripture that recognize the impact of social status
and cultural background in their formulation. The mutual critique between
faith experience and faith statements, what Solivan calls "the existential
aspect of biblical authority," sees Scripture as both *logos* and *pneuma*—reason and Spirit.[15]

In fact, Solivan concludes, Latino Pentecostalism has learned to read
Scripture from the perspective of the nondominant, the poor, who often
eschew the focus on literary aspects of Scripture. "A Pentecostal understanding of Scripture tempered by critical study also questions the other
side of Fundamentalism that is enamored of the letter of the text." This is
the case of fundamentalisms of both right and left, whether focused on literary inerrancy (the "right") or cultural analyses (the "left"), that limit the
conversation to mere literary interpretation. Poor, nonliterate cultures have
taught us to experience Scripture, not just study it or make static claims
about it. "When the Scriptures are reduced to a literary genre entrapped
in history, the results are similar—a dead, lifeless word, far from the living

creative Word of God spoken of by the prophets and experienced by the apostles and the church of the poor."[16] Thus, in Hispanic Pentecostalism, as understood by Solivan, biblical hermeneutics has an expansive understanding that encompasses the written text, a community's experience and living interpretation of that text, and its ultimate goal of personal and community transformation. In addition, the poor lead the way toward such a liberating perspective on the authority of Scripture.

Toward an Ecumenical Latino/a Hermeneutic of Scripture

These Pentecostal foci on experience, community, justice, and an authority demonstrated by transformation of lives are, I would argue, the building blocks toward an ecumenical Latino/a hermeneutic of Scripture. In his review of the emergence of Latino biblical hermeneutics, Francisco García-Treto acknowledges the growing ecumenicity of Latino Protestant and Roman Catholic biblical scholarship that transcends a separation based on Reformation principles:

> Today, within the U.S. Hispano/Latino churches, and specifically at the academic-theological professional level, a new ecumenical openness to cooperation, dialogue, and mutual acceptance has developed between mainline and other Protestant and Roman Catholic biblical scholars, to the extent that a true interpretative community . . . may already be identified.[17]

Rather than doctrinal principles of parent denominations, the focus of Latino biblical hermeneutics from both Catholic and Protestant biblical Latino/a scholars has been on community and the cultural/social nature of that community. Thus, García-Treto argues:

> Just as a transnational Hispanic/Latino consciousness of being a people is emerging and setting a sociocultural agenda in the United States, so a transdenominational consciousness of being an interpretive community reading the Bible from the social location of our people has arisen and is beginning to bear noticeable fruit.[18]

An ecumenical Hispanic/Latino biblical interpretation is emerging from at least the academic circles of biblical and theological scholarship across the

Catholic and Protestant divide, with subsequent impact on the minds and hearts of U.S. Latino/a people of faith everywhere.

One of the fundamental understandings of how Latinos/as read the Bible, therefore, is their engagement in a community of interpretation. Rather than being "lone rangers" in the task of interpretation, Latinos/as read Scripture in light of community. García-Treto explores the concept of "interpretative community" in literary studies and concludes that the "emerging emphasis on contextual or 'social location' readings of the Bible converge" with "the *teología de conjunto* being developed in U.S. Hispanic churches," that is, theology as a function of community implies that "new hermeneutical strategies and standpoints are being put in place."[19] This leads us then to a reading of Luke 24:13–35 that takes into account the creation of a community of interpretation between the travelers to Emmaus and Jesus, and between these same travelers, now transformed by their encounter with Jesus, and the rest of the disciples in Jerusalem.

Luke 24:13–35: An Exegetical Narrative

This is one of the most dramatic encounters in all of Scripture. Two grieving, confused pilgrims to the Jewish Passover in Jerusalem *and* pilgrims of the Jesus movement intensely discuss the events of the weekend just passed. Their beloved leader has been executed and as they left for home— Emmaus, some seven miles from Jerusalem ("six stadia")—they heard news of an empty tomb. The reader already knows what they do not know: indeed there is an empty tomb and news of a resurrection. Several women disciples and even Peter have been witness to this (Luke 24:1–12). However, for these travelers, this is just hearsay. Nonetheless, they proceed to discuss the events. Who are these two disciples of Jesus ("two of them," 24:13) and what happened to them on their trip to Emmaus? In what follows, I provide an overview of the narrative, with some relevant comments and questions for our consideration about this "way of justice" from a Latino Protestant perspective.

A Narrative Overview

This is the very day of the resurrection, and indeed all of Luke 24 seems to be set in one full day, from the resurrection (24:1–12) to the encounter on the road to Emmaus (24:13–35) to Jesus's appearance before the disciples in

Jerusalem (24:36–53), in which he gives them the final commission to wait for "power from on high" (24:48). Surrounding these miraculous events of resurrection, appearance, and commission in Luke's narrative is all the discussion taking place between the various parties. In our passage, the two travelers discuss with each other the momentous events they have just experienced (24:14). Then a stranger joins them and asks about what they have been discussing. I should say the fellow traveler is a stranger to them, but not to us, because Luke tells us that it is "Jesus himself." For the two travelers, Jesus's question surprises them and challenges them at the same time. In the Greek, Luke puts the question in a vivid way: "What are these words you exchange with each other [literally, "you throw at each other"], while walking" (24:17). The question epitomizes the nature of dialogue in community. One talks while walking, one engages in dialogue about life and faith while carrying out the normal circumstances of the day, what Ada María Isasi-Díaz calls "*lo cotidiano*." In this case, the walking and discussion occur during a return from a religious pilgrimage. True, it has been a pilgrimage like no other. A beloved leader has been slain, and the conversation back home is one of both amazement and sadness. When Jesus, the stranger, asks the question about what they have been talking about, the two "stand sadly," the text tells us, no doubt reflecting on all the negative things they have experienced the last few days, with only a flicker of hope in this notion of an empty tomb.

A word about who these two individuals might be is in order. They are simply referred to as "two of them," the "them" most likely referring to "the eleven and all the rest" (24:8). Later we find out the name of one of them—Cleopas, who finally does answer the question Jesus raises about what they have been discussing (24:18). We know of no other disciple of this name, except perhaps the husband of Mary, the latter a witness to the crucifixion according to John (John 19:25). There the name is listed as Clopas, a Semitic as opposed to Greek name like Cleopas. However, as Sharon Ringe points out, "the experience of immigrants in any age points to just such variation in names when people move from one language context to another." So both names, "Cleopas" and "Clopas," could be a reference to the same disciple.[20] The more intriguing question is who his companion was. Many have speculated that this was a married couple and this was a situation like many in which women remain nameless (although not in John's Gospel!).

Yet Jesus joins and addresses both of them: "While they talked and discussed, Jesus came near and went with them" (24:15). While the reader knows the identity of the new traveler, Luke gives us an interesting piece of information: "Their eyes were prevented from recognizing him" (24:15). The mystery lingers for these two disciples for the moment, but disciples who read Luke's narrative know some answers. This is Luke's goal in this passage: even though Jesus is no longer with us, he is still knowable, sometimes even more so than those who walked with him while he lived on earth. Resurrection makes possible recognition for all, always.

In fact, what makes it possible for these disciples to recognize finally that the stranger is Jesus (24:31) is some exchange of knowledge (24:32)—theirs (24:18–24) and his (24:25–27)—that they have acquired in the encounter, as well as the experience of seeing him break bread (24:30).

What the Disciples Know: 24:18–24

The disciples think they know more than this stranger. When Jesus asks what they have been exchanging words about, Cleopas responds, "Are you the only stranger living in Jerusalem who does not know what has happened in Jerusalem in these days?" Again, even the readers know more than they do, and so does Jesus, of course, who responds, nonetheless, "What things?" Cleopas responds with a Lukan version of the gospel story, noting how "Jesus of Nazareth" was a "prophet mighty in word and deed before God and all the people" (24:19). Despite this divine service to God's people, religious and political leaders of the community conspired against him, and Jesus was crucified (24:20). This, of course, is the news that made them sad (24:17).

Further, there was the sense of hope that Jesus had engendered, because they believed he would be the one "to redeem Israel" (24:21). Some scholars read this reference as the expectation of redemption from the imperial domination of their land. Nonetheless, even though three days have passed since he was killed, and hope seemed smashed, "some of our women" have seen an empty tomb (24:22) and heard from "angels" that Jesus was alive (24:23). Other witnesses went to the tomb as well and saw what the women saw. Thus the events detailed in Luke 24:1–12 are summarized by Cleopas and his companion. And even though they are telling this story to the very Jesus whom the angels proclaimed was alive, they finish this recounting with the declaration, "but they [the various witnesses to the empty tomb] did not see him." Once again the reader is drawn to this narrative by what they know in contrast to what the disciples know. Even though these are living witnesses, their knowledge at that point is limited compared to this next generation of believers. Thus there is some need for interpretation about what the travelers have just seen and experienced.

What Jesus Knows: 24:25–27

Jesus interprets his life, ministry, death, and resurrection differently from these and other first witnesses. Just as Cleopas seems to chastise their traveling companion for his lack of knowledge (24:18: "Are you the only stranger in Jerusalem who does not know . . .?"), Jesus challenges the lack of correct scriptural interpretation. In this way, the narrative also challenges the reader to get the facts straight. The story of Jesus was foretold by the very prophets to whom the disciples compare Jesus. It is just that folks are too "foolish and slow to believe in their heart all the things which the prophets spoke" (24:25). Among these prophetic truths is the reality of suffering for the Christ. In this way, the words of resurrected Jesus identify him with Israel's messianic expectation. Death is part of that suffering, which Luke identifies with "entering his glory" (24:26). The rest of how Jesus interprets Israel's Scriptures for this new postresurrection reality is summarized by Luke with the affirmation that Jesus used all the Scriptures, from the stories of Moses through all the Prophets and Writings, to demonstrate what "the things concerning himself" really meant. So interested are the two disciples in what Jesus has to share with them that they cannot bear to let him continue his journey, so they invite him into their home once they arrive in Emmaus, even though Jesus seemed quite willing to keep going (24:28–29). However, this show of hospitality on the part of these weary pilgrims opens up even greater opportunities for knowledge and recognition.

A Meal of Recognition: Luke 24:30–32

The liturgical imagery in these three short verses is striking. After reclining to eat with them, Jesus "takes the bread, blesses it, breaks it and gives it to them" (24:30). These actions echo most directly the exact same actions at the feeding of the five thousand earlier in Luke when Jesus, "taking the five loaves and the two fish and looking up to heaven . . . gave thanks and broke them. Then he gave them to the disciples to set before the people" (Lk 9:16, *New International Version*). A close parallel is more recent in the Lukan narrative, Jesus's last supper with his disciples, when "he took bread, gave thanks and broke it, and gave it to them, saying, 'This is my body given for you; do this in remembrance of me'" (Lk 22:19). The cumulative effect of these actions at table (no doubt Jesus broke bread with his disciples at various times with similar actions) was to clear the cloudiness in the eyes of Jesus's hosts. They had traveled with him for miles, listened to his interpretation of the Scriptures with regard to the meaning of the life, ministry, and death of Jesus, as much as he listened to theirs, and now, finally, at table, by blessing, breaking, and sharing the meal in a particular way, "their eyes were opened and they recognized him" (24:31a). The strange thing is that he immediately vanishes from their sight (24:31b). Once again, the narrator indicates to his readers that physical experience of Jesus is not necessary for authentic recognition.

Indeed, the two hosts do not dwell on his sudden disappearance. They dwell instead on their sudden recognition, which may not have been so sudden after all. "Did not our hearts burn in us as he spoke to us on the road and opened up the scriptures to us?" (24:32). Already in the "opening up of the scriptures," there was an opening up of their vision about who was traveling with them. However, scriptural interpretation was not enough without the experience of table, the experience of eating and being in community, taking the bread, blessing it and sharing it. Medical Mission Sister Miriam Therese Winter called this scene in Emmaus "eucharist with a small 'e'" because it reflects the power of recognition and creating community around table fellowship.[21] When Latino/a communities put emphasis on meals and fiestas as community building exercises of faith, they are not far from this notion of "eucharist with a small 'e'" nor far from the spirit of recognition and community exemplified by this meal in Emmaus.

Recognition Leads to Mission: Luke 24:33–35

Recognition is not complete without mission. Even though it is late in the day, the two disciples set out for Jerusalem to let their cohorts in the faith know that they have seen Jesus, however briefly with actual recognition of who he was, and just briefly when they realized who he was. How a full day's journey is possible in the evening of the same day is beyond the narrative interest of Luke. He just wants his readers to know that in one day a lot has happened: resurrection, testimony, travel, teaching, table fellowship, and recognition. Without missionary witness by those in the know to those in the dark, the day is not complete. And so the two weary travelers journey back from Emmaus to Jerusalem, energized by the news: Jesus has been raised.

Those already identified as "the eleven" by Luke are gathered with other disciples also bearing witness to a resurrection appearance. Thus they proclaim what will become a gospel truth: "Truly, the Lord has risen" (24:34a). Moreover, of all the important witnesses of this truth, it is important in Luke's narrative, in the Gospel as well as in Acts, that Peter (called Simon here, as also in Luke 4:38, 5:1–10, 6:14, and 22:31) has borne witness to the risen Lord. His leadership in the early Church relies on such experience, although not even Luke's Gospel includes a narrative description of such an encounter at the empty tomb or in Jerusalem. Paul also recounts the early Church's affirmation of Peter's seminal experience of the risen Lord as recorded in this kerygmatic text: "and that he appeared to Peter, and then to the Twelve. After that, he appeared to more than five hundred of the brothers at the same time, most of who are still living, though some have fallen asleep" (1 Cor 15:5–6, *New International Version*).

Emboldened by these testimonies, and by their own experience of the Risen One, both when they didn't realize it as well as when they did, the travelers from Emmaus recount their experiences focusing on the encounter on the road to Emmaus as well as the experience at table. On the road, the then unknown Risen One opened the Scriptures to them, but it was in the breaking of bread at table fellowship that his true identity was revealed to them. As one commentator has noted, the passage about the journey to Emmaus is about how Jesus comes to our recognition through "a revelatory process," rather than just necessarily a physical appearance.[22] In fact, while interpreting the meaning of his death to them, he was unknown, yet facts about him became known. When at table fellowship, it was the experience of seeing him break, bless, and give bread that revealed his true identity. "The scene is almost a mime, therefore, in which the unknown fellow traveler is recognized by his actions."[23]

All this they share with their fellow disciples, adding to the testimonies of resurrection already known and experienced. The themes echoed throughout the text, of speaking and reporting, of appearances and recognition, of fellowship and breaking of bread, are all recollected in this final text of the pericope: "And they reported the things that happened to them on the road and how they recognized him in the breaking of the bread," a fitting end to a dramatic text in this very eventful final chapter of the Gospel of Luke.

Lessons in Latino/a Protestant Hermeneutics

What have we learned from the reading of this narrative about Latino/a Protestant hermeneutics? First of all, scriptural interpretation is critical for authentic understanding. Jesus "opened" the Scriptures to his fellow travelers, and they sensed that there was something special in their encounter. However, it was not until he created community with them, by eating, that the true identity of the stranger was revealed. Scriptural interpretation, mere facts and information, without experience and encounter between human beings seeking faith and transformation, is insufficient. Latino/a Pentecostals, Protestants, and Catholics as well have known this intuitively. More recent biblical scholarship, by means of a variety of new methodologies, including reader-oriented approaches and postcolonial studies, have legitimized these concerns for the experience of the reader as equally important in the proper interpretation of Scripture. Without the experience of table fellowship, the two traveling disciples would not have had their eyes opened to the true identity of Jesus and the meaning of his life, ministry, death, and resurrection.

The Way of Justice

Finally, Latino Pentecostal, Protestant, and Catholic interpreters of Scripture have emphasized the goal of justice and transformation in scriptural study. In this passage, what "saddens" the Emmaus travelers the most, besides the tragic death of their leader, is that Israel would not be "redeemed" from its status as an imperial subject. Justice denied would be their lot in life. Their one great hope was extinguished by the domination system overwhelming their land. Yet, even in the most dire circumstances, when all hope seemed lost, resurrection happens, empty tombs are discovered, the faithful (in this case initially, only the women) bear witness, hope for justice is restored. Not only that, but mission begins and the community is revived, so much so that disciples meet, talk, and plan. "Truly the Lord is risen," they proclaim. Empire does not have the last word. In this sense, the road to Emmaus ultimately becomes the way of justice.

∼

Notes

1.   The following discussion on Latino Pentecostal hermeneutics is adapted from my earlier essay, "*Sola Scriptura* and Latino Protestant Hermeneutics:

An Exploration," published in *Building Bridges, Doing Justice: Constructing a Latino/a Ecumenical Theology*, ed. Orlando O. Espín (Maryknoll, NY: Orbis Books, 2009), 69–87.

2. Eldin Villafañe, *The Liberating Spirit: Toward an Hispanic American Pentecostal Social Ethic* (Grand Rapids, MI: Eerdmans, 1993), 123.

3. Ibid., 205, 206.

4. Eldin Villafañe, *Beyond Cheap Grace: A Call to Radical Discipleship, Incarnation and Justice* (Grand Rapids, MI: Eerdmans, 2006), 57–81.

5. Ibid., 66.

6. Ibid., 75–76.

7. Samuel Solivan, *The Spirit, Pathos and Liberation: Toward an Hispanic Pentecostal Theology* (Sheffield, UK: Sheffield Academic Press, 1998), 72.

8. Ibid.

9. Ibid., 93–94.

10. Ibid., 93, n. 1.

11. Ibid.

12. Ibid., 95.

13. Ibid.

14. Ibid.

15. Ibid.

16. Ibid., 96–97.

17. Francisco García-Treto, "Reading the Hyphens: An Emerging Biblical Hermeneutics for Latino/Hispanic U.S. Protestants," in *Protestantes/Protestants: Hispanic Christianity within Mainline Traditions*, ed. David Maldonado Jr. (Nashville: Abingdon, 1999), 164.

18. Ibid.

19. Ibid., 161.

20. Sharon H. Ringe, *Luke*, Westminster Bible Companion (Louisville, KY: Westminster, 1995), 287.

21. Miriam Therese Winter, *Eucharist with a Small "E"* (Maryknoll, NY: Orbis Books, 2005).

22. See Robert C. Tannehill, *Luke*, Abingdon New Testament Commentaries (Nashville: Abingdon, 1996), 352–58.

23. Alan Culpepper, "Luke," in *New Interpreter's Bible: A Commentary in Twelve Volumes*, ed. Leander Keck et al. (Nashville: Abingdon, 1995), 9:479.

$8.$

The Word of God, Wellspring of Life

Juan I. Alfaro

~

On joining the Royal Spanish Academy, the great Spanish orator Juan Donoso Cortés delivered a presentation entitled "Academic Address on the Bible" which for more than a century crystallized Hispanics' vision of faith about the Bible. Donoso Cortés began by saying:

> There is a book, the treasure of a people, which today is but a fable and the derision of the earth, which in times past was the star of the East, where all the great poets of the western regions of the world have gone to drink of its divine inspiration and from which they have learned the secret to lifting hearts and enrapturing souls with superhuman and mysterious harmonies. That book is the Bible, the book par excellence.[1]

Over the course of the last few decades, the Bible has become the book par excellence of the Christian communities of the Americas. For more than forty years, the Hispanic community in the United States has walked with the Lord Jesus to Emmaus, listening to his voice as he has again opened the meaning of the Scriptures. We will present here the biblical journey of the Hispanic people in the United States during the years that followed the Second Vatican Council (1962–1965). The Hispanic community has sought to engage in a pastoral reading of the Word of God in order that it may give them life and serve as guide and sustenance. It is the Word, wellspring of life, that impels to salvific action in communion with Jesus and which communicates peace and joy. It is the word of love that gives security and hope, affirming all the good that exists in the culture of Hispanic peoples.

The Second Vatican Council's Dogmatic Constitution *Dei Verbum* marked a biblical awakening in the entire Catholic Church, especially in the communities of Latin America, and subsequently, almost by extension, among the Hispanic peoples of the United States.[2] This awakening, as had already been pointed out by Cardinal Joseph Ratzinger, had already been prepared for, for many years, by experts in Sacred Scripture, especially in Europe, since before the Council.[3] The great pontifical encyclicals about the Bible, and, during the Council, the 1964 "Instruction on the Historical Truth of the Gospels," issued by the Pontifical Biblical Commission, opened doors and encouraged new academic studies of the Bible: Leo XIII, *Providentissimus Deus* (1893); Benedict XV, *Spiritus Paraclitus* (1920); Pius XII, *Divino Afflante Spiritu* (1943).

The efforts to spread the Word of God resulted in numerous encounters and biblical circles, as well as the publication of new translations of the Bible.[4] In the preconciliar period, as was done for centuries, while in Europe people "read" the Bible in stained-glass windows and stone-sculpted images in cathedrals; in Latin America schools of religious painting and art were flourishing with an infinity of portraits and works of art that familiarized people with the biblical stories. These sought not only to teach the basic content of those narratives, but primarily to motivate and provoke in the faithful a response of love and faith. For Hispanics, sacred art was characterized by very lively images, with plenty of blood, to stimulate the piety and devotion of the faithful. Later, catechisms and doctrinal summaries became more common, with less biblical content and with an emphasis on memorization of contents. Ordinary people's ability to become familiar with the content of the Bible was limited, through books of "sacred history" with numerous images and pictures that would aid the people in getting to know some of the "historical" sections of the Bible. In the twentieth century, as a response to Modernism and to the teachings of the Catholic Church, biblical publications of French and German origin, of a more popular type, emerged to "prove" that "the Bible was right." A presentation of the Bible that was more of a challenge and sustenance, rather than mere information, was lacking.

The final content of the Dogmatic Constitution on Divine Revelation, *Dei Verbum*, took shape throughout the Council as new insights emerged during the discussions that took place about other conciliar themes: from a focus on the inspired Word as source of revelation alongside tradition, to considerations of the Word as the providential and sacred history of the people of Israel, and finally the Word presented as the history of salvation of all peoples, because Israel should be viewed as the official model and pattern of how God relates to all peoples. It was emphasized that the Word was to be read in relation to the events and the signs of the times in which God continues to reveal himself in the history of nations. A challenge for our times had to be how to accompany the Christian community so that it would increasingly discover the hand and the action of God in today's story.

The New Biblical Awakening after the Council

Among Hispanics in the United States, the opening of the Mexican American Cultural Center (MACC) in San Antonio, Texas, was a cultural, pastoral, and biblical event for all Hispanic communities in the country. The opening of MACC had been insistently requested by PADRES, the National Association of Hispanic Priests, after a successful biblical retreat with John Linskens, C.I.C.M., at the seminary in Santa Fe, New Mexico, in 1971. The following year, MACC opened its doors, offering annual biblical and pastoral courses in which many Hispanic leaders and pastoral agents participated from around the country; they gathered at MACC to familiarize themselves and be enriched by new methods of interpretation and of application of the Bible to the Christian life. Pastoral theologians and biblical scholars of great international renown were invited to offer courses that enriched and motivated the life and participation of the faithful with expressions of faith, and gave direction to the pastoral enthusiasm that was being generated. John Linskens and Juan Alfaro were the resident biblical scholars who offered courses on biblical themes; the Austrian Johannes Hoffinger, S.J., who had been sent as a missionary to China and the Philippines, and who even before the Council was a pioneer in the renewal of catechesis in accord with its biblical roots; professors from the Pontifical Biblical Institute in Rome, Luis Alonso Schökel, S.J., and Juan Mateos, S.J., were invited to share the biblical vision of the Council; Alfonso Nebreda, S.J., came from Japan to provide magnificent contributions to biblical catechesis; José María Calle, S.J., of the Pastoral Institute of East Asia in Manila, Philippines, helped to complement the work of Nebreda. Jacques Audinet, well-known pastoral theologian from the Sorbonne and the Institut Catholique (Catholic Institute) of Paris, enriched participants with his methodology for biblical pastoral ministry. From Latin America came professors who helped provide a new perspective to the aspirations of Hispanics in the United States:

Pablo Richard, Roberto Viola, S.J., Eloisa Choury, Francisco Aguilera (who became auxiliary bishop of Mexico City), and Ricardo Ramirez, C.S.B., who became the second director of MACC and was later consecrated as the first bishop of Las Cruces, New Mexico.

From the beginning, Virgilio Elizondo, a priest of the diocese of San Antonio, founder and first director of MACC, had a providential vision of MACC founded on the Word of God. His love for Sacred Scripture led him to work on a doctoral thesis at the Institut Catholique of Paris, "Mestizaje, Cultural Violence and the Proclamation of the Gospel." A popular version of his doctoral thesis was published with the title *Galilean Journey: The Mexican-American Experience*, which directly invited Hispanics of Mexican descent to reread the Gospels so as to see themselves called and challenged in a special way to become new missionaries of gospel values for the American people of the United States.[5]

Early in 1974, MACC held a conference on National Catholic Rural Life, with bishops and delegates from rural areas of the United States. At that conference, MACC professors offered participants a biblical vision of the promised land as an instrument and sacrament of the liberation of the people of Israel from Egypt. Each family in Israel was to possess a portion of the land, inalienably, that would give them security, independence, sufficiency, and dignity. In many regions of our world, up to now, the possession of a piece of land continues to be an instrument of security and sufficiency for many families, especially the poor. The biblical presentations at that conference awakened a hunger and a desire to understand better how the Bible speaks to the problems and challenges of our times. The participants unanimously asked for the publication of the texts of the biblical addresses presented during the conference. Soon after, MACC began to receive invitations from various areas of the country to assist them in better understanding how the Bible speaks to today's challenges.

From the beginning, MACC employed the methodology born of the Second Vatican Council and developed at the meeting of the Latin American Episcopal Conference (CELAM) in Medellín, Colombia, in 1968, with its three steps of see, judge, and act, seeking to recover the biblical language that would help express the fundamentals of the faith of the Mexican American people. Popular rituals such as *posadas, piñatas, pastorelas*, biblical dramas, and celebrations of Holy Week, patronal feast days, and Corpus Christi, were occasions to establish people in the history of faith of the God who has spoken to us in the Bible.

The Medellín conference had a tremendous impact on the development of the biblical movement in the United States. The announcement of the convocation of the Second Vatican Council by Pope John XXIII led many to dream of the renewal of the Church in the twentieth century. An *aggiornamento* of the Church was expected, an updating of the themes and challenges presented to us by the times we lived in. The pope spoke repeatedly of his hope that the Council would help the Church open herself to the modern world, to our separated brethren, and to the poor. Openness to the modern world and to our separated brethren made good progress during the Council; an opening to the poor was less evident. Belgian Cardinal Leo Joseph Suenens, one of the Council moderators, during one of his last interventions, underlined that the Council had not responded adequately to the urgent clamor of the poor and that this would be seen as a clear omission in the conciliar documents. Some thought the popes had already addressed this adequately in the encyclicals *Pacem in Terris* and *Populorum Progressio*, both promulgated during the Council. The bishops of South America felt this absence in the conciliar documents, and immediately following the Council they convened at Medellín, where the most important viewpoints for their continent were openly discussed. The vast majority of participants at the Medellín conference had been council fathers in Rome. They understood well the spirit of the Council and the hopes it had awakened. Medellín affirmed the power of the Word that convenes and promotes communities, and invites them to a commitment to justice and to a commitment to the poor. In Medellín, a biblical movement began, destined to become the soul of the pastoral ministry and life of the Latin American people.

The Medellín conference had echoes in the United States when many poor communities began to search the Bible for inspiration and direction in promoting the justice and the respect they desired and deserved in the heart of the North American society and Church. Theologians and biblical scholars who came to MACC invited communities to see the examples and the struggles of Israel as models to seek and promote their own liberation.

Inspired by the example and the success of MACC with its biblical and pastoral courses, other pastoral centers were soon established for Hispanics in various regions of the country, opening their doors to the theologians and biblical scholars invited by MACC. In New York, Mario Paredes opened the Northeast Pastoral Center, and in Miami Mario Vizcaino, Sch.P., opened the Southeast Pastoral Institute. Other pastoral centers were temporarily opened in California, Chicago, and Ohio. The exchange of professors between the new pastoral centers and MACC contributed to providing a relatively united vision and hope to the pastoral and biblical emphases of many Hispanic communities in the country.

From the start, it was emphasized to the Hispanic people that they were now the new People of God, and that the Bible, as the Council taught, was a book that belonged to them and which they should access with faith and without fear (see *Dei Verbum* § 22). Besides transmitting the history and the experience of God by the people of Israel, the Bible was a book that transcended the borders of Israel to offer the revealed models of God's divine pedagogy with men in general (see *Dei Verbum* § 14). Each people has lived or is living its Old Testament, with its own peculiar experiences of God, and Hispanics in the United States are living their experience of the Gospel and the action of Christ in their own lives. The Bible, with Israel and the apostles, was presented and seen as a model to discover and interpret the action of God among Hispanic people today. It was very important to teach people how to interpret life in light of the Bible and how to interpret the Bible in the light of the life of faith.

The October 2008 Assembly of the Synod of Bishops on "The Word of God in the Life and Mission of the Church" reaffirms this vision of the Bible as a model of the relationship of God and people when it quotes the prophet Isaiah saying: "Blessed be my people Egypt, and the work of my hands Assyria, and my inheritance Israel" (Is 19:25). The prophet Amos was sterner still when he reminded Israel of the obligations that their election by God entailed: "Are you not like the Ethiopians to me, O men of Israel, says the Lord? Did I not bring the Israelites from the land of Egypt as I brought the Philistines from Caphtor and the Arameans from Kir?" (Amos 9:7). In the Acts of the Apostles Luke shows that God had shown toward all nations a providence like that which he had shown toward the people of Israel, given that all God's actions were aimed at having all peoples seek and find God, as was the history of Israel: "He made from one the whole human race to dwell on the entire surface of the earth, and he fixed the ordered seasons and the boundaries of their regions, so that people might seek God, even perhaps grope for him and find him, though indeed he is not far from any one of us" (Acts 17:26–27). The Old Testament can be read as a description of how God did this with Israel so that the people would seek and find him.

This vision of the Bible and of the Gospel was affirmed by the theological emphasis of the documents of the Medellín conference.[6] In the United States, the presentation of the insights of Dom Helder Cámara, archbishop of Recife, Brazil, in his booklet titled *El Desierto Fértil* (*The Fertile Desert*) had a tremendous effect.[7] Dom Helder invited us to reread the biblical stories keeping in mind the experiences of other groups and cultures, given that the hand of God has been present in the history of all nations, even if in the Bible alone do we find the revealed interpretation of that action of God amid a concrete and particular people. Dom Helder reminded us that the voice of God has found a response in many persons of faith and vision in their own times, who sacrificed for the good of their people:

> The first one to be so called by God was Abraham. He did not hesitate for an instant. He started out immediately. He had to face difficult trials. . . . Jews, Christians, Muslims all know the story of their father in faith. What is he called in other religions? . . . May non-Jews, non-Christians, non-Muslims allow us to give to these minorities called to serve, the Abrahamic name. There is no problem if every race and every religion gives him an equivalent name responding to their best disposition and particular tradition.[8]
>
> It is said of Abraham, and of other fathers in faith and guides of multitudes, that one day they will hear the call of God. This call of the Lord: can we hear it too?[9]

Bearing in mind that everything good comes from God, after the Council there were biblical scholars from Asia who sought the providential hand of God in the richness of the spiritual values of the ancient sacred books of India and China. This is affirmed by the final message of the Synod on the Word when it states:

> The Christian also finds common harmony with the great religious traditions of the Orient that teach us, in their holy writings, respect for life, contemplation, silence, simplicity, renunciation, as occurs in Buddhism. Or, as in Hinduism, they exalt the sense of the sacred, sacrifice, pilgrimage, fasting, and sacred symbols.[10]

Biblical history invites us to reread the history and experiences of other groups and cultures in light of our own Bible. Along these lines, as already stated, Virgilio Elizondo invited the Mexican American people to see themselves as included and called to reread the history of the first steps of the Gospel in the Mexican American community of our day and age. Jesus continues working and living among us, and we are privileged to respond to his call.

During this same period, Ernesto Cardenal published *The Gospel in Solentiname,* in which he invited his readers to make the Gospel a part of their lives, reading it from the perspective of the aspirations of the poor and as Good News for the poor.[11] The author underlined that just as St. Joseph and the Virgin Mary listened to the Good News from the lips of the shepherds in Bethlehem, so too can we listen and learn from the new modes that flourish among the poor and simple in order to update the Word of God in every particular environment.

In the early 1970s, Rodolfo "Corky" Gonzáles published *I Am Joaquín / Yo Soy Joaquín,* which resonated within Chicano circles and seemed to parallel some of the biblical lines of interpretation, especially among young people.[12] Gonzáles identified himself with figures from Mexican and Mexican American history of the past, be it Montezuma, Cuauhtémoc, Father Hidalgo, Benito Juárez, or others. He saw himself as a part of his forebears and felt called to be much more then they. In a similar fashion, in the Bible he saw Jesus as the new Adam creating a new humanity; the new Abraham, pioneer and model of our faith in the Letter to the Hebrews; the new Moses who promulgated his law in the Sermon on the Mount; the Son of David, greater than Solomon and the prophets, and wiser than all wise men. Jesus, in the plan of God, is the origin and the goal of the history of all peoples. As nations come to know Christ, they will recognize how the hand of God was present in their history. It could be said that until every nation attains to the knowledge of Christ, each nation is living its old testament, even without knowing it. After the revelation of Christ, every believer throughout time is living his personal gospel, in such a manner that each may feel called to write a fifth gospel based on their personal experience of being a witness of Christ, of the action of Jesus in their life. With this in mind, many Hispanics went on to see in their own history and in the biblical history the foundation for their current vision of their social and religious situation. The publication of the third edition of the *Biblia Latinoamericana,* with photographs of Dom Helder Cámara and Martin Luther King Jr., in the introduction to the Prophets, and with an image of the Mexican hero Pípila at the beginning of the book of Judges, was the source of much controversy, but it also led many to see their own story reflected and founded in the Bible.[13]

In the early years of the biblical awakening, a large number of Hispanics began to take ownership of the Bible and make it a part of their history. Due to the experience of oppression or discrimination that many felt, the book of Exodus, with the experience of the people of Israel in Egypt, became a key theme of many articles and simple publications. The Canticle of Mary, the *Magnificat,* also inspired many to fight in favor of the lowly, the disregarded, and the poor. Many turned to the experience of Israel during the Babylonian captivity to reread the experience of Hispanics who felt as captives now, though they were in their own land.

When in 1977 the Second Hispanic *Encuentro* was held in Washington, DC, among leaders of Hispanic communities across the country there was already a strong sense among the participants of being the People of God in present-day history. For ten years, many Hispanic groups considered themselves called to be "prophetic voices" in the midst of the North American society. The National Pastoral Plan for Hispanic Ministry approved by the National Conference of Catholic Bishops during its general assembly in Washington on November 18, 1987, inspired the publication of a bilingual book entitled *Prophetic Vision,* which affirmed the call of the Hispanic people in the United States to play their part in society and the Church.[14] In this book, explicit reference was made to an episode in the history of Israel (Num 11:16–30) when Moses, inspired by God, chose seventy-two judges to share his mission. Two of those judges, Eldad and Medad, also received the spirit of Moses, despite having been absent when the spirit was communicated to the group. In response to the objection of some at hearing that the two were prophesying in the camp despite not having been present, Moses exclaimed: "Would that all the people of the Lord were prophets!" (Num 11:29). Already from the Second Hispanic *Encuentro* in Washington many Hispanic groups seemed to feel called to be prophetic voices amid the North American society, and especially within the Church, so that their voice could resound calling the Church to change, to conversion.

Characteristics of the Hispanic Interpretation of the Bible

From the first moment when the Bible began to be spread and hunger for the Word became self-evident, brought about by God (Amos 8:11), groups and biblical studies associations multiplied. Soon principles and values emerged, fruit of a long experience with the Word from the time of the first missions, which were to be a source of unity among groups along the same lines and the teachings of the Church.

First, following a very ancient Hispanic tradition brought by the missionaries and continued until our own day and age, it was very important to seek guidance for daily life on the basis of biblical texts. In antiquity, St. Benedict composed his Rule as a practical way of living out the Bible. St. Isidore of Seville, who was the master of Hispanic theology for centuries, also underscored the importance of knowing how to make the teachings of the Bible a part of one's life so as to understand them better. The "moral" sense of Scripture, affirmed during the Scholastic age, had as its foundation the belief that the Bible is not only a rule of faith, but also a rule of conduct for people. Even the allegorical interpretations of biblical texts sought to make the Bible part of life, helping us understand the Christian life. Later on, due to the pressures born of the Inquisition and in the aftermath of the Protestant Reformation, it no longer seemed that important to see the Bible as the only source of "truths," given that, for that, we had the Magisterium of the Church to guide the interpretation of the Bible, especially through preaching. The Bible was aimed at prayer and daily life; thus, the Bible was to be seen, not as a book in which to find biblical quotes with which to learn formulas of faith that would help maintain the orthodoxy of the faithful, but rather to focus on orthopraxis, oriented to Christian living of the faith in charity, seeking norms to guide the life of the faithful. This connected well with the Hispanic tradition of associating the Bible with life rather than with formulas and dogmas that had to be learned by memory, a practice that had become prevalent since the days of the Protestant Reformation.

Besides, it was necessary to underscore that the Bible is the Word of God and the spiritual sustenance of believers, given that "man does not live on bread alone" (Mt 4:4). Extreme care was needed to avoid making the biblical bread into a book of proofs of prejudices and personal agendas, demonstrating how some are right and others are wrong; above all, it was important to avoid converting the bread and biblical sustenance into stones and quotes, oftentimes out of context, with which to attack other groups, be they Catholic or Evangelical.

The Bible, especially the message of Jesus, should be seen as an urgent call to conversion and change, not only at the individual level, but at the collective and social as well, in terms of work for justice, hope, peace, and solidarity, leading to the elimination of structures of injustice. The Bible was to be seen as a book filled with challenges and calls. Due to this, some Bible study groups were labeled dangerous and subversive because they saw in the Bible challenges to the social reality in which they found themselves. The footnotes of the *Biblia Latinoamericana,* which became very popular during that period, were seen by some in the United States and in countries in South America as subversive and dangerous; some people were assassinated for having a copy of that Bible. As Pope Benedict XVI reminded us in his encyclical *Spe Salvi,* the Bible, the Gospel, is not a communication of truths and of things that can and must be known, but rather it is effective and creative, destined to make things happen and change the life of the reader (*Spe Salvi* § 39). In the final document of *Aparecida,* fruit of the meeting of Latin American bishops with the Holy Father in Brazil, we are reminded that biblical reading and study aims at helping people open themselves up, not to something *of* the Messiah, but to the very Messiah, the path to growth into "the full stature of Christ" (Eph 4:13), a process of discipleship, of communion with the brethren, and of commitment with society (*Aparecida* § 24).

The history of the people of Israel has been studied and reread by many Hispanics in light of their present-day experience. The people of Israel in the Old Testament were always a people that could have been considered Third World. For centuries Israel found itself trapped by power and the interests of the powerful nations of its time: Egypt, Assyria, Babylonia, Persia, Greece, and Rome. It was a poor nation at the mercy of international politics. Though its leaders were required to anchor themselves in justice and their Covenant with God, they frequently sought political alliances that repeatedly led them to disaster; the poor carried the weight of the tributary taxation. In modern times, tensions between the East and the West left many poor countries at the mercy of the interests of the powerful. Many nascent Christian base communities started to emphasize that now, like then, it was time to anchor ourselves in the values of justice and fraternity called for by the prophets, and in the challenges of love presented in the Gospels. Some went so far as to suggest that to understand the biblical prophets it would be more advantageous to live in a Christian base community in Latin America that sought to live the challenges of the Bible than to travel to a German university to study the Hebrew language. This was due to the fact that they saw a social and faith affinity with ancient Israel. Truly, our forebears were the patriarchs, the prophets, and the apostles whose spirit continues to live in the Hispanic people. Given that the Bible was written as "good news to the poor" (Lk 4:18), it was necessary to keep in mind that all authentic biblical study would need to also become good news to the poor, for it was expected that it would lead scholars to a commitment in favor of the poor. This was especially expected in the North American society, in which many preachers seemed to distort the Bible to convert it into good news for the rich, disregarding the poor. Samuel Ruiz, bishop of Chiapas, who was totally committed to the marginalized and the poor, published a small book entitled *Teología Bíblica de la Liberación* (Biblical Theology of Liberation) in which he warned that if the rich, according to the Gospel, will enter the Kingdom of Heaven as by a miracle, another miracle will be needed for the rich (and for whomever plays party to them) to understand the Book of the Kingdom without obscuring the revelation of this Kingdom.[15] In speaking about the poor and the rich, one speaks not solely in material terms given that the rich of the world, who do share with the poor and make their causes their own, are in some ways poor in spirit, deserving of blessedness.

The theme of the Bible and the poor was stressed in the October 24, 2008, "Message to the People of God" from the Synod of Bishops, at the conclusion of the Twelfth Ordinary General Assembly of the Synod of Bishops:

> The Christian has the mission to announce this divine word of hope, by sharing with the poor and the suffering, through the witness of his faith in the kingdom of truth and life, of holiness and grace, of justice, of love and peace, through the loving closeness that neither judges nor condemns, but that sustains, illuminates, comforts and forgives, following the words of Christ: "Come to me, all you who labour and are overburdened, and I will give you rest" (Mt 11:28).[16]

The synod was very prudent in not calling to mind the judgments and condemnation of the rich and powerful in the Gospel according to Luke and in the Letter of James; furthermore, in Saint John, it is Jesus's own word that condemns those who do not receive it.

In this first period of the biblical movement among Hispanics in the United States, during the 1970s, a family-based catechesis that came from Puebla, Mexico, began to penetrate several areas. Ricardo Ramírez, C.S.B., director of MACC and later the bishop of Las Cruces, New Mexico, promoted this catechesis. The method used had a strong biblical dimension: starting with listening to the Word, followed by meditating on it, making it part of life and prayer, celebrating it, and culminating in the proclamation of the Word. In many places this family catechesis became an opportunity for in-depth biblical study among parents and their children, with a deep prayer dimension and *Lectio Divina*. To these groups could be applied the following words from the synod's "Message to the People of God":

> The family, enclosed between the domestic walls with its joys and sufferings, is a fundamental space where the word of God is to be allowed to enter. The Bible is full of small and great family stories, and the Psalmist depicts with liveliness the serene picture of a father sitting at the table, surrounded by his wife, like a fruitful vine, and by his children, "shoots of an olive tree" (Ps 128) . . . "the first preachers of the faith" (*Lumen Gentium* § 11).[17]

In the same final message, the bishops continue to underline the important role of the family in the transmission of the biblical message:

> Every home should have its own Bible and safeguard it in a visible and dignified way, to read it and to pray with it, while, at the same time, the family should propose forms and models of a prayerful, catechetical, and didactic education on how to use the Scriptures, so that "young men and women, old people and children together" (Ps 148:12) may hear, understand, glorify, and live the word of God.[18]

At Puebla in 1979, the Latin American Bishops' Conference promoted the biblical movement and the biblical apostolate, connecting the Word with evangelization. Some features of family catechesis were reinforced, reaffirming the fundamental characteristics of access to the Word of God: listening, deepening, celebrating, proclaiming, giving witness to the Word, and denouncing situations of sin, in order to achieve personal conversion and help build a new society.[19] A number of observers from the United States were present at Puebla, aware that the results of the conference would have significant repercussions on the pastoral ministry of Hispanics in this country, especially in insisting not so much on the interpretation of the Bible, but on interpreting the Bible in light of life.

During the 1980s, numerous requests began to arrive at MACC for courses and conferences to teach simple and practical methods with which to approach the study of the Bible in Hispanic parishes. Between 1982 and 1990 courses were offered each summer along these lines, and teams from MACC would travel to other dioceses of the United States offering simple methodologies within reach of the people. During this period, there was great collaboration with the pastoral centers in New York and Miami. Methods were developed for study with books, themes, individual texts, and especially following the See-Judge-Act method. It was important to teach groups how to ask vital questions for life and for the pastoral care of their communities, given that many were surrounded by studies with a strong fundamentalist perspective or which focused on superficial and trivial questions and "Bible trivia" games that were totally disconnected from the life of faith of persons and from the biblical message.

The See-Judge-Act Method

In many parts of Latin America, the See-Judge-Act method was deemed as the most appropriate to ensure that the Bible truly become a source of life for the study groups. Due to its simplicity and efficacy it was adopted in various forms by many groups, because it was a method that produced transformative results. This method of study generally includes sessions that last approximately an hour, with twenty minutes for each of the steps. It often happens that at the end of the hour, participants are left with a desire to study and understand more, as opposed to being jaded, as can happen with some methods that take much longer. All the study sessions, regardless of the method, should begin with prayer and a dialogue about the "news about the poor," the positive and negative things that happen in the heart of the barrio or the community that do not make it to the newspapers. These news stories serve as the basis for moving to some specific charitable action or commitment at the end of the session. A few examples can help us understand how the method works. If we take as an example the first chapters of Genesis, we will see the simplicity and efficacy of the method.

Taking the priestly narrative of creation in the first chapter of Genesis, the participants are invited, in the first step (*See*), to share examples and cases, from a faith perspective, where they have "created" something, be it a dress, a dish, a card, an ornament, or any other object. They may be asked to remember who or what they were thinking about in the process of creating it; what their expectations were when they gave it to or shared it with its addressee; how their work of "creation" was received, whether it was accepted with gratitude or silence. In the second step (*Judge*), they are invited to read and listen to a biblical text, paying attention not only to the content, but also to the words that are repeated. Members explain to one another what may not have been understood about the text. In this manner they come to see that the narrative is extremely artificial, that God creates by speaking or pronouncing ten words; that God "called" what he was creating; that God "saw" that all he created was good. In light of their reflection and experience as they "see," participants begin to discover above all else the greatness and the love of God, how he must have been thinking of us while creating things; and, finally, that God, after having created all things, gave it all as a gift to the couple he created; God created in order to reveal his love. In the third step of the method (*Act*), we consider how we receive and use this creation God has given us. As a result of this study, one community developed a local ecological program, having learned that everything that surrounds us is a gift from our loving Father whom we offend at times by filling trash bags with his great gift.

In the narrative of the temptation of Adam and Eve, after we share and *see* the various ways in which people are tempted and justify their falls (think of this society which consumes unnecessary things, fooled by the deceit of marketing strategies), we move on to *judge*, to read and meditate on the temptation of Adam and Eve in order to discover generally that we act just like them, with the same excuses and lack of repentance they exhibited. In the third step (*Act*), participants can share the ways in which we can avoid the many temptations that surround us.

In the story of Cain and Abel, one can begin to share in detail and *see* the common experiences of violence that afflict many communities. The reading of the biblical text, taking notice of the verbs and, above all, of words that are repeated, often brings the participants to *judge* and think about how we too might have a dormant Cain within each of us, which we must control to prevent him from springing up. In the *act* section the group can reflect on ways in which individuals and society can prevent outbreaks of violence from occurring.

Other themes that interest many Hispanics might include the story of the Tower of Babel and the confusion of tongues, and its antithesis, the day of Pentecost; the vocation and migration of Abraham and the trials that accompanied him, given that many immigrants now live in a similar situation; the story of Joseph of Egypt; and many more. The miracles and stories of the Gospels offer many opportunities for study, as they have a very meaningful message that speaks to today's realities.

Study According to Themes and Texts

Biblical study according to themes can be developed adapting the See-Judge-Act method. Once the theme has been chosen, you can find in a thematic Bible some texts from Scripture that touch upon the theme. Participants begin by sharing their experience of faith as it relates to the chosen theme (be it vocation, conversion, sacrifice, love, patience, etc.), and then read some biblical texts that touch on the theme, paying attention to verbs and special terms in the narratives. The most important point in this method of study is the questions the participants ask about the texts. They ought to be pastoral questions that take into account the experience of faith of the participants. If we take as an example the theme of vocation in the Bible, after sharing known cases of people who have embraced a vocation in their life and have made sacrifices in order to pursue it, the group can read several texts of biblical vocations, noticing the variety and diversity of details we find in the Bible. God does not often call people directly, often using intermediaries instead. God calls people of all social classes and with totally different qualities; God calls them in the midst of their daily activities and sometimes even in their dreams. The aim of any call is always the formation and direction of the people of God. No one is called for personal and exclusive gain. The lives of persons called by God very often change radically, being considered "consecrated" to their mission. The last part of the study is dedicated to discerning how to help people discover their vocation and how to encourage them to follow that call.

With ordinary communities, the study of texts can be adapted to the needs and the capacity of the group. One simple approach is to invite the participants to listen to biblical text, after which they can respond to questions about the words or ideas that they may not have understood well; then each participant is asked to choose a verse or idea from the text read that he or she considers most important or has the greatest impact, reflecting on it, and pointing out the reasons why he considers it such. Then each is asked to briefly write down that thought or idea, with an assessment in a few words that they will share with the other participants in the study. It is surprising to see how in this method all participants are both teachers and disciples. At the end, the person who serves as facilitator of the group can provide a summary of the fruits shared and reflect with members on what the text is asking of the participants today.

Biblical Fundamentalism

Biblical fundamentalism has had limited influence on Bible studies in Hispanic communities. We must keep in mind that currently fundamentalism has become a phenomenon with cultural, political, economic, and ethical dimensions. There are tendencies that claim to be right and certain, while declaring others to be in the wrong. For most, biblical fundamentalism has been separated from its Protestant roots regarding fundamental truths that needed to safeguard biblical revelation, and has become a way of approaching biblical texts from a literal and an ahistorical point of view, with no relation to the literary and historical context that gave rise to the text at hand.

It has become common practice to teach Hispanic communities that the most important thing when approaching a biblical text is not so much to ask simply what it says or what it says to me, but rather what was the author wanting to transmit to the readers, what attitudes did he desire to awaken in them, and how does this text continue to speak to us today. The question as to whether what is related in the text actually happened or not historically is relegated to second or third place, because what is sought here is to discern the message of God in what the author said and in what the text says to us today.

Fundamentalism loses its power and attractiveness in Hispanic communities when pastoral questions are raised about the texts that take the reader beyond the text to discover its theological and pastoral dimensions, how the text can become part of their life of faith. In our experience with Bible study groups, the deficiencies of fundamentalism are more clearly seen through practical examples, with biblical passages well known to our people, so that people may see what might be positive about fundamentalism, and all that is lost when other riches in the text are overlooked; one could almost say a fundamentalistic reading of Scripture in some ways is to grasp at straws. In presenting the Bible to people, we must keep in mind that the Word lives in the faith and love of the believing community, whom we wish to familiarize with three levels of interpretation:

1. A literal level that focuses on the text and sometimes seeks to find definitive affirmations of faith
2. A theological and revelatory level that seeks to discover the mind of the author and whether there is something more that the author intends to communicate through the text
3. A level of pastoral actualization in which we let the text live, seeking to make it part of the faith experience of the reader

In order to help people understand this process we have sometimes turned to the texts of the Gospel according to St. Luke, well known to the people, related to the joyful mysteries of the Rosary; simple people can appreciate what fundamentalism misses and, at the same time, they can begin to learn how to situate the Bible into their own lives, as the documents of Puebla suggest.

Thus, the joyful mystery of the Annunciation to Mary, on the literal level, can lead the reader to appreciate the angel's announcement with the twofold promise that Mary would become the mother of the Son of David, whose kingdom will have no end, as they also appreciate the second promise made by the angel, that her son shall be called Son of the Most High. From the literal level, the reader is then invited to look at the narrative from a more theological level or perspective. In the Hispanic tradition, the first joyful mystery is often called the incarnation of the Son of God because one must consider that on that day the coming of the Holy Spirit upon Mary and the incarnation of the Son of God in her womb was more important than the coming of the angel to Mary. The reader is also invited to meditate on what type of person Mary must have been to whom the Spirit and Jesus came that day: Mary was a simple woman obedient to the plan of God, the woman who made the desires and yearnings of the poor her own, as she proclaims in her canticle, the Magnificat. The pastoral level of the text is made present as the reader is invited to reflect on who today resembles the Mary of the Gospel, people of simple faith who are yearning for the presence of God/Jesus in their lives, and for liberation from the many pressures they suffer in present-day society.

In the second joyful mystery, at the literal and fundamentalist level, one can appreciate the Visitation of Mary to her cousin Elizabeth, discovering the attitudes and faith values, love, and hope which the text reveals. Also one could note that the text suggests two visits: a visit between the two women and a visit between the two children in their mothers' wombs. One could reflect also on the three beatitudes contained in the text, regarding the faith of the women and the content of Mary's canticle, the Magnificat. At the theological level, the reader can be invited to think about the type of person whom Jesus comes to visit, who experiences the great joy celebrated in this mystery; it is John the Baptist, the last and greatest of the prophets. One could think about how the child leaps for joy in his mother's womb as he experiences the salvation announced by the prophets and awaited for centuries, now becoming a reality with the presence of the Savior in the life of John. At the pastoral level of application to today's life, the reader can meditate on the prophets of today, people who are ardently committed to change in society and in the Church, who need the presence of Jesus in their life and commitment so that they might continue fighting and working with joy and hope, despite whatever opposition and difficulties they may encounter on their journey.

In the third joyful mystery, the birth of Jesus in Bethlehem, at the literal level one could ponder how amidst human, political, and religious powers, it is the power of God that directs human history; one could meditate on the simplicity, poverty, and humility of the Holy Family under those circumstances. At the theological level, one could ask who experiences joy and gladness in that event: it is the poor and humble, the shepherds, chosen by God once again, who carried the Good News to others. At the pastoral level, one could ponder and pray for people today that are like the shepherds, lowly people who live with great sacrifices, oftentimes ignored or unappreciated by society, people to whom we hope Christ will come again to fill with joy.

In the fourth joyful mystery, the presentation of the child Jesus in the Temple, at the literal level, one could ponder Joseph's and Mary's fidelity to the Law, the presence of Jesus as a poor person among the poor, bringing the offering of the poor to the temple. At another level, more theological, one could ponder the significance of the two individuals who experience a special joy at the presence of their Savior: Simeon and Anna. The two were elderly and for many years had awaited the fulfillment of the promises God had made to them; they were symbols of faith and fidelity. At a pastoral level, one could think of the many who today are awaiting the saving action of God in their lives and whose experience would suggest that God seems always to come late, though he never fails those who place their hope in him.

In the fifth joyful mystery, when one reads and meditates on the child Jesus lost and found in the Temple, at a literal level one could meditate on the agony of the parents as they search for their lost child; also, one could meditate on the mysterious response Jesus gave to their question. Young people can be reminded that, when they complain that their parents do not understand them, Jesus too lived that, but despite that, he obeyed them. At a more theological level, one can meditate and think about what the Evangelist may have communicated in this presence and absence of Jesus that already foreshadowed the suffering of his disciples during the three days of his Passion and death. At the pastoral level, readers can be invited to reflect on a common Christian experience of the presence and absence of Jesus in the spiritual life of believers. In the four previous mysteries we have seen that in each, Jesus came to visit different types of people who seem to have a symbolic role; but the experience which people of faith tend to have sooner or later is that Jesus seems lost to them (as happened to St. Teresa of Avila), and some feel they have lost their faith. That is the moment to meditate and ask Jesus to allow himself to be found once again by those who are truly his.

The Future and *Lectio Divina*: Challenges

In the past several years, we have been blessed by the appearance of new texts and commentaries on the Bible that are accessible to ordinary people. The United Bible Societies have helped with the publication of various editions of the Bible approved by various Catholic bishops. *La Biblia Católica para los Jóvenes,* which is much more than an adaptation of the same Bible published in English, with its attractive appearance, has taken into account the culture and challenges that affect Hispanic youth in the United States, and has been well received in the United States and throughout Latin America. Its introductions, illustrations, and supporting teaching tools, along with the pastoral commentaries, can more directly reach the hearts of our young people because it responds to many of their interests. *La Biblia de Nuestro Pueblo* is highly recommended for its explanatory notes at the reach of common people, in addition to being attractive due to its affordable price. At present, under the direction of CELAM and the Unites States Conference of Catholic Bishops, a new translation of the Bible is under way which will be known as *La Biblia en la Iglesia,* with the hope that it will be of great benefit for Catholics across the American continent. This Bible aims at offering a good interpretation of the texts for our people, one that might assist in our dialogue or communication with God (prayer), and also help in the Church's witness through its proclamation, evangelization, catechesis, and the transformation of society. To this end, the notes to the pericopes will receive great care and special attention so that, as often as is possible, they might include tips for prayer (*Lectio Divina*) and evangelization. A goal of the Assembly of the Synod of Bishops on the Word has been to promote worldwide the practice of *Lectio Divina,* the meditative reading of the Word of God which was spoken of in the instruction by the Pontifical Biblical Commission, on "The Interpretation of the Bible in the Church."[20] *Lectio Divina,* which was so fruitful for centuries in the monasteries of many contemplative orders, is being proposed as an ideal model with which to enrich the spiritual life of men and women today. Santiago Silva Retamales, auxiliary bishop of Valparaíso, Chile, who is in charge of the Biblical Center CEBIPAL-CELAM, has been a promoter of this new, yet ancient, manner of rereading Sacred Scripture. In order for the prayerful and ecclesial reading of the Bible to produce fruit, the Sacred Scriptures suggest at least three approaches:

- An attentive and respectful reading of the text, seeking to discover what God intended to communicate to us, remembering that God speaks to us in the Scriptures through men and in human language that is conditioned by the historical moment in which the biblical text was composed
- An updating of the meaning of the biblical message for here and now through the spiritual exercise of meditation and prayer. In dialogue with God, the Word is made current through reflection, analysis, comparisons, and questioning that shed light on present-day life with its multiple problems and challenges. God continues to speak to and question the reader today about the circumstances of his life
- The action and work of the Holy Spirit, which aids in the contemplative gaze of God and, from him, of reality, in such a way that it allows us to recognize God always and in all things; contemplating God with spiritual joy in all people, seeking his will in all that we live

Lectio Divina must lead the believer to a personal encounter with Jesus, the Son of God, the Face of the Father, the source of our discipleship, and, at the same time, to the missionary zeal for a new evangelization that is enculturated in the reality within which we live.

The question raised by Pope John Paul II at the start of the Third Millennium will always remain a valid one: In what way is the Word of God the inspiration of our Christian existence, as was asked by the Council's Dogmatic Constitution *Dei Verbum*? It will also remain everyone's responsibility to ensure that the Scriptures are Good News to the poor today when so many try to make the Scriptures Good News to the rich in order to secure their positions, instead of questioning their values and structures. The task indicated in the Pontifical Biblical Commission's "Instruction on the

Interpretation of the Bible in the Church" also remains: seeking to make the biblical passages say the same thing God and the inspired authors intended them to say to their generation.[21]

In his intervention at the Synod of the Word, Mons. Silva Retamales emphasized:

> not only when one reads the Word, but also when one allows it to read us, not only when we favor the encounter of man with the Scriptures, but also the encounter of the Word with human words, the mutual interpretation between Word and life makes its proclamation significant for those who seek to know where "to stay" (Jn 1:39), where to place their lives so that they might have meaning. . . . We read the Scriptures from the vantage point of who we are and are called to be. The Word of God generates processes of humanization; the identity that the encounter with the Word brings about is lived in the ecclesial community and is testified in its mission. . . . We need to return the Scriptures to their original context: communities that welcome the Word, celebrate it, and announce it as the principle of a new order.[22]

It will always be a challenge for experts and scholars of the Word of God to recognize that the key to the Scriptures that they have received in their academic formation is intended, not as a means to become part of a closed circle of experts who play tennis with their back-and-forth questions and answers, but as a means by which they might open the Scriptures to common people, so that they may understand and participate more fully in God's designs for humanity and experience the joy that the Word of God brings to the life of the believer.

~

Notes

1. Juan Donoso Cortés, "Discurso Académico sobre la Biblia," April 18, 1848 (Bogotá: Zalamea, 1889).
2. See the comprehensive article on this topic published by the Coordinator of the Catholic Biblical Federation for Latin America and the Caribbean (Federación Bíblica Católica para América Latina y el Caribe) Gabriel

Naranjo Salazar, C.M., in *Medellín: Teología y pastoral para América Latina* 35, no. 37 (2009): 5–36.

3. Joseph Ratzinger, "Dogmatische Konstitution über die göttliche Offenbarung (Constitutio dogmatic de divina Revelatione '*Dei Verbum*')," in *Das zweite Vatikanische Konzil. Dokumente und Kommentare, Lexikon für Theologie und Kirche*, ed. Heinrich Suso Brechter et al. (Freiburg: Herder, 1967), 2:497–528, 571–81.

4. Among these translations were *Torres Amat, Nácar-Colunga,* and *Bover-Cantera* from Spain, as well as of *Biblia Comentada* by Mons. Juan Straubinger of Argentina.

5. Virgilio P. Elizondo, *Galilean Journey: The Mexican American Promise* (Maryknoll, NY: Orbis Books, 1983).

6. Consejo Episcopal Latinoamericano, Documentos Finales de Medellín (1968), http://www.mscperu.org/biblioteca/1magisterio/america_lat/bl_medellin.htm (in Spanish).

7. Helder Cámara, *El Desierto Fértil* (Salamanca, Spain: Sígueme, 1972).

8. Ibid., 18.

9. Ibid., 25.

10. Message to the People of God of the XII Ordinary General Assembly of the Synod of Bishops (October 24, 2008), 14, http://www.vatican.va/roman_curia/synod/documents/rc_synod_doc_20081024_message-synod_en.html.

11. Ernesto Cardenal, *The Gospel in Solentiname*, trans. Donald D. Walsh (Maryknoll, NY: Orbis Books, 2010).

12. Rodolfo "Corky" Gonzáles, *I Am Joaquín / Yo Soy Joaquín*, http://www.latinamericanstudies.org/latinos/joaquin.htm.

13. *La Biblia Latinoamericana*, 3rd ed. (Madrid: Ediciones Paulinas, 1972).

14. S. Galerón, R. M. Icaza, and Rosendo Urrabazo, *Prophetic Vision: Pastoral Reflections on the Pastoral Plan for Hispanic Ministry (Visión Profética: Reflexiones pastorales sobre el plan pastoral para el ministerio hispano)* (Kansas City, MO: Sheed & Ward, 1987).

15. Samuel Ruiz, *Teología Bíblica de la Liberación* (Mexico City: Librería Parroquial, 1975), 11.

16. "Message to the People of God," at the conclusion of the Twelfth Ordinary General Assembly of the Synod of Bishops (October 24, 2008), 13, http://www.vatican.va/roman_curia/synod/documents/rc_synod_doc_20081024_message-synod_en.html.

17. Ibid., 12.

18. Ibid.
19. Consejo Episcopal Latinoamericano, Documento de Puebla, III Conferencia General del Episcopado Latinoamericano, 1305, http://www.uca.edu.ar/esp/sec-pec/esp/docs-celam/pdf/puebla.pdf.
20. Pontifical Biblical Commission, "The Interpretation of the Bible in the Church" (March 18, 1994), *Origins* 23, no. 29 (January 6, 1994): 497–524; also available at http://www.ewtn.com/library/CURIA/PBCINTER.htm.
21. Ibid.
22. I personally received the text of this intervention from my friend, Bishop Silva Retamales.

9.

"Hearts Burning Within Us"

The Bible in Nahuatl
and the Evangelization of a New World

Jaime Lara

~

N*ahuatl* is the ancient language of the Mexica, known to us more com-
monly as the Aztecs. It also refers to the larger world of pre-Hispanic
Mesoamerica, the matrix culture of many Latinos in the United States of
America. But much of what this chapter covers will also be applicable to
Hispanics from the Caribbean and Central and South America.

Here I am highlighting the biblical culture out of which Hispanic Catholicism has emerged. I hope to dispel a myth propagated by some fundamentalist Protestant and Evangelical groups, namely, that Catholics in Latin
America never had the Bible and that Latino Catholics are ignorant of it. A
simple survey of baptismal records, for example, will show that, in addition
to the names of all the Christian saints, Latino Catholics bear the names of
all the major and minor characters of the Old and New Testaments. How
many Anglo Christians are ever baptized "Melchizedek" or "Uriel"? Those
names are quite common in Spanish-speaking Catholic America. Or how
many Anglos are serenaded on their birthdays with the morning psalm of
King David (Psalm 58)? Hispanics are.[1] But there are more historical reasons for my statement, as we shall see.

Moreover, I hope to show that the Hispanic Catholic approach to Scripture is entirely consistent with the long history of the Bible as "the Church's
liturgical book and treasure house."[2]

The Bible as Book

I begin by asking three questions about the book we call "the Bible": What was a Bible on the eve of the discovery of America? Where did you get one? And who could read it? These questions may not at first appear relevant, but they will have wider implications for the use of biblical texts and for knowledge of the Scriptures in the Americas.

To begin quite generally, a book today is a different sort of thing from a book in the Middle Ages.[3] The production of a book was an incredibly expensive, labor-intensive process. Book production involved the death of animals from whose hides the parchment would be made through a process of curing and scraping. It involved the creation of inks from plants and quill pens from the feathers of birds, as well as the painstaking copying of texts, often adorned with hand-painted illustrations, and all packaged in hand-wrought leather bindings. As a result, a book was an extremely precious commodity, far beyond the economic means of even the well-to-do layman.

With regards to the Bible in particular, the first thing to realize—and one that will certainly shock fundamentalists—is that there was no Bible in the early Church or Middle Ages in the sense of a single volume containing the whole of the Hebrew and Christian Scriptures. A complete Bible would have required over 1,500 parchment pages. Binding such a tome together in a single volume would produce an unusable text, too heavy even to lift, and easily damaged.[4] Instead, a complete Bible would usually be divided into nine volumes, and even these would be rare. It is doubtful that, in the Middle Ages, all Christian communities had all fifty-two books of the Old and New Testament; most parish priests never owned a complete Bible before modern times.

More commonly, books of Scripture were circulated in even smaller volumes, like the four Gospels in one tome and the letters of St. Paul in another. It was only on the eve of the invention of movable type in the fifteenth century that small complete Bibles with miniscule handwriting could be purchased; but only in large cities, like Paris, that had universities and professional scribes.[5] I mention this because some of these rare medieval Bibles made their way across the Atlantic Ocean in the sixteenth century and can be found today in colonial libraries in Mexico and Peru, a sign of biblical interest by the first missionaries.[6]

Moreover, until the early modern period, the biblical text occurred without the kind of navigational apparatus to which we are accustomed:

numerical chapters and verses. And so, the text was not subject to the kind of dissection into discrete units that we think of as useful for "Bible study."[7]

The Bible as Sound

This is not to say that the complete text was unknown, but biblical texts were encountered in other ways: as liturgical texts and as embedded within larger theological commentaries. As liturgical texts, biblical passages would be found in Gospel Books, lectionaries, and psalters. Gospel Books, when not in use, were frequently kept in the tabernacle together with the consecrated host, and that fact indicates a certain attitude toward the physical book itself.

For the first 1,500 years of Christianity, the Bible was the Church's liturgical book; and this is an absolutely crucial point for understanding a Catholic approach to Scripture. As such, the Scriptures were encountered by most Christians in *oral* form, either spoken or sung. Members of religious orders heard the biblical pericopes sung in Latin during the Divine Office, or read to them as *Lectio Divina* during meals in their refectories.[8] The laity heard Scripture passages sung or read in Latin at every Eucharist, and then translated or paraphrased in the vernacular for the sermon. To relate to a text primarily by hearing is a different relationship with that text from one of merely reading. For one thing, reading is a typically private and independent exercise open to misinterpretation, while hearing the Bible in public is a communal experience that already situates the Scriptures in a context for interpretation. Hearing suggests a posture of attentiveness, placing the hearer at the text's disposal, while reading black type on white paper with paragraphs and numerical dissections controls how the text is appropriated, placing the biblical text at the disposal of the reader.

The Bible as Sight

More importantly for the New World and the formative period of Hispanic Catholicism, the Bible was always heard and read by "the witness of the eyes," as Bishop Eusebius of Caesarea would say.[9] There is a Spanish proverb that explains the highly visual nature of Hispanic liturgical practice: *Ojos que no ven, corazón que no siente* ("The heart cannot feel what the eyes do not see"). We might say the same for the Bible in a Catholic context.

From the earliest days, Christians knew the history of salvation through stories and images. The overwhelming evidence of the third-century house churches and catacombs, for example, would have us believe that every Christian man, woman, and child knew certain biblical passages of the Good Shepherd, Noah's Ark, the Sacrifice of Isaac, Moses and the Red Sea, Daniel in the Lion's Den, the Three Youths in the Fiery Furnace, and the Visit of the Magi *through pictures* precisely because these represented the most often-read pericopes of their liturgical gatherings.[10]

From the Carolingian period onward it was common practice to display the illustrated Bibles opened on altars; this seems to be the primary way that the book of Revelation, for example, was known to the faithful.[11] The art of the medieval cathedrals, churches, and chapels was thoroughly biblical with giant wall murals, stained-glass windows, and carved wooden altarpieces wherein even the most obscure Old or New Testament personage or story might prove a useful model of virtue or vice. The sheer quantity of images demonstrates that the medieval layman and woman were probably more visually literate than we are today.

Nor were the visual arts a dumbing down to the illiterate *rustici*, as some have mistakenly suggested.[12] Preachers, for example, had a useful tool in the so-called *Biblia pauperum*, an illustrated book that paired, on each page, two Old Testament stories that foreshadowed the central New Testament event (see figure 1). This was complemented with quotes from four prophets placed above and below the central scene. The intricate Latin text in Gothic script, and the often-

Fig. 1. *Biblia pauperum* (1480). Page exegeting the Transfiguration of Christ. (Courtesy of the Beinecke Rare Book and Manuscript Library, Yale University.)

arcane correspondences between stories, shows that this was no Bible for the poor and unlettered, but was an early "Homily Help" for preachers in their preparation of the Sunday sermon.[13] It stimulated their visual imagination and allowed them, in turn, to conjure up word-images in their hearers. This was a tried-and-true procedure of homiletic *ekphrasis*—the graphic, often dramatic description of a visual work of art—used in the Old World as well as the New[14] (see figure 2).

My point is that this attitude toward the Scriptures continued even after the invention of printing in the late 1400s.[15] While it is true that the Gutenberg Bible was the second book ever printed with movable type,[16] we should not think that printed Bibles were any less expensive or inaccessible. Bibles continued to appear as multi-volume works, they were still labor-intensive to produce and correct, and they were a commodity of the few who were

Fig. 2. Diego Valadés, *Rethorica Christiana* (1579). Friar preaching with pictures of the Passion. (Courtesy of the Beinecke Rare Book and Manuscript Library, Yale University.)

capable of reading. Most Catholics and Protestants were illiterates well into the nineteenth century; it is a myth to think that general literacy occurred as soon as William Tyndale translated the Scriptures into English in 1525, or Martin Luther translated them into German in 1534.[17] The Bible still had to be read out loud to most believers either in church or at home, which is to say that the Scriptures continued to be experienced primarily as *sound* rather than as print. And both Catholics and Protestants hesitated to put the sacred texts into the hands of unschooled readers for fear of political upheavals caused by misreading of the text, especially the book of Revelation. For example, King Henry VIII, head of the Anglican Church and of the Protestant Reformation in England, prohibited the reading of the Bible by women, farmers, and day laborers.[18]

Four Modes of Exegesis

Neither the Renaissance nor the Protestant Reformation essentially changed the manner of exegeting Scripture that was inherited from the Fathers and formulated in the medieval period.[19] Well into the eighteenth century, Catholic and Protestant intellectuals read and explained the Bible on four levels of exegesis that were schematized as tree-like, with root and branches. The four senses of Scripture were history, typology, morality, and anagogy.[20] The first and root sense was the historical or the literal; then came the spiritual "branches." The second sense, the *typological*, signified the fulfillment of an Old Testament person or event in the New Testament; it was an explanation in terms of foreshadowing Christ, the Church, or the sacraments. The typological sense of the Old Testament is evident in the Emmaus story (esp. Lk 24:25–27): "Then Jesus said to them, 'Oh, how foolish you are, and how slow of heart to believe all that the prophets have declared!' . . . Then beginning with Moses and all the prophets, he interpreted for them the things about himself in all the scriptures" (i.e., in the Hebrew Bible).

The third sense of Scripture, the *moral* sense, provided an ethical meaning applied to men and women in the here and now, and to the salvation of the individual soul; while the fourth sense, the *anagogical*, provided an eschatological explanation that elevated the thoughts of the hearer from visible to invisible things, to a higher truth and to an eternal fulfillment of God's plan.[21] I will return to this schema below because it was used in the evangelization of the Aztecs.

On the eve of the discovery of America, the history of the Bible was intertwined with three epoch-making developments: the invention of printing, Renaissance humanism, and the Protestant Reformation. In the late Middle Ages Parisian biblical scholars, like the Franciscan Nicholas of Lyra, had even consulted Jewish rabbis regarding the correct interpretation of Hebrew words and objects in an effort to improve the historical, literal understanding.[22] With pseudo-archaeological interest, these scholars began to illustrate Bibles with what they considered accurate maps and drawings of cities and buildings as they had appeared in the times of David, Solomon, or Ezekiel (see figure 3). These illustrated Bibles traveled with the Franciscans, Dominicans,

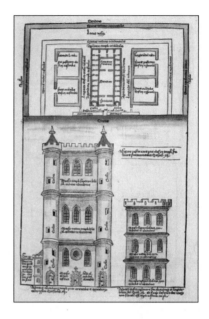

Fig. 3. Nicholas of Lyra, *Postilla super totam bibliam* (1493). Illustrations of Ezekiel's utopian temple complex. (Private collection.)

and Augustinians to New Spain (Mexico). The drawings were later used for the first Christian architecture in the Spanish colonies of the Americas. For example, Ezekiel's utopian restored city of Jerusalem (Ezekiel 40–48) served well for the idealistic "new Jerusalem society" that the friars wished to install in the Americas, far from the European doctrinal conflicts and wars of religion. But, as I attempted to show in a book on early architecture in New Spain, Ezekiel's text also offered a ground plan for a rectilinear urban grid—an idealized cityscape for the colonies—and for outdoor worship spaces that suited the new Christians of the Americas. Thus, even New World architects could find practical solutions for sacred space in the biblical texts[23] (see figure 4).

Humanism, the intellectual movement of the fifteenth century that placed a new importance on human will and creativity, involved a concern for historical and linguistic accuracy that led scholars to go back to the Hebrew and Greek sources.[24] But more important was the rediscovery

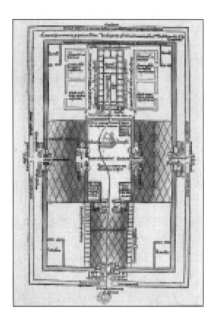

Fig. 4. Nicholas of Lyra, *Postilla super totam bibliam*. Ground plan of Ezekiel's temple and courtyard used in the New World for the design of missionary conversion centers.

of the ancient language of Christ himself, Aramaic. In Spain, Cardinal Francisco Ximénes de Cisneros supervised the production of the *Polyglot Bible* (also known as the *Complutensian Polyglot*) at the University of Alcalá in 1514.[25] One reason why it employed Aramaic in its translation was so that it could be used to communicate directly with Christ upon his Second Coming to earth.[26] Around the turn of the sixteenth century and shortly thereafter the return of Christ was thought to be near. The Fifth Lateran Council (1512–1517) concerned itself with the prophetic signs of the times and declared that the discovery of a *Novus Orbis* (New World) was but one of several "proofs" that the End of Days was approaching. This eschatological anxiety is demonstrated by the fact that more commentaries on the book of the Apocalypse appeared around the year 1500 than during the previous three centuries.[27] The Sibylline Oracles received new interest and an early printing.[28] Prophecy and reform were the hallmark of Catholic biblical preaching of the day.[29]

Christopher Columbus, Biblical Exegete

Onto this scene came Christopher Columbus and, with his explorations, a New World later called America. In 1502 Columbus wrote the *Libro de las Profecías* (The Book of the Prophecies).[30] It is a masterful compilation of biblical texts, oracles, and commentaries, as well as speculations on geography and eschatology. Columbus combed the Scriptures for every passage he could find with the word *islands*, especially those mythical islands of

Seba, Ophir, and Tharsis mentioned in relation to Solomon (and his mines) because he believed that he had now discovered them.[31] He found the core of this insular exegesis in the Prophets and the Psalms, for example in Psalm 72:10: "The kings of Tharsis and the islands shall pay him tribute: the kings of Sheba and Seba shall bring gifts." This verse he exegeted as referring to the Spanish monarch, King Ferdinand, who funded his voyages. In Psalm 97:1, "The Lord is king, let the earth rejoice: let the many islands be glad," Columbus understood the reference to be to the islands of the West Indies that he explored on four voyages.[32]

The explorer seems to have been obsessed by Psalm 2, applying verses 7 and 8 both to the Spanish monarchy and to himself: "The Lord said to me: 'You are my son. It is I who have begotten you this day. Ask and I shall bequeath you the nations, and put the very ends of the earth in your possession.'" Columbus's baptismal name, Christopher (meaning "Christ-bearer"), and his distinctive Trinitarian signature, hint at his understanding of himself as an individual with a divine mission. Quoting the prophet Isaiah, chapter 61, he claims that he is none other than the prophet of the Last Days, the one foretold in Scripture to bring the Good News to the nations, and thus, by his voyages, to initiate the final age of world history.[33]

There even arose an eschatological desire on the part of Europeans to read the world-discoverer himself, Christopher Columbus, into the biblical prophecies. In 1516, a *Polyglot Psalter* was published in Genoa. Psalm 19:4 reads as follows: "No speech, no word, no voice is heard, yet their span extends through all the earth, their words go out to the utmost bounds of the world." It is at this place in the text that the printer added an entire *vita* of Columbus and his accomplishments that runs on for several more folios.[34] Christopher Columbus was himself exegeted into the book of Psalms.

We usually think of the explorer as seeking a new route to China, and that is true in part; but it was the Jerusalem of the Bible that Columbus was really after.[35] It is no surprise that Columbus should begin his book with an explanation of the classic four senses of Scripture mentioned above specifically related to the exemplum "Jerusalem," because his stated goal was to discover a new route to the Holy City for a last crusade.

The fourfold interpretation of Holy Scripture is clearly implicit in the word *Jerusalem*. In a historical sense, it is the earthly city to which pilgrims travel. Typologically, it indicates the Church in the world. Morally, Jerusalem is the soul of every believer. Anagogically, the word means the Heavenly Jerusalem, the celestial fatherland and kingdom.[36]

Columbus, and the missionaries who followed him, even speculated that the human beings they discovered in these strange lands might be the descendants of the Lost Tribes of the Jews mentioned in the book of Esdras—a belief that would naturally color the missionaries' use of the Bible in those domains.[37]

Close Encounters of the Biblical Kind

The discovery and colonization of the New World has usually been analyzed in terms of military, political, or economic factors. But one could also view the sixteenth-century encounter as a collision of sacred texts: the People of the Book meeting peoples who also had, in one form or another, holy books and sacred poetry. Scriptures were not unknown to the native peoples of the New World. All the great civilizations, like the Aztecs, Incas, and Mayas, had some means of recording sacred stories and events, although not in alphabetic script. The Incas, for example, had *quipus*, colored cords with knots that could be read by a *quipucamayoc*, cord-reader. Still a mystery to us, the quipus seem to have been quite sophisticated in the information that they could record because native catechists even used them in the Catholic evangelization.[38]

The Aztecs, on the other hand, had their own system of pictorial writing in color in screenfold books (see figure 5). For the Nahuatl speakers, sacred writing was *in tlilli in tlapalli*, the painted "Red and the Black" of their pictographic codices. That expression, "the red and the black," could denote sacred speech, as well as being a metaphor for wisdom.[39] When the natives looked over the shoulders of the friars to inspect their leather-bound books, as they no doubt did, they spied the very same sacred colors: black type with rubrication on white paper, frequently accompanied by black and red images. This was the standard visual format of printed Bibles and ritual books used in America, all of which became the new "Red and the Black," the new wisdom of the new religion.[40] The phrase *in tlilli in tlapalli* was also used to indicate the Gospels and the writings of the Hebrew prophets.[41] Gazing upon these sacred colors, the friars chanted, processed, and performed rituals—as had the Aztec priests in their temples before them. For visual readers of pictographs and ideographs, like the Mexica, the picture was truly worth a thousand words, and they expected texts *to be* images.[42] When shown pages of printed type by Hernán Cortés in 1519, the reac-

Fig. 5. Aztec screenfold book, *Codex Fejérváry-Mayer* (before 1521).
Liverpool Museum, MS Mayer 12014. (Werner Forman/Art Resource, NY.)

tion of the Aztec literati was "Why do they not speak?" meaning why are there no readable pictures? In that context, a printed Bible would have been "voiceless."

Therefore, the first missionaries used images as a means of communicating the Scriptures and Christian doctrine. In New Spain, visual material soon appeared. Only a handful are extant today, though many more must have once have existed, wore out, and been discarded.[43] For example, we can translate the pictographs of the Lord's Prayer here (see figure 6) and see that the visual text is actually much richer than the written version. (The alphabetic script is a later addition.) The pictographs incorporate the Nahuatlan notion of *xochitl*, flowers, as sacred objects in the Mexica paradise of Tlalocan. *Xochitl* also stood for the concept of joy and moral goodness, righteousness, and here it is woven into the Christian belief in a God who enjoys his kingdom by inhaling the aroma of flowers. The Lord's Prayer has been thoroughly assimilated to Aztec culture. Reading from left to right:

Oh, our Father!
In heaven, God the Father is found.
Noble people worship the Name.
The faithful request on earth the kingdom that is in Heaven.

On earth, may God the Father breathe in the flowers!
In the Christian world, may the flowers multiply!
The faithful kneel to receive the sacred tortilla,
which God the Father gives to Christians each day.
May the faithful have tortillas on their tables.
May God the Father point out venial sin to the faithful
who come to Him with devotion.
May the faithful go with devotion to God the Father
who looks down on the soul overcome by mortal sin.
May God the Father defend and protect
the fearful and afflicted faithful
with the sword and the Cross
as they beg Him protection
from the cowardly Evil One who runs away.
Let there be flowers! (=Amen).

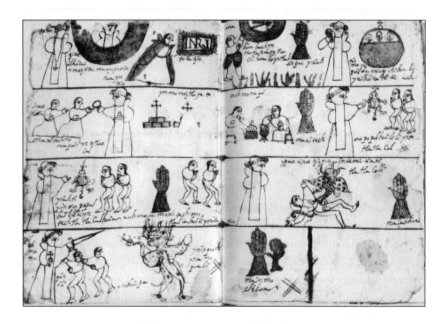

Fig. 6. *Egerton Manuscript 2895.* The Lord's Prayer.
The British Library. (Used with permission.)

The Nahuatl Bible

Instruction through the eyes was very powerful, but it was also imprecise. As educated and logocentric Europeans, the friars no doubt preferred the written word to the pictographs, and this brought up the problem of translation. Once the friars learned the indigenous languages—which took several years—they began to create grammar books and vocabulary lists, together with catechisms written in the native language using alphabetic script.[44] Translations of Bible verses into Indian languages also existed, but only fragments of them have survived to our day. We know of native people who had their own copy of the four Gospels or even the book of the Apocalypse in an Indian language; but almost all were collected and destroyed by the Inquisition.[45] One such fragment has only recently come to light (see figure 7). *Nahuatl Manuscript 1692* is a translation of several verses of the Acts of the Apostles dealing with the soulful conversion of Saint Paul on

Fig. 7. *Nahuatl Manuscript 1692.* Nahuatl translation
of portions of the Acts of the Apostles (c. 1525–1550).
(Courtesy of the Schøyen Collection, National Museum of Norway.)

the road to Damascus—a timely topic for recent converts. The manuscript is written on paper made from the bark of the fig tree and displays Aztec hieroglyphs together with Spanish-Nahuatl script. It is the earliest extant biblical text in Nahuatl yet found.[46]

It is doubtful, however, that the whole Bible was ever translated or made available to natives; nor was it necessary. The basic biblical texts were those employed as proof texts in the conversion process, and those used as lectionary pericopes for Mass. The latter are what we encounter in the work of friar Bernardino de Sahagún, his *Evangeliarium, Epistolarium et Lectionarium Aztecum*, probably composed around 1540 or shortly thereafter. It contains the Epistle and Gospel readings in Nahuatl for all the Sundays of the year and major feast days.[47] Another early translation of the Epistles and Gospels has come down to us with the title *Incipiunt Epistolae et Evangelia*.[48] Since the custom was to have the preaching in the atrium before the Mass, the vernacular Bible readings were proclaimed from an outdoor pulpit.[49]

A paraphrase of biblical and hagiographical stories is contained in another of Sahagún's productions, the *Psalmodia Christiana*, which was in use as early as the 1560s. This songbook was composed in the Nahuatl language in an effort to replace the pre-Conquest hymns that were still dear to the indigenous population; but it was also designed physically to look like an illustrated Bible.[50] These biblical songs, which were to be sung while dancing in the churchyards, include a brief catechism, basic prayers, the Ten Commandments, and compositions that follow the liturgical year from the feast of the Circumcision (Jan. 1) to the Nativity (Dec. 25). The style of the songs attempts as closely as possible to follow the rhythms, metaphors, and characteristics of ancient Nahuatl poetry.[51]

As yet no linguistic scholar has seriously examined these texts, and a detailed analysis is lacking. A cursory glance, however, reveals that the translators made some adaptation to the Mexica worldview. For example, to clarify the meaning of the phrase in the Lord's Prayer: "Forgive us our trespasses *as we forgive* those who trespass against us," the translators rendered it "Forgive us our trespasses *only after* we have forgiven others"; a significant change of meaning, in my opinion.

Likewise, the Indian neophytes apparently had difficulty understanding the biblical phrase "the Son of Man" found in the book of Daniel and in the Gospels, so Sahagún and his assistants replaced the expression with "the Son of the Virgin [Mary]," making it overtly Christological. In that context it might have even lent itself to a type of Christian cannibalism, reminiscent of the ritual cannibalism that had been practiced before the coming of the Europeans. John's Gospel, chapter 6, verse 53, reads in Nahuatl: "Unless you eat of the flesh of the Son of the Virgin [Mary] and drink his blood, you will not have life in you," thus making Christ's words about eating a human being even more carnal.[52]

The Theatrical Bible

If art was one way in which the spoken word has always been made visible, then the theatrical arts have given it three-dimensionality. Theater began to be used immediately at the inception of the evangelization. It appealed to the native peoples who were accustomed to theatrical performances in their ancient religion and temples where the myths were enacted. A survey of sixteenth-century drama in New Spain shows that, like music and art, it had two purposes: moral indoctrination and eschatological preparation. Being that the conversion of the New World was thought to be the remote beginning of the end of the world—as prophesied in the Bible—there was thus an urgent need to convert, baptize, and prepare for the end.[53] Amerindian converts were instructed by biblical and extra-biblical dramas such as the *Fall of Adam and Eve*, the *Sacrifice of Isaac*, the *Annunciation to the Virgin*, the *Destruction of Jerusalem*, the *Reconquest of the Holy City*, the *Prophecies of Daniel*, the *Last Judgment*, and similar presentations with extensive vernacular narration. All the actors were natives speaking Nahuatl. In addition, there were theatrical performances within liturgical celebrations and, vice versa, liturgical moments within theatrical performances. Real sacramental baptisms of children, for example, took place during performances of a play entitled *The Life of John the Baptist*.[54]

One particular performance treated the delicate topic of human sacrifice, which had been an essential part of the religious worldview of Aztecs, Mayas, and Incas. For the Aztecs, human sacrifice was understood as reciprocity in a cosmic balancing act, necessary to keep the sun in orbit and the world in existence. It was the first practice that the friars stumbled upon, to their horror, and one that colored the first century of the evangelization; but they also recognized that it had been done for pious reasons, and they could laud the religious instinct without, of course, condoning the practice.[55] During the 1538 Corpus Christi pageant, *The Sacrifice of Isaac* was performed. It was taken from Genesis 22, wherein Abraham complies with God's request that he slit the throat of his only son and burn him as a holocaust sacrifice[56] (see figure 8). In the Nahuatl text of the play, Abraham tells the boy: "My beloved son, you will need to turn into ashes, for I am going to make a sacrificial offering of your body." Since courage in the face of voluntary death was a high value in Mexica military society, Isaac replies stoically: "Do not cry, O my beloved honored father, for it is with very great happiness that I receive death at your hands." The patriarch even promises Isaac and the Mexica audience that if they follow his example in obeying God's inscrutable will, they will rejoice and be happy!

Fig. 8. Tecamachalco, Puebla. *The Sacrifice of Isaac.* Painting on fig paper glued to the ceiling of the undercroft. (Author's photo.)

One might rightly note that this was an ambivalent and dangerous message to the spectators, who only recently had given up human sacrifice.[57] It possibly invited them to repeat and succeed at what Abraham had set out to do: sacrifice a human being by slitting his throat and immolating his body. Indeed, Mexica children, like Isaac, were commonly sacrificed in this way to the water god Tlaloc in the springtime to bring the rains; and some forms of Aztec sacrifice had involved decapitation and burning the human oblation, as Abraham planned to do with Isaac.[58]

In pre-Contact days, elements of burning were associated with the temple sacrifices because those humans who became divine in the surrender of their hearts were temporarily converted into receptacles of divine fire. This was literally so because, at the Aztec ceremony of the fifty-two-year cosmic renewal, the New Fire had to be kindled in the chest cavity of the sacrificial victim[59] (see figure 9). (Indeed, "their hearts were burning within them.") Human sacrifice effected a Mesoamerican sort of "transubstantiation" because in the process the victim became a true icon of the god and was divinized.[60]

Certainly it was risky to have the Judeo-Christian God—on stage—request the death of Abraham's only son, but it appears that the friars were willing to take the risk in order to make a typological exegesis of the Old Testament story, that is, a Christological link to the sacrifice of Golgotha and to the sacrificial meaning of the Eucharist itself. The Abraham and Isaac episode, as presented in Nahuatl translation, operated as the harbinger of a new cosmic economy of human sacrifice for Aztec-Christians, one now transferred to that of Jesus on the cross and the altar table.[61] After all, the play was performed as part of the Corpus Christi procession in the presence of the Eucharist in its sunburst monstrance (see figure 10). Sacred sunlight and blood were now transposed in a Christological reworking.

The rehabilitation of human sacrifice by the missionaries for the once-and-for-all sacrifice of Calvary seems deliberate. The new biblical sacrifice of the cross was presented as superseding the former human sacrifices of the Mexica, even while it continued their metaphors. When Sahagún and

Fig. 9. Bernardino de Sahagún, *Historia general de las cosas de la Nueva España*, ed. Francisco de Paso y Troncoso, 1905. Aztec New Fire ritual. (Public domain.)

Fig. 10. Huejotzingo, Puebla. Modern Corpus Christi procession with eucharistic monstrance. (Author's photo.)

his native assistants translated the word *Golgotha* (Hebrew for "skull hill") in the Gospels, they chose the Nahuatl words *quaxicalli tepeuh*, literally "mounds of skulls," with connotations of the sacrificial Aztec skull rack that had stood in the courtyard of the temples or even of the bowls into which the fresh hearts were tossed.[62]

The Billboard Bible

Open-air theatrics and preaching were common for the New World friars. Pulpits, preaching balconies, and sonic shells were constructed outdoors for the weekly hour-long sermon that preceded the eucharistic celebration (see figure 11). It was here that the vernacular translations of the Bible were most in need.

One of the most difficult concepts to communicate to the Aztec neophytes was that of personal moral responsibility for their deeds, and the resulting reward or punishment that would occur in this world or in an eter-

Fig. 11. Actopan, Hidalgo. Open-air chapel. (Author's photo.)

nal life after this one. Pre-Columbian Amerindians had neither the notion of eternity nor that of sin in our Western theological sense of the word. In Mexica mythology, after death, one traveled to inhabit either one of the thirteen above worlds or one of the nine below worlds, but only temporarily; personal and cosmic annihilation would eventually win out. In terms of human conduct, there were transgressions of established behavior, often thought to have been the result of outside causality, but personal responsibility and its consequences were unknown.[63] Therefore, the Christian missionaries had to find ways to demonstrate to the neophytes that their freewill choices, and their actions in themselves, were either good or evil, and would have consequences in a hereafter that continued perpetually, *in æternam*. This was done verbally in the friars' preaching and catechesis by recounting the biblical stories of the Fall of Adam and Eve and the promise of redemption. For example, Bernardino de Sahagún paints a beautiful verbal picture of heaven, taken from Revelation 21, in his Nahuatl-language collection of daily meditations, *The Daily Exercise*, that would appeal to an Aztec sense of pleasure and enjoyment in the "highest heaven":

> Enormous is the mercy that God has there in the empyrean heaven for good Christians! . . . There, in the interior of heaven, he has gathered all pleasures, all riches. By faith, we know that there, above the moon, the sun, the stars, there in the highest place is a very great city called Celestial Jerusalem, which God our Lord constructed at the same time that he founded the world. It is made all of gold and precious gems, but not like those of this world. They are much more precious, beautiful, marvelous, and dazzling. Saint John the Evangelist and Saint Paul saw the design, the size, the wonders of this great city of the Celestial Jerusalem . . . and we keep their words which are written in the Holy Scriptures. Saint John spoke of many things in his divine book called the Apocalypse, a discourse perfectly amazing, perfectly enjoyable. . . . This city, the Celestial Jerusalem, is great, there is none like it in this world! Its plants, trees, flowers, and fruits do not grow here in this world; they are much more attractive, aromatic, tasty, and fulfilling. . . . There it is always summertime; and in many parts of the city there are patios, large spacious patios, and well-made houses with marvelous ornamentation. There is nothing like it in this world! And all its paved streets are gold and translucent like crystals, emeralds, and amethysts!

Then Sahagún moves from the topic of the heavenly city to the doctrine of the Beatific Vision:

> The souls of those who live there actually see God the Father, Son, and Holy Spirit. . . . Our own eyes will see the precious body of our Lord Jesus Christ, true God-Man. . . . There we will be with the only deity, *Dios*. Absolutely no one will take away our joy, our delight, our complete contentment; and eternal life will be in our bodies which will outshine the moon, sun, and stars wherever we go, wherever we soar like the eagle.[64] There is absolutely nothing of the same intensity [on earth] . . . Saint John spoke of many more things in the twenty-first chapter of the Apocalypse, but he could not describe them completely. Let us take care while we live in this world, so that by a just and holy life we may be worthy to see the wonders of God.[65]

This colorful passage—with its familiar references to the multiple levels of heaven, to an orderly urban center with patios and aromatic flowers, to the soaring eagle, and to baubles, bangles, and beads—would appeal to the Aztec imagination with its very concrete religious aesthetic. But the new faith would still need to be visualized through the fine arts.

Traditionally, the most common way to demonstrate the Christian concept of eternal life was by visual images of Christ's return, using the Resurrection and "last judgment passages" in Matthew 25 and Revelation 14, and the resulting reward or punishment in heaven or hell[66] (see figure 12). The preaching balconies and shells were often lined with colorful paintings of these themes. The murals acted as giant billboards advertising the new religion, supporting the moral preaching, and visualizing the new doctrine. We find paintings linked to positive practices like correct Christian worship, or to negative images of sins considered common to the native peoples—such as idolatry, drunkenness, and sexual deviance. One estimate holds that there must have existed more than 300,000 square meters of wall space for didactic mural art in the combined mendicant evangelization centers.[67]

In the open-air chapels of Actopan and Xoxoteco, white Europeans, as good role models, venerate the eucharistic host and teach natives to do likewise (see figure 13). But in the same chapel other Europeans, negative role models, are committing the seven deadly sins and creating scandal, and are placed precariously close to the jaws of a monstrous hellmouth (see figure 14). Thus evangelization art was instructional and illustrative of the

Fig. 12. Calpan, Puebla. Facade of an outdoor processional chapel. The resurrection of the dead and the Second Coming of Christ. (Author's photo.)

Fig. 13. Actopan. Pagan worship versus Christian worship. (Author's photo.)

Fig. 14. Xoxoteco, Hidalgo. Pulque
drinkers and devils. (Author's photo.)

Word proclaimed in the Nahuatl sermons, sermons that were also warning native peoples of the bad example of conquistadors and colonists.[68] One of Sahagún's Nahuatl sermons is based on the Gospel parable of the Separation of the Sheep and Goats (Mt 25:31–46). But there was one problem with a straightforward translation of the parable because, when Sahagún made the translation, there were few sheep and goats in New Spain, but plenty of pigs. They were quickly reproducing, devouring the native crops, and becoming a pest. It translates this way:

> Very frightening, terrifying things will occur, when [Christ] will come and judge people. . . . And then he will invite those to his right, the good ones, the pure ones. . . . The good and pure ones will enter into heaven. And then he will call those on his left, the bad ones, the impure ones. . . . "Move away, leave me, go there to *mictlan*, and enter into the flames. . . . You shall suffer, have pains forever!"
>
> You grow fat, you eat very much, you sleep a lot, you get drunk, you just care for your body. The Devil raises you as a pig, stuffs you in order to kill you when you grow really fat, to bring you there to *mictlan*.[69]

Note that the anagogical and moral exegeses of Scripture have come to the fore in this paraphrase. Missionary literature of the sixteenth century is also full of examples linking pre-Contact worship with the idolatry of the Old Testament Canaanites. Was not the Bible, after all, filled with condemnations of false solar cults and ritual cannibalism (Ez 5:10 and 8:16), like that practiced by the Aztecs? Did it also not condemn the worship of plumed and slithering animals (Dt 4:15–24 and Ez 8:10) that seemed like eyewitness accounts of Aztec deities and devotions, proleptically written ages ago? Hence—in the friars' minds—the need for a constant spiritual crusade to extirpate the demonic practices and to safeguard the Indian neophytes for the kingdom of Christ.[70] Art reinforced this war of good against evil with a plethora of warrior angels seen on church facades and in murals. The three archangels mentioned in the Bible—Michael, Gabriel, and Raphael—are omnipresent in the colonial world. Fighting angels became extremely popular with the militaristic Aztec machismo.[71]

Conclusions

The Bible as sound, sight, stage performance, and selected texts was present in the New World from the very start of the evangelization process and permeated every activity of the missionaries. Their urtext was the Great Commission of Matthew 28:16–20: "All authority has been given to me in heaven and on earth. Go, therefore, and make disciples of all the nations, baptizing them in the name of the Father and of the Son and of the Holy Spirit, teaching them to observe all things that I have commanded you; and behold, I am with you always, even to the end of the age" (understood to be soon).

The first book of the Bible, Genesis, brought the Amerindians into the Judeo-Christian metanarrative as fallen son and daughters of Adam and Eve, equal in that sense to the Europeans. The "middle book" of Holy Writ, that of the prophet Ezekiel, provided a model for a utopian society in the New World, and even for religious buildings that functioned well for a people accustomed to worshipping outdoors in temple compounds.[72] The last book of the Christian Scriptures, the Apocalypse, predicted the earthquakes and plagues that would devastate the New World as the End of Days approached.[73] The Ten Commandments, and the Gospel parable of a Last Judgment and reward or punishment, provided a visualization of resurrection, individual moral responsibility, and eternal consequences.

Lastly, I wish to suggest that the Bible as story—heard, seen, and enacted—especially its episodes of self-sacrifice and sacred blood, has penetrated the religious culture of Latin America to its very core.[74] It is the Word of God that we still hear, see, and enact today, especially in the two poles of the Hispanic liturgical year, Christmas and Holy Week (see figure 15).

Fig. 15. Cholula, Puebla. Modern Passion play. (Author's photo.)

Questions for the Reader

1. If the Bible has traditionally been experienced as sound rather than as print, then what does that imply for our lectors, for their preparation, and most of all, for their delivery of the biblical word on Sunday morning in church?

2. What do our clergy and catechists need to do to prevent Latino Catholics from falling into the trap of biblical literalism and fundamentalism (think of TV evangelists)? How do we communicate the fact that certain books, chapters, and passages of the Bible should be taken as poetry and metaphor rather than as literal or scientific data?

3. How do we encourage reading the Bible as serious poetry? And how do we encourage homilists to give poetic inspiration rather than mere historical exegesis or moral harangue?

4. If the Bible was more often seen rather than read, and made its impact on the eyes and heart, how biblical is the visual art of our Latino Catholic congregations? How consistent is it with the Gospel stories, parables, and exemplars? What might that demand in terms of replacing certain images in our worship spaces?

Notes

1. The birthday song, *Las Mañanitas*, begins with the line: "*Éstas son las mañanitas que cantaba el Rey David / Hoy por ser día de tu santo, te las cantamos a ti . . .*" (This is the morning psalm that King David sang / Because today is your saint's day we're singing it for you. Wake up!). Cf. Psalm 58.

2. This was the theme of the 2008 General Assembly of the Synod of Bishops in Rome, entitled "The Word of God in the Life and Mission of the Church."

3. I have based this section on Beryl Smalley, *The Study of the Bible in the Middles Ages* (London: Blackwell, 1959); the excellent articles in *The Bible as Book: The First Printed Editions*, ed. Paul Saenger and Kimberly van Kampen (London: British Library, 1999); and Stephen Joel Garver, "Inventing 'The Bible': Revelation, Theology, Phenomenon, and Text," http://www.joelgarver.com/writ/phil/bible.htm.

4. One medieval Bible was so large that it was considered to be one of the Seven Wonders of the World. See Paul Needham, "The Changing Shape of the Vulgate Bible in Fifteenth-Century Printing Shops," in *The Bible as Book*, 53–70.

5. Ibid.

6. I have examined copies in Mexico City, Puebla, Lima, Arequipa, and Cuzco.

7. Paul Saenger, "The Impact of the Early Printed Page on the Reading of the Bible," in *The Bible as Book*, 31–51.

8. Ibid., 32.

9. "The evidence of our eyes makes instruction through the ears unnecessary." Eusebius, *The History of the Church from Christ to Constantine*, trans. Geoffrey Arthur Williamson and Andrew Louth (London: Penguin Classics, 1989), 315.

10. There is no reason to think that the biblical wall paintings in the third-century house church of Dura-Europos (Syria) or in the Roman catacombs were exceptional. As the evidence of the murals and mosaic encountered in early synagogues proves, neither Jews nor Christians of the early Common Era ever took the Second Commandment literally or as prohibiting visual art. See, for example, Sister Charles Murray, "Art and the Early Church," in

Studies in Early Christianity, ed. Everett Ferguson et al. (New York: Garland, 1993), 215–57; and Robin Jensen, *Understanding Early Christian Art* (London: Routledge, 2000), passim.

11. See the introductory notes to John Williams, *The Illustrated Beatus: A Corpus of the Illustrations of the Apocalypse* (London: Harvey Miller, 1994/2003).

12. Gregory the Great's famous phrase, "What writing offers to those who read it, a picture offers to the ignorant who look at it," has as much to do with the cost of books as luxury items of the rich as with the general illiteracy in his day.

13. On this topic, see Avril Henry, *Biblia Pauperum: A Facsimile and Edition* (Ithaca, NY: Cornell University Press, 1987).

14. On "visual preaching," see Jaime Lara, *Christian Texts for Aztecs: Art and Liturgy in Colonial Mexico* (Notre Dame, IN: University of Notre Dame Press, 2008), 41–56.

15. For this section I have relied on Jerry Bentley, *Humanists and Holy Writ: New Testament Scholarship in the Renaissance* (Princeton, NJ: Princeton University Press, 1983); *The Bible in the Renaissance: Essays on Biblical Commentary and Translation in the Fifteenth and Sixteenth Centuries*, ed. Richard Griffiths (Aldershot, UK: Ashgate Publishing, 2001); and *Biblical Interpretation in the Era of the Reformation*, ed. Richard Muller and John Thompson (Grand Rapids, MI: Eerdmans, 1996).

16. The first book ever printed with movable type appears to have been a collection of the Sibylline Oracles (the *Sibyllenbuch Fragment*). This fact will be important for the eschatological dimension of the discovery of America, as I explain below. See Malcolm Brown, "A Beam of Protons Illuminates Gutenberg's Genius," *New York Times*, May 12, 1987.

17. On Luther's translation and biblical polemics, see John Flood, "Martin Luther's Bible Translation in Its German and European Context," in *The Bible in the Renaissance*, 45–70.

18. See Anthony Kenny, introduction to *The Bible as Book*, 1–5; and Vincent Strudwick, "English Fears of Social Disintegration and Modes of Control," in *The Bible in the Renaissance*, 133–49.

19. Richard Muller, "Biblical Interpretation in the Era of the Reformation: The View from the Middle Ages," in *Biblical Interpretation in the Era of the Reformation*, 3–22.

20. The last three senses of Scripture are considered by some to be examples of *eisegesis*, a reading *into* the text, rather than exegesis.

21. Henri de Lubac, *Exégèse médiévale: Les quatre sens de l'écriture*, 4 vols. (Paris: Aubier, 1959–64).

22. On Lyra's life and influence, see Charles-Victor Langlois, "Nicolas de Lyre, frère mineur," *Histoire littéraire de France* 36 (1927): 355–400; Herman Hailperin, *Rashi and the Christian Scholars* (Pittsburgh: University of Pittsburgh Press, 1963) 61–71; and Bentley, *Humanists and Holy Writ*, 21–31.

23. On the topic of biblical buildings copied in the New World, see Jaime Lara, *City, Temple, Stage: Eschatological Architecture and Liturgical Theatrics in New Spain* (Notre Dame, IN: University of Notre Dame Press, 2004), esp. 111–49.

24. Guy Bedouelle, "The Bible, Printing and the Educational Goals of the Humanists," in *The Bible as Book*, 95–99.

25. Julián Martín Abad, "The Printing Press at Alcalá de Henares: The Complutensian Polyglot Bible," in *The Bible as Book*, 101–15. The momentous event was recorded in a now-lost painting by the artist Pedro Ibarra Ruíz (112, n. 4).

26. Richard Popkin, "Jewish Christians and Christian Jews in Spain, 1492 and After," *Judaism* 41 no. 3 (1992): 248–68.

27. Bernard McGinn, "Reading Revelation: Joachim of Fiore and the Varieties of Apocalypse Exegesis in the Sixteenth Century," in *Storia e figure dell' Apocalisse fra '500 e '600*, ed. Roberto Rusconi (Rome: Viella, 1996), 11–36.

28. See note 16.

29. See Michael O'Connor, "The Ark and the Temple in Savonarola's Teaching," in *The Bible in the Renaissance*, 9–27; John O'Malley, *Praise and Blame in Renaissance Rome: Rhetoric, Doctrine, and Reform in the Sacred Orators of the Papal Court* (Durham, NC: Duke University Press, 1979); and Marjorie Reeves, *Prophetic Rome in the High Renaissance Period* (Oxford: Clarendon Press, 1992).

30. Christopher Columbus, *The* Libro de las Profecías *of Christopher Columbus*, ed. and trans. Delno West and August King (Gainesville: University of Florida Press, 1991). The handbook of biblical sources, as he calls it, was composed with the help of his son, Ferdinand, and his personal chaplain, Fray Gaspar Gorricio. An English translation only appeared in 1992.

31. On Columbus as an exegete, see John Fleming, "Christopher Columbus as a Scriptural Exegete," *Lutheran Quarterly* 5 (1991): 187–98; and Hector Avalos, "Columbus as Biblical Exegete: A Study of the *Libro de las Profecías*," in *Religion in the Age of Exploration: The Case of Spain and New Spain*, ed. Bryan Le Beau et al. (Omaha: Creighton University Press, 1996), 59–80.

32. Columbus, *Libro de las Profecías*, 7–40; 261, n. 18. The medieval commentaries that he used all claimed that the island nations were real locations to the west of Europe, and that they would receive the Gospel message near the end of time. With this biblical confirmation, the explorer developed a geo-eschatology to describe the relationship between geographic lore and a theology of the End Times.

33. Alain Milhou, *Colón y su mentalidad mesiánica en el ambiente franciscanista español* (Valladolid, Spain: Casa-Museo Colón, 1983), 79ff. and passim.

34. This polyglot psalter, entitled *Psalterium Hebreum, Grecum, Arabicum et Chaldaeum* (Genoa, 1516), contains the complete *vita* of Columbus immediately after verse 5 of Psalm 19. I used the copy in the Bancroft Library of the University of California, Berkeley. See Adriano Prosperi, "New Heaven and New Earth: Prophecy and Propaganda at the Time of the Discovery and Conquest of the Americas," in *Prophetic Rome and the Renaissance*, ed. Marjorie Reeves (Oxford: Clarendon Press, 1992), 279–303, esp. 281, n. 4.

35. See Lara, *City, Temple, Stage*, 59–63 and notes.

36. Columbus, *Libro de las Profecías*, 101.

37. For the supposed Jewish origins of Native Americans, see Lee Eldridge Huddleston, *Origins of the American Indian: European Concepts*, 1492–1729 (Austin: University of Texas Press, 1965), especially 33–47 and 83–128; "Tribes, Lost Ten," *The Jewish Encyclopedia*, 12 vols. (New York: Funk and Wagnall, 1901–1906), 12:249–53; Lynn Glaser, *Indians or Jews? An Introduction to Manasseh Ben Israel's "The Hope of Israel"* (Gilroy, CA: R. V. Boswell, 1973), 3–32; and Ronald Sanders, *Lost Tribes and Promised Lands: The Origins of American Racism* (Boston: Little, Brown, 1978, 1992), 43–46. Early Puritans in New England also shared this belief; see Djelal Kadir, *Columbus and the Ends of the Earth* (Berkeley: University of California Press, 1992), 178–92. Perhaps for some related reason, the apocryphal Fourth Book of Esdras was included in the Gutenberg Bible; see Needham, "The Changing Shape," 56.

38. Frank Salomon, *The Cord Keepers: Khipus and Cultural Life in a Peruvian Village* (Durham, NC: Duke University Press, 2004). The Inca-Christian catechist, Felipe Guaman Poma de Ayala, and others used them. See Thomas Abercrombie, *Pathways of Memory and Power: Ethnography and History among an Andean People* (Madison: University of Wisconsin Press, 1998), 260. The Jesuit José de Acosta, in *Historia natural y moral de las Indias* (1590), documented their use in confession. "I saw a handful of these strings, which an Indian woman carried and in which was written a general

confession of her entire life, and through them she confessed, as I would do with a handwritten paper, and I even asked about certain little strings that seemed somewhat different from the others, and they were certain circumstances required to confess some sins fully."

39. Elizabeth Hill Boone, *Stories in Red and Black: Pictorial Histories of the Aztecs and Mixtecs* (Austin: University of Texas Press, 2000), 21. The Nahuatl-Christian historian Domingo de San Antón Muñón Chimalpáhin Cuauhtlehuanitzin (1579–1660) used the same expression, *in tlilli in tlapalli*, for the Hebrew prophets of the Old Testament. See *Codex Chimalpáhin: Society and Politics in Mexico*, ed. Arthur Anderson and Susan Schroeder (Norman: University of Oklahoma Press, 1997), 2:153.

40. For example, Fray Pedro de Gante's *Doctrina cristiana en lengua mexicana* (1553) was printed in red and black, as were the several editions of Alberto Castellani's *Liber sacerdotalis* (first edition, 1523), the ritual book that was used in the New World for the administration of the sacraments. See Lara, *Christian Texts*, 36–37. It seems no coincidence that some of the friary murals were painted in black grisaille with red details.

41. Bernardino de Sahagún, *Exercicio quotidiano* (before 1574), in Anderson and Schroeder, *Codex Chimalpáhin*, 162–65.

42. On this topic, see Elizabeth Hill Boone, "Pictorial Documents and Visual Thinking in Post Conquest Mexico," in *Native Traditions in the Postconquest World*, ed. Elizabeth Hill Boone and Tom Cummins (Washington, DC: Dumbarton Oaks, 1998), 149–99.

43. Juan Guillermo Durán, *Monumenta catechética hispanoamericano (siglos XVI–XVIII)*, 2 vols. (Buenos Aires: Facultad de Teología de la Universidad Católica Argentina, 1984), 2:92–144.

44. Ibid., 151–64.

45. The fear of vernacular Bible translations was as much a political policy of the Spanish authorities under Philip II as the doctrinal anxieties of the Tridentine Holy Office of the Inquisition. On the topic of vernacular translations, see Susanne Klaus, *Uprooted Christianity: The Preaching of the Christian Doctrine in Mexico Based on Franciscan Sermons of the 16th Century Written in Nahuatl* (Bonn, Germany: Anton Saurwein, 1999), 37–40.

46. *MS. 1692*, titled "Conversión de Sanct Pablo," in the Schøyen Collection of the National Museum of Norway. Jaime González Rodríguez, "La difusión manuscrita de ideas en Nueva España," *Revista Complutense de Historia de América* 18 (1992): 92–94, speaks of an "underground" circulation of

hand-copied Bible manuscripts that the Franciscans were producing. This may be one of them.

47. Bernardino de Sahagún, *Evangeliarium, Epistolarium et Lectionarium Aztecum Sive Mexicanum* [c. 1540] (Milan, Italy: Jos. Bernardoni Johannis, 1858). For the Gospel reading on Good Friday, Sahagún harmonized the Passion narratives of all four evangelists to create one continuous story.

48. It is found in the Newberry Library of Chicago (*Ayer Manuscript 1476*). See John F. Schwaller, *A Guide to Nahuatl Language Manuscripts Held in United States Repositories* (Berkeley, CA: Academy of American Franciscan History, 2001), #74.

49. As far as we can tell from similar practices elsewhere, the priest would go to the pulpit, the place for vernacular preaching, and would read either the Nahuatl Epistle and Gospel of the day or just the Gospel, with no ceremonies. This allowed the preacher to comment on what was just heard.

50. Bernardino de Sahagún, *Psalmodia Christiana* (before 1585), trans. Arthur Anderson (Salt Lake City: University of Utah Press, 1993).

51. It appeared to some that there were linguistic characteristics similar to spoken Hebrew or Aramaic. Indeed, an analysis of ancient Nahuatl poetry shows the use of many of the same lyrical devices as the Hebrew psalms: repetition, parallelism, internal rhyme, and cantillation; and, of course, some chroniclers believed in a Jewish origin of the Amerindians. See Miguel León-Portilla, *Native American Spirituality* (New York: Paulist Press, 1980), 47.

52. The earliest reference to Christian cannibalism is found in Justin Martyr's *First Apology*, c. 150 CE; and in the thirteenth century Jacques de Vitry could write in *De sacramentis*: "And just as we have died through appetite in Adam, so shall we recover life through the taste of Christ, 'as whence arose death, thence shall life re-arise." Quoted in Milad Doueihi, *A Perverse History of the Human Heart* (Cambridge, MA: Harvard University Press, 1997), 19; see also 68–74.

53. On this subject, see Lara, *City, Temple, Stage*, esp. 59–89.

54. Toribio de Motolinía, *History of the Indians of New Spain*, trans. Elizabeth Andros Foster (Westport, CT: Greenwood Press, 1973), 104–5.

55. Surveying the history of human piety, Bartolomé de Las Casas could praise the religious instinct that led to offering human oblations: "The nations who offered human beings in sacrifice to their gods had attained a more noble and worthy estimation of their gods and therefore possessed superior understanding and a clearer rational judgment than all other nations.

And those who gave their own children in sacrifice for the well-being of the people outstripped other nations in religious devotion." *Apologética histórica sumaria*, in *Fray Bartolomé de las Casas, Obras completas*, ed. Vidal Castelló (Madrid: Alianza, 1992), 183.

56. The text is found in Barry Sell and Louise Burkhart, *Nahuatl Theater* (Norman: University of Oklahoma Press, 2004), 1:146–63.

57. Human sacrifice continued sporadically and covertly in some rural areas.

58. Philip Arnold, *Eating Landscape: Aztec and European Occupation of Tlalocan* (Niwot: University Press of Colorado, 1999), 83, 154–58.

59. Kay Read, *Time and Sacrifice in the Aztec Cosmos* (Bloomington: Indiana University Press, 1998), 170. The New Fire ceremony was the "ritual echo" of the cosmogonic myth of the "Birth of the Fifth Sun," in which the deity Nanahuantzin had immolated himself to bring about the new and last era of world history.

60. On this notion of Aztec "transubstantiation," see Lara, *Christian Texts for Aztecs*, 77–80 and notes.

61. Viviana Díaz Balsera, "Instructing the Nahuas in Judeo-Christian Obedience," in *Nahuatl Theater*, 1:107.

62. Sahagún, *Evangeliarum*, 200: "*Golgotha, onan quaxicalli tepeuh toc . . .*"

63. Louise Burkhart, "Doctrinal Aspects of Sahagún's Colloquios," in *The Work of Bernardino de Sahagún: Pioneer Ethnographer of Sixteenth-Century Aztec Mexico*, ed. Jorge Klor de Alva (Austin: University of Texas Press, 1988), 71.

64. The eagle was a divinity in the Aztec pantheon; it was he who carried the hearts of sacrificial victims to the divine sun in his *cuauhxicalli* box. The eagle also played an important part in Christian lore. According to Gregory the Great's exegesis of Ezekiel, the eagle is the only animal that can look directly into the sun without harm; thus, Gregory says, Christ the Solar Eagle is the only human being who has seen the dazzling glory of divinity.

65. Bernardino de Sahagún, *Adiciones, Apéndice a la Postilla y Ejercicio Cotidiano* [1579], ed. Arthur Anderson (Mexico City: UNAM, 1983), 80–83.

66. For the European tradition, see Ives Christe, *Jugements derniers* (Paris: Zodiaque, 1999). Aztecs had some idea of judgment by a divinity. Tezcatlipoca, for example, was believed to judge human beings; he punished arrogance and rewarded self-control, but the judgment only occurred in this life and the ancient religion added no notion of an after-life verdict.

67. Constantino Reyes-Valerio, *Arte Indocristiano* (Mexico City: Instituto Nacional de Antropología e Historia, 2000), 379–82.

68. A collection of Sahagún's sermons is found in the Newberry Library of Chicago, *Ayer MS 1485*. See Klaus, *Uprooted Christianity*, 56–113.

69. Translated in Klaus, *Uprooted Christianity*, 64–65. Mictlan was the lowest level of the Mesoamerican underworld.

70. Robert Ricard, *The Spiritual Conquest of Mexico*, trans. Lesley Bird Simpson (Berkeley: University of California Press, 1966), 75–108. Fray Andrés de Olmos, author of a *Tratado de Hechicerías y Sortilegios*, was an expert on sorcery and demonology both before he came to Mexico and after. He was probably responsible for much of the theological information about the demons that appear so often in the catechetical murals. Fray Geronimo de Mendieta called him the "font from which all the streams of the knowledge [of pre-Columbian religion] flow." According to Jacques Lafaye, *Mesías, Cruzadas, Utopías: El judeo-cristianismo en las Sociedades Ibéricas* (Mexico City: Fondo de Cultura Económica, 1988), 122, Fray Andrés composed the early Nahuatl drama *The Last Judgment*.

71. There are more images of armed angels, archangels, cherubim, and seraphim in Hispanic art than in all of coeval European art. See *Gloria in Excelsis* (New York: Center for Inter-American Relations, 1988), 58, 62.

72. On the theme of the book of Ezekiel as the "middle book" of the Bible, see my forthcoming chapter, "Halfway between Genesis and Apocalypse: Ezekiel as Message and Proof for New World Converts," in *After Ezekiel: Essays on the Reception of a Difficult Prophet*, ed. Andrew Mein and Paul M. Joyce (London: T&T Clark, 2010), 137–57.

73. The chroniclers recorded natural catastrophes in an apocalyptic light.

74. I treat this at greater length in *Christian Texts for Aztecs*, 229–54.

10

Pope Benedict XVI, the Bible, and the Synod on the Word of God

Archbishop Nikola Eterović

~

Introduction

The Holy Father Pope Benedict XVI has great experience with synods, resulting from the fact that he has participated in seventeen out of the twenty-two synodal assemblies that the Catholic Church has celebrated thus far. As Bishop of Rome, head of the episcopal college and president of the Synod of Bishops, he has presided over two ordinary general assemblies, namely, the Eleventh Ordinary General Assembly which took place in the Vatican October 2–23, 2005, on the topic "The Eucharist: Source and Summit of the Life and Mission of the Church" and which culminated in the publication of the Post-Synodal Apostolic Exhortation *Sacramentum Caritatis.* Pope Benedict XVI also presided at the Twelfth Ordinary General Assembly of the Synod of Bishops which was held, again in the Vatican, October 5–26, 2008, on the topic "The Word of God in the Life and Mission of the Church." My chapter will concentrate on this synod and on the specific contribution made by the Holy Father, Pope Benedict XVI.

It is useful to point out that before becoming the Bishop of Rome, the 264th successor of St. Peter, Cardinal Joseph Ratzinger participated in fifteen synodal assemblies. As Archbishop of Munich and Freising, he took part in two ordinary general assemblies, in 1977 and 1980. During the 1980 synodal assembly on the Christian family, he was general rapporteur. Appointed by the servant of God Pope John Paul II as Prefect of the Congregation for the Doctrine of the Faith, Cardinal Joseph Ratzinger participated in five ordinary general assemblies, in 1983, 1987, 1990, 1994, and 2001, and the Extraordinary General Assembly of 1985, as well as seven special assemblies of the Synod of Bishops, all except that for the Netherlands in 1980. Cardinal Ratzinger was also president-delegate for the Ordinary General Assembly of the Synod of Bishops in 1983 on the topic "Penance and Reconciliation in the Mission of the Church." He was a member of four ordinary councils of the General Secretariat of the Synod of Bishops, those in 1980, 1983, 1987, and 1990, respectively and two extraordinary councils in 1983 and 1997 of the same General Secretariat. Therefore, the Holy Father's great esteem for the Synod of Bishops and synodality in the Church in general comes as no surprise. In fact, he has stated that "the synodal dimension is constitutive of the Church; it consists of a coming together of every people and culture in order that they become one in Christ and walk together, following him, who said: 'I am the way, and the truth, and the life' (John 14:6)."[1]

The topic of the Word of God has always had a certain fascination for the Holy Father. As a young *peritus* or expert at the Second Vatican Council, he took part in the very lively discussions on the Dogmatic Constitution on Divine Revelation *Dei Verbum*. He also published his observations on this important conciliar document.[2] In all his theological works, the Bible has a preeminent place. Therefore, it came as no surprise that the Holy Father's love for Sacred Scripture and his deep awareness of the problems of biblical hermeneutics would become evident during the synodal assembly on the Word of God.

A synod is characterized by three periods: a time of preparation, the actual celebration of the synod, and then a period in which the synod's results are implemented. The first two phases have a time frame, while the third does not. In fact, it is hoped that the implementation of this past synod might be the concern not only of the Holy Father—and most certainly of all pastors of the Church—but possibly also of the lay faithful, who love the Word of God.

As regards the centrality of the Word of God in the Holy Father's thought, Pope Benedict XVI made a very significant statement at the beginning of his Pontificate: "My real program of governance is not to do my own will, not to pursue my own ideas, but *to listen*, together with the whole Church, *to the word and the will of the Lord*, to be guided by Him, so that He himself will lead the Church at this hour of our history."[3] The Lord's will, namely, his commandment to love God and neighbor, is perceived primarily by means of Sacred Scripture. Pope Benedict XVI himself said: "There is nothing more beautiful than to be surprised by the Gospel, by the encounter with

Christ. There is nothing more beautiful than to know Him and to speak to others of our friendship with Him. . . . Loving means giving the sheep what is truly good, the nourishment of God's truth, of God's word, the nourishment of his presence, which he gives us in the Blessed Sacrament."[4]

In this chapter, I would like to briefly indicate the contribution of Pope Benedict XVI to the work of the synod on "The Word of God in the Life and Mission of the Church." In doing so, I shall principally concentrate on citations from the Supreme Pontiff, divided into two sections: one treating citations from the liturgical celebrations and one discussing those coming from outside of the liturgy. I shall then make some final observations.

To begin, I would first like to make a distinction concerning the expressions "Word of God," "tradition," and "magisterium," which, in turn, will allow a better understanding of the biblical thought of the Holy Father.

The Word of God, Tradition, and the Magisterium

The celebration of the Twelfth Ordinary General Assembly of the Synod of Bishops led to a clarification of the various meanings of the expression "Word of God." The concept has many meanings or "voices," as in a symphony. Pope Benedict XVI himself recalled at the conclusion of the synod's work: "The *Instrumentum laboris* spoke of the polyphony of Sacred Scripture."[5] The synod permitted the participants to experience the beauty and richness of the Word of God "in the polyphony of faith, a symphony of faith, with many contributions, also by the fraternal delegates."[6]

The Word of God can be said to be "symphonic." It is par excellence Jesus Christ, the Word of God-Made-Flesh (see Jn 1:1, 14). Since "all things were created through him and for him" (Col 1:16), the created order (*liber naturae*) reveals God and becomes his Word. This is particularly the case in human beings, who are created in the image and likeness of God (see Gn 1:27). After original sin darkened the conscience and mind of humanity, God, nonetheless, desired in his infinite goodness to reveal himself in salvation history. His words, spoken through chosen men who were inspired by the Holy Spirit, are recorded in the seventy-three books of the Bible, forty-six in the Old Testament and twenty-seven in the New Testament. Sacred Scripture is then the authentic and great manifestation of the Word of God. The whole Bible looks to the coming of the Messiah, Jesus Christ, the Incarnate Word, who is the fulfillment of God's revelation and God's final, definitive Word, who gives a fullness of meaning to the Bible. Under the wise guidance of the Holy Father, the synod fathers were able to deepen this symphonic meaning of the Word of God, which harmoniously converges in the person of Jesus Christ.

It must be said that Sacred Scripture, read in the living tradition of the Church and authentically interpreted by the Church's magisterium, was constantly present in the presentations of Pope Benedict XVI. The Church's living tradition is distinct from Sacred Scripture, even if it be intimately bound to it. Tradition reveals the Church's life: worship, holiness to its supreme act in martyrdom, charity, the transmission of oral and written doctrine, and the teaching of the Fathers and doctors of the Church.[7] Jesus Christ entrusted to the Church's living magisterium the office of interpreting the Word of God in an authentic way. This magisterium, however, "is not above the Word of God, but serves it, teaching only what has been handed on, listening to it devoutly, guarding it scrupulously and explaining it faithfully, in accord with a divine commission and the help of the Holy Spirit, and draws from this one deposit of faith everything which it presents for belief as divinely revealed."[8]

Presentations of the Holy Father during the Synod

Presentations during Liturgical Celebrations

According to Pope Benedict XVI, "the privileged place where the Word of God resounds and edifies the Church—as was repeatedly mentioned in the synod—is undoubtedly the liturgy. This is where it appears that the Bible is a book of the people and for the people; . . . the Bible remains a living Book with the people, its subject, who read it. The people cannot exist without the Book, because in it they find their reason for being, their vocation and their identity."[9] The Bible is an inheritance passed on to its readers to make present in their lives the history of salvation, which finds testimony in its pages. In virtue of the Holy Spirit, the faithful gathered in liturgical assembly hear Jesus Christ who speaks, when the Bible is read in Church and when the Covenant which God renews with his People is accepted. Of all these liturgical celebrations, special reference is given to the Eucharist, the source and summit of the life of the Church, which comprises two parts, the table of the Word of God and the table of the Eucharist, both of which are united to such a point as to form one act of worship.[10]

During the synod, participants were also able to experience this reality expressed in an exceptional way by the Bishop of Rome. The pope presided at four Masses, addressing the faithful in as many homilies. Besides those at the opening and closing of the synodal assembly, Pope Benedict XVI celebrated the Eucharist on October 9 to commemorate the fiftieth anniversary of the death of the Servant of God, Pope Pius XII, and on October 12 for the canonization of four *beati*: Gaetano Errico (1791–1860), Mary Bernard Bütler (1828–1924), Alfonsa of the Immaculate Conception (1910–1946), and Narcisa di Gesù Martillo Morán (1832–1869). In these two significant events, the Holy Father voiced his appreciation, along with that of the synod fathers, for the efforts of Pope Pius XII in fostering a greater awareness of the Word of God in the Catholic Church. In fact, with his Encyclical *Divino afflante Spiritu* (1943), Pope Pius XII "established the doctrinal norms for the study of Sacred Scripture, bringing to the fore its importance and role in Christian life."[11] With this encyclical, Pius XII showed an openness to the scientific research of biblical texts and, in particular, developed the idea of literary genre to better understand the original sense of both the Old and New Testaments.

In his canonization homily, Pope Benedict XVI highlighted the exemplary lives of the four *beati* from various countries (Italy, Switzerland, India, and Ecuador), who realized the ideal of holiness by endeavoring to live in conformity to God's will, which they came to know through the Gospel of Jesus Christ. In fact, the Word of God is a constant invitation from God, like that addressed to the faithful in the Old Testament: "You shall be holy; for I the Lord, your God, am holy" (Lv 19:2) and in the New Testament: "You, therefore, must be perfect, as your heavenly Father is perfect" (Mt 5:48). Pope Benedict XVI, referring to the Word of God in the readings of the liturgy (see Is 25:6–10; Mt 22:1–14), described the canonization of the *beati* by using the biblical image of those invited to a banquet, dressed in a wedding garment, stating that "it is a joyful image because the banquet accompanies a wedding feast, the Covenant of love between God and his People."[12]

Particular attention should be given the two homilies in conjunction with the celebration of the synodal assembly on the Word of God. In his homily opening the synod, the Holy Father pointed out that the purpose of the work session was together to seek ways "on how to make the Gospel proclamation increasingly effective in our time. We all know how necessary it is to make the Word of God the center of our lives, to welcome Christ as our one Redeemer, as the Kingdom of God in person, to ensure that his light may enlighten every context of humanity: from the family to the school, to culture, to work, to free time and to the other sectors of society and of our life."[13]

Inspired by the Word of God that was proclaimed at the Eucharist closing the synodal assembly, the Supreme Pontiff drew attention to the unbreakable bond between the loving listening of God and the disinterested service of the brethren. According to St. Paul, the experience of the Christians of Macedonia teaches that love of neighbor is born from docilely listening to the Word of God (see 1 Thes 1:6,8). As a result of the synod, the Church became more aware of this bond, which implies following three pastoral priorities. In the first place, "the Church's principal task, at the start of this new millennium, is above all to nourish herself on the Word of God, in order to make a new evangelization."[14] It consists in making every effort to realize the two loves of God and neighbor. In fact, the Word of God reminds us that "the fullness of the law, as all of the divine Scriptures, is love."[15] To fulfill this vocation well—a vocation to which all are called—requires prayer, so that, in obedient listening to the Word of God, the Church might experience a new Pentecost, an authentic spiritual renewal which, under the guidance of the Holy Spirit, will become a source of great pastoral zeal and a new missionary dynamism. In this regard, a particularly striking example is offered by the Blessed Virgin Mary, who listened, meditated upon, and lived the Word of God (see Lk 2:19).

Presentations during the Liturgy of the Hours

The liturgy facilitates dialogue between the people and the Lord. In liturgical prayer the faithful call upon God in the very words which God himself addressed to his Church through Sacred Scripture. "The Word issued from the mouth of God and witnessed in the Scriptures returns to him in the form of a prayerful response, a response that is lived, a response that wells up from love (see Is 55:10–11)."[16] The Holy Father gave proof of this dialogue during the Liturgy of the Hours, celebrated at the synod each day. This prayer, composed of psalms and passages from the Old and New Testament, is obligatory for members of the clergy—particularly the hours of morning and evening prayer—but it is also recommended to the lay faithful, who are called to recite it personally or in community.

In commenting on certain passages from Psalm 118, the psalm used during mid-morning prayer, the Holy Father emphasized, among other things, the solidity of the Word of God, which is a veritable reality and the foundation of all things. Everything was created by the divine Word in such a way as to make reality a *creatura Verbi*. At the same time, each person is called to serve the Word. Through the human words of Sacred Scripture we ought, in virtue of the grace of the Holy Spirit, continually to discover the Word of God, the Person of Jesus Christ, the Word-Made-Flesh (see Jn 1:14). Therefore, knowledge of the Scripture is not so much a literary phenomenon as it is an existential exegesis. "It is the movement of my existence. It is moving towards the Word of God in the human words."[17] God alone is infinite; his Word is also universal and knows no boundaries. "Therefore by entering into the Word of God we really enter into the divine universe."[18] We enter into the communion of the universal Church, the communion of all our brothers and sisters and the communion of all humanity. The Word of God comes to us with a face, that of the person of Jesus Christ. He takes the initiative in turning to us, opening his heart, and calling us through Baptism to become part of his Mystical Body. The Word of God is like a ladder which permits us, along with Jesus Christ, the Word of God par excellence, to ascend and descend into the depths of his love. From this conception comes a sense of Christian realism. "The realist is the one who recognizes the Word of God, in this apparently weak reality, as the foundation of all things."[19]

During the celebration of evening prayer on October 18, the Holy Father gave a brief greeting, after having attentively listened to the homily that the Ecumenical Patriarch Bartholomew I of Constantinople preached to the synod fathers in the Sistine Chapel. Pope Benedict XVI expressed deep joy at the experience of communion and a genuine, profound unity, even if not as yet complete. This unity also came from an awareness of sharing the same Church Fathers, a fact which made them "brothers." Thus, referring to the address of the Ecumenical Patriarch, the Bishop of Rome emphasized that he is "nourished by the spirit of the Fathers, by the Sacred Liturgy, and for this very reason, [he is] also strongly contextualized in our time with a great Christian realism that made us see the challenges."[20] The Word of God, found in the words of Sacred Scripture, is a light for all, also allowing them to come to grips with present-day problems.

Other Presentations

Prior to the opening of the synodal assembly on the Word of God, the Holy Father Pope Benedict XVI dedicated three reflections to this important synodal event before reciting the *Angelus*. This traditional prayer of the

Catholic Church uses biblical passages (Lk 1:26–38; 39–45; 2:1–7) to renew wonder in the mystery of the Incarnation of Jesus Christ, the Word-Made-Flesh (see Jn 1:14), who is made present as the faithful recite the prayer.

As a pilgrim at the Marian shrine of Pompeii, Italy, the Holy Father prayed that the Ordinary General Assembly of the Synod of Bishops on the Word of God might "bear the fruits of authentic renewal in every Christian community."[21]

At the end of the closing liturgy of the synodal assembly, before the *Angelus* prayer, Pope Benedict XVI highlighted that, in the course of their reflections, the synod fathers focused on the Word of God which is Christ, who guides and enlightens his Church. To be able to encounter the Lord Jesus through human words requires allowing oneself to be guided by the Holy Spirit, who guided inspired men in their composition of the Bible. In this regard, three classic criteria should be kept in mind for an ecclesial understanding of Sacred Scripture: "every text must be read and interpreted keeping in mind the unity of the whole of Scripture, the living tradition of the Church and the light of the faith."[22]

On various occasions, Pope Benedict XVI has recommended the prayerful reading of Sacred Scripture, especially *Lectio Divina*. This practice starts with the literal sense of the text and then proceeds to a discovery of its spiritual sense, which can be allegorical, moral, or anagogical. Addressing the subject, the pope said: "Scientific exegesis and *lectio divina* are therefore both necessary and complementary in order to seek, through the literal meaning, the spiritual meaning that God wants to communicate to us today."[23]

The Integral Reading of Sacred Scripture

During the General Congregation of October 14, the Holy Father made a presentation on the relation between the historical-critical method and the theological method in the interpretation of the Bible. He recalled how, while engaged in writing his book *Jesus of Nazareth*, he became aware that scientific exegesis is well developed even in the Catholic Church, but the theological method is almost absent, bringing very grave consequences.[24]

Instead, *Dei Verbum* § 12 states that a proper exegesis of Sacred Scripture requires two distinct yet correlated levels in methodology. The first is the so-called historical-critical method, which is necessary from the very nature of the history of salvation, culminating in the Incarnation of the Word of God in the Person of Jesus Christ (see Jn 1:14). "The history of salvation is not mythology but rather true history, and is therefore to be studied alongside serious historical research methods."[25] The second methodological level is necessary so as to interpret well words which are simultaneously the human words and the divine Word, given "that Scripture is to be interpreted in the same spirit in which it was written."[26] *Dei Verbum* also referred to three decisive steps in understanding the divine aspect, namely, the theological sense of Sacred Scripture; interpret the text keeping in mind (1) the unity of all Scripture, (2) the living tradition of the Church, and (3) the analogy of faith. "Only where the two methodological levels, both historical-critical and theological, are observed can one speak of a theological exegesis which is adequate to this Book."[27]

Many exegetes and theologians deserve our gratitude for their studies, which have proved of great assistance in discovering the profound sense of Sacred Scripture. A major effort, however, needs to be undertaken so that similar results can be attained in biblical interpretation on the theological level. In doing so, two serious consequences, caused by the absence of a theological hermeneutic of Scripture, will be avoided. The first consists in considering the Bible only as a book of the past, incapable of speaking to the people of today. Following this line of thinking, biblical exegesis runs the risk of considering the Bible as purely historical or literary writing. A second negative consequence, which is even more serious, is the disappearance of the hermeneutic of faith, mentioned in *Dei Verbum*. In such a case, the hermeneutic of belief gives way to "a hermeneutic that is secularist, positivist, the key fundamental of which is the conviction that the divine does not appear in human history."[28] This hermeneutic denies the historicity of the divine events in the Bible, reducing them exclusively to the human level.

Therefore, the life and mission of the Church and the future of the faith demands overcoming the dualism between exegesis and theology, which unfortunately is oftentimes present at the academic level, including centers for the formation of future candidates to the ecclesial ministries. "Biblical theology and systematic theology are two dimensions of one reality, which we call theology."[29] Theologians and exegetes need to work together so that the study of Scripture, on the one hand, is not reduced simply to the historical aspect of the inspired text and, on the other, does not lose its force in contemporary theology. In fact, "when exegesis is not theological, Scripture cannot be the soul of theology, and vice versa; when theology is not essentially scriptural interpretation within the Church, then this theology no longer has a foundation."[30] Consequently, exegetical study needs to broaden its horizon and attentively follow the principles laid down in *Dei Verbum*.

The reflections of Pope Benedict XVI, which found a place in propositions 25, 26, and 27, were approved almost unanimously by the synod fathers and thus will be included in the Post-Synodal Apostolic Exhortation on the Word of God. These elements are of great importance in ensuring a full, Christian grasp of the Word of God, understood in the obedience of a faith that grows through the action of the Holy Spirit, who is present in a particular manner in liturgical celebrations. Making use of the complementary relationship between the historical-critical method and the theological method will avert the erroneous reading of Sacred Scripture, namely, a fundamentalism that ignores "the human mediation of the inspired text and its literary genre,"[31] and which is often proposed by various sects that promise on various occasions "an illusory happiness through the Bible, often interpreted in a fundamentalistic way,"[32] and the danger of a selective reading, which leads to "a vague spiritualism or pop-psychology."[33] Both such erroneous readings are to be avoided, because they leave the Word of God void or deprive it of either a literary, historical meaning or its spiritual and divine aspect.

Final Observations

I will conclude with some pertinent reflections from Pope Benedict XVI.

Synodality in the Church

At the end of the synod's work, the Bishop of Rome stated: "The Synod is nearing its end, but the walking together under the guidance of the Word of God continues. In this sense, we are always at a 'synod,' walking together towards the Lord with the Word of God to guide us."[34] These words of Pope Benedict XVI show his high regard for the Church's synodal character. As he himself has said, synodality is a part of the Church's life, inasmuch as it represents the road for all Christians—and even all people of goodwill—to walk in following Jesus Christ, the Word of God, who desires that all peoples, races, languages, and cultures be one (see Jn 17:22–23) in his Mystical

Body (see Eph 4:4). "Walking in synod" also includes in some way those who recognize the Bible as an important literary work, indeed, as the great code of universal culture. However, even in this case, the Bible "should not be stripped of the divine element, but must be read in the same Spirit in which it was composed."[35]

The Word of God, then, continues its course in the Church and history (see 2 Thes 3:1). In this act of walking together in the pilgrimage of faith, primacy is given to the Word of God, which continues to guide the Church. Illumined by the Holy Spirit, the Church must seek to discover, through the words of Sacred Scripture, the Word of God, the Person of Jesus Christ, the Divine Word Incarnate. In his homily at the beginning of his pontificate the Holy Father spoke of the primacy of the Word of God and the Gospel as the program of his pastoral activity as Bishop of Rome and Universal Pastor of the Church. *Dei Verbum* also emphasized that the Church's magisterium is in service to the Word of God, which, with the assistance of the Holy Spirit, "is devoutly listened to, scrupulously guarded and faithfully explained."[36]

The Ecumenical Dimension

Other members of churches and Christian communities, not yet in full communion with the Catholic Church, also walk with us on the path toward synodality. On various occasions, the Holy Father has thanked fraternal delegates for their participation at synods. In a special manner, he expressed his gratitude to the Ecumenical Patriarch Batholomew I of Constantinople, the first ecumenical patriarch to take part in a synodal event. His presence was a visible sign of ecumenical dialogue between the Catholic and Orthodox churches, which, in a spirit of friendship, is growing in recent years. Protestant denominations are also associated. Christians' shared veneration for Sacred Scripture assists ecumenical dialogue and hastens the road to full communion.

In his address to the synod fathers, Patriarch Bartholomew I also made reference to the last document of the International Mixed Commission for Theological Dialogue between the Catholic Church and the Orthodox Church on the topic "Ecclesial Communion, Conciliarity and Authority." Recalling this fact with approval, Pope Benedict XVI expressed the conviction that this document "certainly unfolds a positive prospect of reflection on the relationship that exists between primacy and synodality in the

Church. This is a matter of crucial importance in relations with our Ortho-dox brethren and will be the subject of examination and exchanges at the next meetings."[37]

Ecclesial Communion

Every synodal assembly is a powerful experience of ecclesial communion. This was the case above all at the Twelfth Ordinary General Assembly "because it focused on what illumines and guides the Church: the Word of God: Christ in person."[38] The communion shared by the synod fathers with their head the Bishop of Rome was manifested each day in listening, prayer, reflection, and the rediscovery of the richness and depth of the Word of God. Communion also results from a common awareness of the grace and joy of being disciples of Jesus Christ and servants of his Word. The original meaning of the term "Church" means "to be called." It is not surprising, then, that "we experienced the joy of being gathered together by the Word and, especially in the liturgy, found ourselves on our way within it, as in our promised land, which gives us a foretaste of the Kingdom of Heaven."[39]

The School of Listening

According to Pope Benedict XVI, the synodal experience was "also a school of listening." Synodal methodology calls for listening to each other. In the course of the assembly, 223 synod fathers spoke for five minutes each. After taking into account the time of the other presentations,[40] the participants at the synodal assembly listened for about thirty hours. Listening, even though apparently passive, has great potentiality. Concretely, listening led to a better understanding of Sacred Scripture. By listening, the synod fathers could better perceive "the relationship between the Word and words, that is, between the Divine Word and the Scriptures that express it."[41] In fact, "we listened to each other and we learned how to listen to the Word of God in a better way. We experienced the truth of the words of St. Gregory the Great: Scripture grows with the one who reads it."[42] Listening to the experiences of the participants coming from various parts of the world, facing every-day realities, with different situations of life each day, "one can discover the potential, the riches hidden in the Word of God. . . . One is opened in a new way also the sense of the Word which was given us in the Sacred Scrip-tures."[43] Therefore, the Word of God remains always alive and effective (see

Heb 4:12); no one can exhaust it, because it is infinite, like Jesus Christ himself, the Incarnate Word.

There is yet another important aspect to this idea of listening. "In listening to each other, we may hear the Lord better. And in dialogue of hearing, we then learn the deeper reality, obedience to the Word of God, conforming to our thought, our will to think turning to God's thought and will."[44] This obedience, instead of attacking freedom, develops all possibilities and makes a person truly free.

Cultural Renewal

The Synod of Bishops resulted in a rediscovery of the importance and contemporary character of the Word of God. "What we take too much for granted in our daily lives, we thus realize once again in its sublimity: the fact that God speaks, that God answers our questions."[45] God always speaks in the present, his Word is addressed to each one personally, but "precisely because the Word is so personal, we can understand it correctly and completely only as part of the 'we' of the community established by God."[46] Therefore, the synod assembly permitted the Church to experience a new Pentecost even today, namely, the multiplicity of ways of experiencing God and the world, the richness of culture and the variety of its manifestations in various languages. Nevertheless, "we also learned that Pentecost is still 'on the way,' still incomplete: there are many languages that still await the Word of God contained in the Bible."[47] Pope Benedict XVI expressed his hope that the "experiences and the fruits of the Synod may have a constructive influence on the life of the Church: on our personal relationship with the Sacred Scriptures, on their interpretation in the liturgy and catechesis, as well as in scientific research, so that the Bible will not remain a Word from the past, but that its vitality and timeliness will be appreciated and brought to light against the vast horizon of its fullness of meaning."[48]

I ask that you join me in praying along with the Holy Father that "a renewed listening to the Word of God, guided by the action of the Holy Spirit, may cause to spring forth an authentic renewal in the universal Church and in every Christian community."[49]

⁓

Notes

1. Benedict XVI, "*Angelus*" (October 5, 2008), *L'Osservatore Romano: Weekly Edition in English* (October 8, 2008), 1, 4.

2. Joseph Ratzinger, "Dogmatische Konstitution über die göttliche Offenbarung (Constitutio dogmatic de divina Revelatione 'Dei Verbum')," in *Das zweite Vatikanische Konzil. Dokumente und Kommentare, Lexikon für Theologie und Kirche*, ed. Heinrich Suso Brechter et al. (Freiburg, Germany: Herder, 1967), 2:497–528, 571–81.

3. Benedict XVI, "Homily at the Inauguration of the Petrine Ministry of the Bishop of Rome" (April 24, 2005), *Acta Apostolicae Sedis* 97 (2005), 709.

4. Ibid., 710–11.

5. Benedict XVI , "Greetings to Participants of the Twelfth Ordinary General Assembly of the Synod of Bishops at the Concluding Luncheon" (October 25, 2008), *L'Osservatore Romano* (October 26, 2008), 1.

6. Ibid.

7. On the subject of tradition, *The Catechism of the Catholic Church*, referring to the Second Vatican Council's Dogmatic Constitution on Divine Revelation (*Dei Verbum*) § 7, states: "Through Tradition, 'the Church, in her doctrine, life and worship, perpetuates and transmits to every generation all that she herself is, all that she believes. The sayings of the holy Fathers are a witness to the life-giving presence of this Tradition, showing how its riches are poured out in the practice and life of the Church, in her belief and her prayer" (78).

8. Second Vatican Ecumenical Council, Dogmatic Constitution on Divine Revelation (*Dei Verbum*), § 10.

9. Benedict XVI, "Homily at the Conclusion of the Twelfth Ordinary General Assembly of the Synod of Bishops" (October 26, 2008), *Acta Apostolicae Sedis* 100 (2008): 781.

10. See *General Instruction of the Roman Missal*, 28; Second Vatican Ecumenical Council, Constitution on the Sacred Liturgy (*Sacrosanctum concilium*), 56.

11. Benedict XVI, "Homily in Commemoration of Pope Pius XII" (October 9, 2008): *Acta Apostolicae Sedis* 100 (2008): 765.

12. Benedict XVI, "Homily of Canonization" (October 12, 2008), *Acta Apostolicae Sedis* 100 (2008): 768.

13. Benedict XVI, "Homily at the Opening of the Twelfth Ordinary General Assembly of the Synod of Bishops" (October 5, 2008), *Acta Apostolicae Sedis* 100 (2008): 757.

14.   Benedict XVI, "Homily at the Conclusion," 779.

15.   Ibid., 780.

16.   Ibid., 781.

17.   Benedict XVI, "Meditation during Mid-Morning Prayer" (October 6, 2008), *Acta Apostolicae Sedis* 100 (2008): 760.

18.   Ibid.

19.   Ibid., 759.

20.   Benedict XVI, "Address to the Ecumenical Patriarch of Constantinople Bartholomew I" (October 18, 2008), *L'Osservatore Romano: Weekly Edition in English* (October 22, 2008), 7.

21.   Benedict XVI, "*Angelus*" (October 19, 2008), *L'Osservatore Romano: Weekly Edition in English* (October 22, 2008), 1.

22.   Benedict XVI, "*Angelus*" (October 26, 2008), *L'Osservatore Romano: Weekly Edition in English* (October 29, 2008), 1.

23.   Ibid.

24.   The problem of the relation between the historical-critical method and the theological method was presented to English-language audiences by Cardinal Joseph Ratzinger at a conference in New York in 1988. The text is entitled "Biblical Interpretation in Conflict: On the Foundations and the Itinerary of Exegesis Today," in *Opening Up the Scriptures. Joseph Ratzinger and the Foundations of Biblical Interpretation*, ed. José Granados, Carlos Granados, and Luis Sánchez-Navarro (Grand Rapids, MI: Eerdmans, 2008), 1–29.

25.   Benedict XVI, "Address during the Twelfth Ordinary General Assembly of the Synod of Bishops" (October 14, 2008), *L'Osservatore Romano: Weekly Edition in English* (October 22, 2008), 13.

26.   Ibid.

27.   Ibid.

28.   Ibid.

29.   Ibid.

30.   Ibid.

31.   Proposition 46.

32.   Proposition 47.

33.   Benedict XVI, "Message to the People of God of the Twelfth Ordinary General Assembly of the Synod of Bishops," *L'Osservatore Romano: Weekly Edition in English* (October 26, 2008), 6.

34.   Benedict XVI, "Greetings."

35.   Benedict XVI, "*Angelus*" (October 26, 2008).

36. *Dei Verbum*, § 10.

37. Benedict XVI, "Address to the Participants at the Plenary Session of the Pontifical Council for Promoting Christian Unity" (December 12, 2008), *L'Osservatore Romano: Weekly Edition in English* (December 24–31, 2008), 7.

38. Benedict XVI, "*Angelus*" (October 26, 2008).

39. Ibid.

40. The participants in the synodal assembly also listened to twenty-two reports of varying length.

41. Benedict XVI, "*Angelus*" (October 26, 2008).

42. "*Divina eloquia cum legente crescunt*" (Gregory the Great, *Homilia in Ezechielem* 1, 7, 8: *CCL* 142, 87). See Benedict XVI, "Greetings to Participants," 1.

43. Ibid.

44. Ibid.

45. Benedict XVI, "Discourse to the Roman Curia" (December 22, 2008), *L'Osservatore Romano: Weekly Edition in English* (January 7, 2009), 12.

46. Ibid.

47. Ibid.

48. Ibid.

49. Benedict XVI, "Homily at the Conclusion," 779.

11.

"Their Eyes Were Opened"

The Bible and Prayer, a Guided Meditation

Eduardo C. Fernández, S.J.

~

Introduction

This past summer, I did a reading from my first book, *La Cosecha*,[1] which recently came out in Spanish, for our students at the Instituto Hispano at the Jesuit School in Berkeley where I teach. One of the aims of the evening was to give them a sample of some of the contemporary writings of our Latina and Latino theologians. Many were not aware that such writings existed and listened with great interest. Once I finished, in what was the last session of a very long day, pizza smells began to fill the room as I thanked them for their time and interest. But, no, they were not ready to eat! Several asked for the floor as, one by one, they shared why this theology was so meaningful for them: in a nutshell, they could identify with the suffering found in those texts, and at the same time, the hope of the Resurrection, where the darkness of sin and racism which many had experienced when they came to this country did not have the last word.

Needless to say, the session's direction that evening surprised me to no end. Why such an emotional response, often accompanied by tears? In conversation with one of the other professors, Sister Teresa Maya-Sotomayor, C.C.V.I., who had been teaching them the history of Latino Catholics in the United States, helped me to see that taking the long view of the turn of events allowed them to see that their own stories, many filled with much suffering, were not in vain as they were part of a much larger story, one, like that of the Paschal Mystery, which ultimately led them to see the grace of God at work, not only in their lives but also in the larger community.

193

In Luke's Emmaus story, one which can be contemplated from many different angles and in a million and one ways, we hear a similar emotional reaction to the animated presence of Jesus on the road. "Were not our hearts burning (within us) while he spoke to us on the way and opened the scriptures to us?" (Lk 24:32). Here the heart, according to some scriptural scholars, is not only signifying the emotional part of human beings but also the center of intelligence. In the *Instrumentum Laboris* of the 2008 Synod of Bishops, the bishops make the point that faith and understanding are not opposed to each other but both form parts of the same process of coming to believe,[2] or as beautifully described in the text, "having our eyes be opened" as were those of the once discouraged disciples (v. 31).

Some Thoughts on the Bible and Prayer

Our God is constantly trying to reveal Godself to us.[3] We have come to know this tender God especially through the deeds and words of Jesus that we find in the Gospels. Similarly, God speaks to us through other parts of Sacred Scripture. God also comes to us by means of the Church, the extension of Christ in the world. Because we are united in Christ, God also speaks to us through other persons, as well as through the beauty of creation. Moreover, God often speaks to us through the events of our lives, those very things we might rejoice or struggle through, such as the birth of a child or the death of a loved one. Before going further, given much of the focus of this published work, please allow me to say a few words about Latinos and the Bible.

While it is accurate to say that Roman Catholic missionaries who came to the Americas, being persons of their times, did not promote the active reading of Sacred Scripture—in fact, such direct reading was often prohibited without permission—they did not completely ignore the Bible. In fact, some have made the argument "that the Catholic Church's missionary activity has always been Bible-centered, for (1) Scripture served to motivate the missionaries themselves; (2) biblical texts have always played an important role in the church's liturgy; and (3) the Bible has even served as a means of evangelization—although usually in an indirect way."[4] One need only recall the popularity of such biblically based practices as *Las Posadas* and the live *Via Crucis*, or way of the Cross, as examples of how we act out certain Bible stories. Much of our indigenous culture, similarly, also expressed itself by the dramatic performance of mythical stories and dances. There is a certain rubric of corporality which reminds us that we, in many ways, learn through our senses, a perfect complement to the sacramental principle that stresses that God becomes present through sacred symbols and gestures, or doorways to the Sacred.

For the remainder of this chapter and spiritual exercise, I will focus on praying with Scripture, a type of *Lectio Divina* which St. Ignatius proposes in his school of prayer, the *Spiritual Exercises*, a sixteenth-century manual for prayer. While he drew from the great traditions of his time, especially from the Benedictine cultivation of Sacred Scripture, along with the Franciscan gift for integrating all of creation, I will focus on his particular stylization of this sacred practice.

St. Ignatius's Method in the Spiritual Exercises

There is a method of prayer proposed by St. Ignatius that he calls "contemplation." While this word takes on different meanings in the Christian mystical tradition, his use often has to do with inviting the person praying to take a scene from the life of Christ and enter into it, reliving it as if it were actually occurring and the person was a participant in the event.

As a preparation for this type of prayer, he suggests, as would a movie director, that we take the time to do a composition of place, a type of setting the scene. In what he offers as points or guides for meditating on the mystery of the Incarnation, for example, he suggests the following in his *Spiritual Exercises*: first, we get a glimpse of the characters. He writes: "Here it will be to recall how Our Lady, pregnant almost nine months and, as we may piously meditate, seated on an ass, together with Joseph and a servant girl leading an ox, set forth from Nazareth to go to Bethlehem and pay the tribute that Caesar had imposed on all those lands" (*Spiritual Exercises* [hereinafter *SE*] 111).[5] Regardless of whether Joseph and Mary traveled with a servant, a very unlikely reality for a couple of slender means, this inclusion of a maid allows the person praying to enter into the scene. Exhorting the prayer to engage the gift of imagination, he further instructs the person to picture a mental representation of the road from Nazareth to Bethlehem. He writes: "Consider its length and breadth, whether it is level or winds down valleys and hills. Similarly, look at the place or cave of the Nativity: How big is it, or small? How low or high? And how is it furnished?" (*SE* 112).

The inclusion of the servant girl gives him an opportunity to allow the person praying to be actively part of the scene. After acknowledging the presence of the Blessed Mother, St. Joseph, the maid, and the child Jesus, St. Ignatius writes: "I will make myself a poor, little, and unworthy slave, gazing at them, contemplating them, and serving them in their needs, just as if I were there, with all possible respect and reverence. Then I will reflect upon myself to draw some profit" (*SE* 114). Later on, he adds, how the person should consider, observe, and contemplate what the persons are saying and/or doing, such as "journeying and toiling, in order that the Lord may be born in greatest poverty; and that after so many hardships of hunger, thirst, heat, cold, injuries and insults, he may die on the cross! And all this for me! Then I will reflect and draw some spiritual profit" (*SE* 115–16).

This active contemplation of a sacred scene is not unlike St. Francis of Assisi's taking Jesus down from the Cross, although he was in fact risen, or St. Anthony of Padua's being caught up in the presence of the child Jesus in his arms, although he was now an adult. Similarly, St. Teresa of Avila declared that her favorite form of meditation was to be present to Christ as he went through his agony in the garden. The truth is always much bigger than the current facts, for this type of imaginative contemplation acts as a gateway to a sacred encounter with the Lord.[6] To dismiss this possibility of a living, sacred encounter with the Lord who is forever trying to invite us to rest in his arms is to be "so enamored of the truth of history that we miss the truth of mystery."[7]

It is in this spirit that I invite you, the reader, to contemplate the beautiful Gospel story about what happens to the discouraged disciples who are leaving Jerusalem on their way to Emmaus on the first Easter Sunday. In preparing this contemplation, I have drawn from several authors, although, for the sake of the narrative flow, I will not mention them by name.[8]

A Preparatory Exercise

As a college student close to thirty years ago, I remember the power of St. John of the Cross's insightful phrase: the "moment is pregnant with God." Could it really be that God is as close to us as the air we breathe whether we are aware of it or not, and that simply taking the time to be present in the moment helps us to experience that?

In spite of this graced possibility, our minds are often rapid streams of consciousness and it is not easy to become still and know that God is God.

A great help I have found in this regard, both in teaching others to pray in this way, as well as in my own prayer, is to allow the senses to help us relax by getting us out of our heads. The formula is a simple one: we relax when we come to our senses, when we "become as fully conscious as possible of our body sensations, of the sounds around us, of our breathing, of the taste of something in our mouth."[9] In order to help us contemplate the Emmaus story, therefore, I will first guide you through a body sensation awareness exercise taken from Jesuit Anthony de Mello's *Sadhana, a Way to God: Christian Exercises in Eastern Form*:

> Take up a posture that is comfortable and restful. Close your eyes. . . . I am now going to ask you to become aware of certain sensations in your body that you are feeling at this present moment, but of which you are not explicitly aware. . . . Be aware of the touch of your clothes on your shoulders. . . . Now become aware of the touch of your clothes on your back, or of your back touching the back of the chair you are sitting on. . . . Now be aware of the feel of your hands as they touch each other or rest on your lap. . . . Now become conscious of your thighs or your buttocks pressing against your chair. . . . Now the feel of your feet touching your shoes. . . . Now become explicitly aware of your sitting posture. . . .
>
> Once again: your shoulders . . . your back . . . your right hand . . . your left hand . . . your thighs . . . your feet . . . your sitting position. . . . Again: shoulders . . . back . . . right hand . . . left hand . . . right thigh . . . left thigh . . . right foot . . . left foot . . . sitting posture. . . .
>
> Continue to go the round by yourself now, moving from one part of the body to the other. Do not dwell for more than a couple of seconds on each part, shoulders, back, thigh, etc. . . . Keep moving from one to the other . . . You may dwell either on the parts of the body I have indicated or on any other parts you wish: your head, your neck, your arms, your chest, your stomach . . . The important thing is that you get the *feel*, the sensation of each part, that you feel it for a second or two and then move on to another part of the body . . .[10]

A Guided Meditation on the Emmaus Story

Continue to quiet yourself, gently allowing the Lord to guide your thoughts. Do not be in a hurry, but let the scene unfold gradually before you as you try to compose the place. Imagine the road from Jerusalem to the town of Emmaus. Is it hilly or flat? Desert-like or lush with green vegetation? Do trees line the road? Are there houses along the way? What is the temperature like on this spring day?

Having prepared the stage, let the whole scene now come to life. Note the two disciples coming down the road, deep in conversation. What do they look like? Are they male, female, perhaps father and daughter? Husband and wife? How are they dressed? What strikes you about their faces? Can you hear what they are discussing? Why do they seem so distressed? It is not enough for you to observe the whole scene from the outside, as if it were a movie on the screen. You must participate in it. What are you doing there? Why have you come to this place? What are your feelings as you survey the scene and enter into the activity of the day? Do you speak to anyone? To whom?

You gradually notice that a stranger has now joined the conversation. How is he dressed? What does his voice sound like? It surprises you that he does not seem to have a clue as to what has happened recently in Jerusalem. How can he not know about Jesus of Nazareth, the prophet, and about what happened to him in that large city, about his powerful words and deeds and yet tragic end? How is it that this stranger did not know that this Jesus was handed over by the chief priests and rulers to be sentenced to death and crucified? "But we were hoping that he would be the one to redeem Israel; and besides all this, it is now the third day since this took place. Some women from our group, however, have astounded us: they were at the tomb early in the morning and did not find his body; they came back and reported that they had indeed seen a vision of angels who announced that he was alive. Then some of those with us went to the tomb and found things just as the women had described, but him they did not see" (Lk 24:21–24).

The stranger reacts to this account with great passion: "How foolish you are, how slow you are to believe everything the prophet said! Was it not necessary for the Messiah to suffer these things and then to enter his glory?" What are your feelings as you hear the stranger utter these words? What effect has it had on others around you who hear him say these things? Has his tone of voice changed? Listen closely as he continues, slowing explaining what was said about the Messiah in all the Scriptures, beginning with the books of Moses and the writings of all the prophets. Again, what are your feelings as you hear him break open the Scriptures? Can you tell what the others are feeling?

As you start to arrive in the town of Emmaus, it seems that the stranger is intent on going further. What to do? Immediately, however, the disciples hold him back, saying, "Stay with us; the day is almost over and it is getting dark." He accepts the invitation and sits down at table with you and the others. He takes the bread in his weathered hands, says the blessings, breaks it, and shares it.

But this powerful gesture, this breaking of the bread, has awakened something in the two disciples at table with you. Might it be the memory of so many meaningful fellowship meals? Perhaps they remembered at that instant what Jesus had told them about how sharing food with outcasts would be a sign that the Kingdom had indeed come. Now they were doing this very thing by offering hospitality to a stranger. Perhaps things were not as dismal as they might have seemed a few hours ago before encountering this mysterious stranger on the road to Emmaus . . . all of these thoughts are going through your head when you look up and notice the amazement in the disciples' faces as you see from their expressions that they have recognized Jesus in the breaking of the bread! As they do so, he vanishes from their sight!

The room cannot contain their excitement: "Wasn't it like fire burning in us when he talked to us on the road and explained the Scriptures to us?" You, too, recall the feeling that you had as Jesus explained the sacred texts. The decision is quickly made to go back to Jerusalem, that large, impersonal city which had witnessed the death of Jesus. As you return to the road, this time back to Jerusalem, you find yourself enthralled in conversation with these witnesses concerning what happened that afternoon. What could it all mean? Could it really be that through their concern to provide hospitality to a stranger, "the disciples' sadness, foolishness, and slowness of heart" became transformed into joy, insight, and joyful recommitment to Jesus' way?[11]

They walk ahead excitedly, and gradually you find yourself seemingly alone, but not really, for Jesus himself has come to walk with you. He is quiet at first but then slowly engages you in conversation. Talk to him about what you just witnessed. What about you? Is there any destructive discouragement from which you need to be delivered? Physical, emotional, spiritual? Might he be inviting you to see him in others? Whom might they be? Speak to Jesus about it. What does he have to say? Spend a while now in quiet prayer in the company of Jesus.

By Way of Conclusion

The great teachers of this and similar types of prayer remind us that we should not get discouraged if we are not able, as much as we would like, to enter into this type of contemplation. While people often have greater success with further practice, ultimately, it is God who grants the person this ability and different forms of prayer are best suited for different kinds of people. In moments when we feel that we cannot pray, let the words of the great apostle Paul in the eighth chapter of his Letter to the Romans give us comfort: "In the same way, the Spirit too comes to the aid of our weakness; for we do not know how to pray as we ought, but the Spirit itself intercedes with inexpressible groanings. And the one who searches hearts knows what is the intention of the Spirit, because it intercedes for the holy ones according to God's will" (Rom 8:26–27).

Also, the Word of God will bear fruit in its own time and God will speak to us when and how God chooses:

> For just as from the heavens
>   the rain and snow come down
> And do not return there
>   till they have watered the earth,
>   making it fertile and fruitful,
> Giving seed to him who sows
>   and bread to him who eats,
> So shall my word be
>   that goes forth from my mouth;
> It shall not return to me void,
>   but shall do my will,
>   achieving the end for which I sent it. (Is 55:10–11)

May we never cease to trust this promise!

～

Notes

1. Eduardo C. Fernández, S.J., *La Cosecha: Teología hispana contemporánea en Estados Unidos (1972–1998)* (Mexico City: Obra Nacional de la Buena Prensa, 2009). English edition: *La Cosecha: Harvesting Contemporary United States Hispanic Theology (1972–1998)* (Collegeville, MN: Liturgical Press, 2000).

2. XII Ordinary General Assembly of the Synod of Bishops, *Instrumentum Laboris,* "The Word of God in the Life and Mission of the Church" (May 11, 2008), § 26, http://www.vatican.va/roman_curia/synod/documents /rc_synod_doc_20080511_instrlabor-xii-assembly_en.html.

3. Some of these ideas come from the ideas of Armand M. Nigro, S.J., and John F. Christensen, S.J., in a handout "Praying with Scripture" (n.d.).

4. See Timonthy A. Lenchak, S.V.D., "The Function of the Bible in Roman Catholic Mission," in *Scripture, Community, and Mission: Essays in Honor of D. Preman Niles,* ed. Philip J. Wickeri (Hong Kong and London: Christian Conference of Asia and the Council for World Mission, 2002), 3. Here Lenchak is drawing from Eric Fenn.

5. George E. Ganss, S.J., *The Spiritual Exercises of Saint Ignatius: A Translation and Commentary* (Chicago: Loyola Press, 1992). All subsequent quotes from the *Spiritual Exercises* are taken from this translation.

6. See Anthony de Mello, *Sahhana, a Way to God: Christian Exercises in Eastern Form* (New York: Image Books, Doubleday, 1978), 82–85.

7. De Mello, *Sadhana,* 82.

8. Among the authors consulted are Luke Timothy Johnson, *The Gospel of Luke,* Sacra Pagina 3 (Collegeville, MN: Liturgical Press, 1991); Robert J. Karris, O.F.M., "The Gospel According to Luke," in *The New Jerome Biblical Commentary,* ed. Raymond E. Brown, S.S., Joseph A. Fitzmyer, S.J., and Roland E. Murphy, O.Carm. (Englewood Cliffs, NJ: Prentice Hall, 1990), 675–721; Gustavo Gutiérrez, *Compartir la Palabra a lo largo del Año Litúrgico* (Lima, Peru: Instituto Bartolomé de Las Casas y Centro de Estudios y Publicaciones, CEP, 1995), 132–33.

9. De Mello, *Sadhana,* 16.

10. Ibid., 15–16.

11. Karris, "The Gospel According to Luke," 721.

12

"He Interpreted for Them the Scripture"

The Bible and Preaching

Jorge L. Presmanes, O.P.

∽

> Now, that very day two of [the disciples] were going to a village seven
> miles from Jerusalem called Emmaus, and they were conversing about
> all the things that had occurred. And it happened that while they were
> conversing and debating, Jesus himself drew near and walked with
> them, but their eyes were prevented from recognizing them.
>
> —Luke 24:13–16

Introduction

Reminiscent of the disciples' Emmaus experience, I encountered the risen
Christ on my return from a trip to Cuba. Standing in front of me in the
queue for the final security checkpoint at the Havana airport was a young
teenager with his mother. I was moved by the love and the tenderness that
she demonstrated as she caressed her son's tear-stained face and by the way
he clung to her as if by doing so he could postpone the painful separation
that was about to take place. When the time came for him to go through
the security checkpoint, the young man fruitlessly attempted to say his final
good-bye but his grief had overwhelmed him. Gently drying his tears with
her fingers and looking him straight in the eyes, the boy's mother uttered
the words: "*No te preocupes, mi hijo, Dios va contigo*" (Don't worry, my son,
God goes with you).

As I think back to that memorable experience I realize that before my
eyes and in the person of the teenager's mother was the risen Lord calling
her son to faith in a loving and compassionate God who is ever at our side.

The mother's faith-filled words which she hoped would comfort her son as he faced life's challenges without her guidance and support in a distant land proclaim the faith of many in the Latino/a community that God travels with us on our life's journey. For me, the faith event that played out before my eyes at the airport security checkpoint was the locus of God's self-revelation and a dramatic example of human experience as the primary source for Christian preaching.[1]

The paradigm of the theology of preaching presented in the pages to follow is found in Mary Magdalene's encounter with the risen Lord on that first Easter morning:

> Jesus said to her, "Do not hold me, for I have not yet ascended to the Father, but go to my brothers and sisters and say to them, I am ascending to my Father and your Father, to my God and your God." Mary Magdalene went and said to the disciples, "I have seen the Lord." (Jn 20:17–18)

With the five words, "I have seen the Lord," the preaching ministry of the Church commences. Like Mary Magdalene at the tomb, the two disciples on their way to Emmaus encounter the risen Christ. When they finally recognize that their fellow traveler was the risen Lord, their actions mirror those of Mary Magdalene. They immediately return to Jerusalem and recount to the disciples "what had taken place on the way and how he was made known to them in the breaking of the bread" (Lk 24:35).

The declaration that the Lord had risen and was in their midst gave the bewildered disciples the vigor to joyfully persevere in the eschatological mission with which they had been entrusted. Today, Christian preaching, born of the presence of the risen Christ in our midst, continues to engender the hope that moves disciples to work on behalf of the building up of the Church and the Reign of God as envisioned and preached by the Lord Jesus.

Mary Catherine Hilkert correctly claims that to preach is to unveil and point to the presence of the risen Christ in human experience.[2] The preaching that is rooted in God's self-revelation in human experience challenges the training that many preachers, including myself, have received. What we have been taught in seminary training is what we may call a method of adaptation that begins with the scriptural text and its exegesis. The faith tradition that is revealed in the text is then adapted or translated in a way that the intended and fixed message can be effectively communicated to a specific community of culture. Robert Schreiter contends that adaptation as a ministerial practice is "inadequate because of its simplistic and too static understanding of culture—as if a culture can be so easily read that an adaptation can be readily prescribed, and that this process takes place once and for all in an unchanging culture."[3] Here, I suggest that to preach is *not* to adapt the meaning of the Scriptures to a contemporary context. Rather, I argue for enculturated preaching that is fruit of the dialogue between a particular community of culture and the faith tradition.

In the pages to follow I map out an enculturated Latino/a practical theology of liturgical preaching in three movements. I begin with a cursory sketch of a Latino/a method of practical theology. Second, I apply this method to the practice of liturgical preaching. Finally, I offer some practical suggestions for preachers in the Latino/a community, garnered from my own experience.

A Latino/a Practical Theology

From its emergent stages, the primary concern of the *Encuentro* processes and of the methodology of Hispanic pastoral planning was that the ministries respond directly to the concrete reality of Latinos/as and that the participation of *la base* (the grass roots) in the pastoral planning process be prioritized. The methodological cornerstone of the *Encuentro* processes was one that saw praxis as both its initial and final reflection, and in so doing it established a practical theology done from the underside of history and human experience. According to the United States Conference of Catholic Bishops' document *Encuentro & Mission*, this methodology remains a "pastoral discernment that focuses on the needs and aspiration of the faithful, judges that reality in light of the Scriptures and Tradition, and moves into transforming action."[4] Popularly referred to as *ver-juzgar-actuar-evaluar* (see-judge-act-evaluate), this process continues to be the pastoral method of choice of many in the U.S. Hispanic church.

As I see it, there are two preconditions to the effective use of this hermeneutic circle in the pastoral praxis of the Latino/a community. First, the minister-preacher-theologian must be in solidarity with the community. By solidarity, I am referring to *convivencia*—the concrete commitment to minister to and with the community. The second precondition is ecclesiological in nature. The minister-preacher-theologian must be committed to operating within a communal ecclesial context that respects the baptismal dignity and priesthood of all the faithful. Without a commitment to solidarity and community, this Latino/a pastoral circle is irreparably subverted.

Having met the two preconditions, the first movement of the method is *el análisis de la realidad,* which is a comprehensive and multidimensional analysis of the ministry and its social location. From my perspective, one of the most important contributions of Hispanic/Latino/a practical theology is the emphasis it places on a bottom-up communal process that drives all stages of the methodology. Consistent with the preconditions noted earlier, this Latino/a practical theology maintains that *el análisis de la realidad* is to be performed not by the minister alone but by the minister with *la base*— the membership of the community. As *Encuentro & Mission* reminds us, we plan with the people, not for the people.[5]

The second movement in the pastoral circle is the *juzgar* stage. This theoretical step is a critical analysis of the theological tradition as it specifically informs the pastoral questions and issues that arise out of *el análisis de la realidad.* The insights garnered from the dialogue between the ministerial praxis and the theological reflection in the second movement are then verified and tested for *orthodoxy* and *orthopraxis.* Once the insights are tested and verified they are then implemented in the ministerial praxis. In terms of preaching, the revised praxis is the preaching event itself. The final step is a communal evaluation of the revised ministerial praxis. The result of the evaluation then becomes an integral element of the first praxis as the hermeneutical process begins anew.

Ver: The First Praxis in Liturgical Preaching

The process of *el análisis de la realidad* of the faith community is crucial for the preacher for two reasons. First, it enables effective communication in the preaching event. The second reason is because the community itself is the locus of God's self-revelation. In their pastoral statement titled *Fulfilled in Your Hearing: The Homily in the Sunday Assembly,* the U.S. Bishops' Committee on Priestly Life and Ministry remind us of the importance of a comprehensive understanding of the community in order to effectively communicate the gospel message:

> We believe that it is appropriate, indeed essential, to begin this treatment on the Sunday homily with the assembly rather than with the

preacher or the homily, and this is for two principal reasons. First of
all we can point to the great emphasis which communication theorists
place on an accurate understanding of the audience if communication is to be effective. Unless a preacher knows what a congregation
needs, wants or is able to hear, there is every possibility that the message offered in the homily will not meet the needs of the people who
hear it.[6]

For the sake of effective communication, *Fulfilled in Your Hearing* challenges the preacher to use an enculturated approach to homiletics that
places the tradition of faith in a dialogical relationship with the culture of
the assembly.

At the heart of inculturation is a comprehensive understanding of culture. Orlando Espín correctly defines culture as "the dynamic sum of all
that a human group does and materially and symbolically creates in order
to prolong its life in history within geographical contexts." [7] Culture is an
all-encompassing reality that frames every aspect of human knowledge
and action. "No human society and no human individual," says Espín, "can
even dream of the possibility of existing without culture. That dream itself
would be a cultural exercise, made possible precisely by the culture of the
dreamer."[8] Accordingly, and in order for the preacher to achieve an effective
communication of the gospel message, a comprehensive understanding of
the congregation through a multivalent analysis of the culture of the assembly is essential.

The second dialogue partner in the process of inculturation is the tradition of faith. The great Dominican ecclesiologist Yves Congar insightfully
defines faith as "the concrete human response to the universal call from
God to participate in the creation of a new world order rooted in the love
of Jesus Christ through the power of the Holy Spirit."[9] Congar holds that
though the call from God to humanity is universal, it is mediated through
the particularity of culture, lest the call be silenced or misunderstood. He
points to the fact that faith is necessarily bound by culture:

The revealing initiatives of God on the one hand, and the faith which
responds to them on the other do not exist except concretely, and thus
they exist at the meeting points of time and place, of social context, of
expression. The response of faith is not the response of someone, of a
concrete human subject, unless it is given, lived, expressed in the flesh
of a concrete humanity. Thus revelation and the Church are catholic

only in some particular. "Particular" is opposed to "general" but not to "catholic." The particular realizations or expressions of the Catholic Faith are *"pars pro toto," "totum in parte."*[10]

Using Congar's understanding of inculturation, the liturgical homily is then a mouthpiece through which God communicates God's universal call in the context of the particular culture of the assembly. Unlike preaching as adaptation, an enculturated approach to preaching does not make absolute those elements of the tradition that were modeled in one culture and then are translated to another. Instead, in the process of inculturation, faith and culture are placed in a relationship of open dialogue. The fruit of this dialogue is the enrichment of not only the community receiving the preaching, but also the tradition of faith that the preaching event proclaims. Consequently, *el análisis de la realidad* of the congregation in the *ver* stage of the process is essential if the preacher is to effectively enculturate the homily.

According to *Fulfilled in Your Hearing*, the second principal reason why the homiletic process begins with the assembly rather than the preacher or the homily is because in the liturgy "the primary reality is Christ in the assembly, the People of God."[11] The General Instruction of the Roman Missal underscores the revelatory locus that is the worshipping community when it states that "Christ is really present in the very liturgical assembly gathered in his name, in the person of the minister, in his word, and indeed substantially and continuously under the eucharistic species."[12] Thus the preacher begins the homiletic process with the assembly not just because it is critical for effective communication, but because it is the locus of God's self-revelation; it is where the presence of the risen Lord is found.

If Mary Magdalene's proclamation, "I have seen the Lord," or the two disciples recounting of their experience on the way to Emmaus, is the paradigm of Christian preaching, then the homily is the articulation of the presence of the risen Lord among us.

I have argued that a primary and essential task of *el análisis de la realidad* in the *ver* stage of this method in preaching is to search for God's self-revelation in the unique and particular culture of the faith community. Yet this process cannot be done solely by the preacher. It must be a collaborative process between the preacher and *la base*—the community of faith at the grassroots level.

Juzgar: The Theological Reflection in Liturgical Preaching

As I see it, there are two primary texts that inform the preaching event: the Scriptures and the liturgical rite. But these texts will be incomprehensible to the assembly unless they are read from the prism of the congregation. Scripture scholar Fernando Segovia refers to this hermeneutical entry point as the "flesh-and-blood" reader of the text.[13] He correctly holds that the flesh-and-blood reader of the text—or, in the context of liturgy, the hearer of text—must be introduced into the praxis of biblical criticism, because the context of the reading of the biblical text is inseparable from the text itself. The preacher then approaches the texts from Scripture through the hermeneutical lens provided by the communal insights harvested in the *ver* stage of the methodology. While approaching the text from the prism of the assembly, the exegetical work of the preacher must make use of the historical-critical method of biblical interpretation, but always with the awareness that the text itself is found not just, nor primarily, in its written form but in the "relationship that is created between the reader, the writer, and the [written] text."[14] The other text that informs the preaching event and how the biblical text is interpreted is the liturgical rite in which the Word is proclaimed and preached.

As in biblical criticism, liturgy is not celebrated in a vacuum. Someone is praying the Church's liturgical texts in a particular place and time and moment in history. Because of the uniqueness and particularity of time and culture, no other community has or will pray the liturgical text in quite the same way. Together with the Scripture readings, the preacher must study and exegete the rite—the collects, preface, the feast that is being celebrated, the context of the liturgical season, and the other elements of the eucharistic prayer. But the Church's liturgical text must also be analyzed through the prism of the lived experience of the assembly. For the preacher, the exegesis of the liturgical rite is crucial, because it informs the interpretation of the biblical texts in the context of the liturgical celebration. The preaching event is thus the fruit of the insights that are garnered from the conversation between "our narrative," the "biblical narrative," and the "ritual narrative."

An important element of the theoretical stage of the homiletic process is the verification of the insights that flow from the contextual reading of both the Scriptures and the rite. Detractors of the contextual theology approach presented here criticize it as being overly subjective. There is no doubt that uncritical subjectivity is detrimental to the validity of this theological method. As a safeguard against radical subjectivity, the contextual reading of the texts must be verified. Again, I look to the scholarship of Orlando Espín to shed light on this important element of the *juzgar* stage of the process.

Espín's research on Hispanic popular religiosity as locus of revelation suggests that the faith-filled intuitions that underlie popular piety must be verified through the use of a two-prong test. First, the intuitions must be *orthodox*, that is to say that they must be consistent with the Christian tradition's magisterial teaching, the work of the theological community, and the historical development of the interpretation of the Bible. The second verification is *orthopraxis*. The test for orthopraxis assures that the theological intuitions are consistent with the ethical demands of the Gospel.[15] In other words and from a homiletic context, the preacher must make certain that the insights that flow from the contextual reading of both the Bible and the rite are consistent with a Christian ethic that foments the participation of the faithful in the edification of the Kingdom of God.

Actuar y Evaluar:
The Preaching Event and Its Evaluation

When the Latino/a practical theology method is applied to the ministry of liturgical preaching, the revised praxis is preaching from the underside of culture that is the outgrowth of the dialogue between the concrete experience of the liturgical assembly and the biblical and theological tradition. While the theoretical insights in the second step of the practical theology hermeneutic circle are evaluated in terms of orthodoxy and orthopraxis, the homiletic event itself must also be evaluated and verified. This is the task once again of a collaborative venture between the preacher and members of the community.

For eleven years I was the pastor of a large Latino/a parish in Miami. For most of that time I employed a "homily preparation team," which proved invaluable in the implementation of the method in preaching that I have thus far mapped out. The team, composed of six to eight members of the congregation, met every Monday night and had two objectives: evaluation and preparation. The first task of this team was to evaluate the previous day's homily. In this part of the meeting the following questions were addressed: Did the homily adequately address the biblical readings? Was the homily effectively enculturated in the cultural context of the assembly? Did it enable the assembly to hear God's call and respond to it in faith? Did the preacher address *la realidad* of the community? Was the presence of the risen Christ revealed in the community correctly identified and unveiled in the homily?

The answers to these questions then become fodder for *el análisis de la realidad* when the process of pastoral circle begins anew. And it begins in the very homily preparation meeting. In essence, the meeting turns from an evaluative team to a hermeneutical community. In this part of the meeting, the members—who have already read the readings for the following Sunday—become "flesh-and-blood" readers of the biblical texts. Here they attend to the following questions: What does the text say about God? From the perspective of the community, what is the meaning of the text? What are the ethical demands of the text? In light of these insights about God and Christian praxis, where are these insights already visible in the community? How can the preacher communicate these insights in a way that the assembly can hear and respond to them in faith? Equipped with the feedback received from the members of the team, the preacher then proceeds with the homily preparation within the framework of the method in preaching outlined above.

Conclusion

When the Latino/a pastoral circle is the method for liturgical preaching, the homiletic process becomes a hunt for the hidden treasure that is found in the juxtaposition of the presence of the risen Christ in our own historical context and in the tradition of faith as revealed in the Scriptures and the liturgical rite. Mirroring the preaching praxis of the first disciples, the preaching that is the product of the Latino/a pastoral circle is one in which the treasure's bounty is revealed to the community of faith. Through the years, I have searched for and experimented with various homiletic styles and theologies of preaching, but I have yet to find any that surpasses what Mary Magdalene did that Sunday morning and what the two disciples on the way to Emmaus did once they recognized the Lord in the breaking of the bread. They stood before the community of disciples and recounted the hope-filled stories of their encounters with the risen Christ.

⌣

Notes

1. Jorge Presmanes, "The Juxtaposition of Dangerous Memories: Toward a Latino Theology of Preaching," in *Preaching and Culture in Latino Congregations*, ed. Kenneth Davis and Jorge Presmanes (Chicago: Liturgical Training Publications, 2000), 26.

2. Mary Catherine Hilkert, "Naming Grace: A Theology of Proclamation," *Worship* 60 (September 1986): 434. See also Mary Catherine Hilkert, *Naming Grace: Preaching and the Sacramental Imagination* (New York: Continuum, 1997).

3. Robert Schreiter, "Faith and Cultures: Challenges to a World Church," *Theological Studies* 50 (December 1989): 746.

4. United States Conference of Catholic Bishops, *Encuentro & Mission: A Renewed Pastoral Framework for Hispanic Ministry* (Washington, DC: United States Conference of Catholic Bishops, 2002), 21.

5. Ibid.

6. National Conference of Catholic Bishops Committee on Priestly Life and Ministry, *Fulfilled In Your Hearing: The Homily in the Sunday Assembly* (Washington, DC: National Conference of Catholic Bishops, 1982), 3–4.

7. Orlando Espín, "Grace and Humanness: A Hispanic Perspective," *Journal of Hispanic/Latino Theology* 2, no. 2 (1994): 134.

8. Ibid., 135.

9. Yves Congar, "Christianity as Faith and Culture," *East Asian Pastoral Review* 18, no. 4 (1981): 304.

10. Ibid., 305.

11. *Fulfilled in Your Hearing*, 4.

12. General Instruction of the Roman Missal (Third Typical Edition, 2002), § 27.

13. Fernando Segovia, "Toward a Hermeneutics of Diaspora: A Hermeneutics of Otherness and Engagement," in *Reading from This Place: Social Location and Biblical Interpretation in the United States*, ed. Fernando Segovia and Mary Ann Tolbert (Minneapolis: Fortress, 1995), 57.

14. Ada María Isasi Díaz, "By the Rivers of Babylon: Exile as a Way of Life," in *Reading from This Place*, 151.

15. Orlando Espín, "Tradition and Popular Religion: An Understanding of the Sensus Fidelium," in *Frontiers of Hispanic Theology in the United States*, ed. Allan Figueroa Deck (Maryknoll, NY: Orbis Books, 1992), 65–66.

13

Founding a Diocesan Scripture Institute

Felix Just, S.J.

~

Introduction

Anyone who desires to establish a diocesan Scripture institute should be commended and encouraged, given how important the Bible is for the Church. But before we consider *how* this can be done, it is crucial to understand clearly *why* we need something of this sort. The initial explorations need to include a careful reflection on the following questions: What motivates such a venture? What needs have we seen that have inspired this idea? Who are the people we wish to serve? What is the purpose or goal envisioned for such a pastoral endeavor? Being clear about the particular needs and desired outcomes will help greatly in determining the nature, scope, and structure of a Bible institute that your diocese might establish.

Stating the overall goals might seem easy on the broadest level of generality. The Church of Christ is founded upon the Word of God, not understood narrowly as just the printed Bible, but more properly as the Incarnate Word, Jesus the divine Word-Made-Flesh. So a solid theological understanding of the relationship between the trio of Revelation, Tradition, and Scripture (as expressed in *Dei Verbum*, the Dogmatic Constitution on Divine Revelation from the Second Vatican Council) is necessary for helping Roman Catholics avoid a fundamentalist overemphasis on the Bible alone. In Catholic understanding, the Sacred Scriptures are part of the broader stream we call Ecclesial Tradition, which in turn is part of the even broader reality of Divine Revelation. Thus, most Church leaders could readily agree that a desirable goal would be to get more Catholics to read the Bible more often, to understand it better, and to use it more regularly in all aspects of personal and pastoral life (in liturgy, prayer, ministries, etc.). But the *why* question quickly translates to a *how* question: How can we help contemporary Americans, in all their cultural and linguistic diversity, learn about the Christian Scriptures from a Catholic perspective? What can parishes and dioceses do to promote these goals? I would suggest that discussion of these goals would be most effective if they were not treated in isolation, but were part of a more comprehensive diocesan pastoral plan.

Diocesan Pastoral-Biblical Plan

Some dioceses might begin with simple or limited goals in regard to promoting deeper understanding and greater use of the Bible, while other dioceses might have much bigger goals. An initial or limited goal may be to begin by having at least one Bible study or Scripture-sharing group established or available in each parish. A broader goal could be to promote the increased use of the Sacred Scriptures by all parish groups and in all aspects of parish life, not just the specifically identified "Bible study" group(s). An even more expansive goal would be to help all parishioners to understand and use the Bible more regularly and more deeply on their own, in their homes, with their families, and in all aspects of their lives. Short-term and long-term goals need to be discussed and decided before beginning a new diocesan-level program.

Establishing Bible-Focused Groups in Each Parish

The first and most limited of the three goals suggested above, ensuring that some type of Bible study or Scripture-sharing group is available in each parish of the (arch)diocese, would already be a good beginning and a significant achievement, especially if resources and trained leaders are scarce. But why have just *one* group per parish? If a particular parish has only a single Bible study group (meeting Thursdays after the morning Mass, for example), then the vast majority of parishioners might never be able to attend. Ideally, each parish would have many groups meeting at different times, on different days, in different languages, and maybe even in different places. The larger the parish, the more groups would be needed to accommodate people's divergent calendars, circumstances, and interests. Some groups could meet during the daytime and others in the evening, some midweek and others on weekends (not only on Saturdays, but perhaps even on Sundays between or after the Masses).

A parish that has multiple groups meeting at various times, even in different languages, can still foster a sense of overall unity if all of the groups follow the same basic plan. For example, all could focus on the Scripture readings for the following Sunday, or all might study one particular biblical book using bilingual materials available from certain publishers, such as Little Rock Scripture Study. On the other hand, since people have different interests and different learning styles, it might be even more helpful to have different groups with different methodological approaches: some using a *Lectio Divina* style sharing the Lectionary readings, others a "canonical" approach (studying one book of the Bible at a time, using resources such as the *New Collegeville Bible Commentaries*), and still others a more "theological" or "thematic approach" (using resources from the *Threshold Bible Study* or *Six Weeks with the Bible* programs, for example).

The more groups each parish has, however, the greater the need for trained facilitators, people who may not have academic degrees in biblical studies but at least have some basic knowledge of the Bible itself and the Catholic approach to the interpretation of the Scriptures, as well as training and practice in the various skills needed for facilitating small groups.

Promoting Greater Use of the Bible in All Parish Groups and Activities

Since the Second Vatican Council, the Catholic Church has placed greater emphasis on the importance of the Scriptures in the celebrations of all of the Sacraments, not just the Mass. Similarly, the use of the Bible in a Catholic parish need not be limited to the Bible study or *Lectio Divina* group(s) per se, but all parish groups and organizations could be encouraged to incorporate the Scriptures more regularly into all of their regular meetings and activities. This applies not only to the Parish Council, the Liturgy Committee, the RCIA team, or other specifically catechetical ministries, but pertains also to the Knights of Columbus, the Altar Guild, Youth Groups, Social Justice Ministries, and any other organized group within the parish. One might hope that all such groups already begin and end their meetings and activities with a short prayer, but an even more laudable goal would be that all develop a habit of incorporating some Scripture (short biblical readings) into all of their prayers, publications, reflections, retreats, and other programs. To attain this goal, not only would the pastor, the parish staff, and all ministry leaders need to be on board, but it would be useful to recruit and train some other people to function specifically as "Bible Promoters" for their parish. These could either be volunteers or members of the parish staff whose particular interest and responsibility it would be to actively promote the use of the Scriptures by all of the various groups, ministries, and activities of the parish.

Helping All Catholics to Understand and Use the Bible More

To counter the strong and growing attraction of biblical fundamentalism, some broader diocesan-level goals would be to help all Catholics attain a basic understanding of the Bible (not only of its contents and history, but also of an authentically Catholic interpretation of the Scriptures) and to encourage all the faithful to read and pray with the Bible more regularly. To attain such an ambitious and worthy goal, a diocese would need to do more than just establish a Scripture institute. This would require a much broader, sustained, and coordinated effort in each parish and at the diocesan level, and the active promotion and support of the diocesan bishop(s) and local pastors, of diocesan offices and parish staffs. For example, could editors of diocesan newspapers or newsletters and of parish bulletins add even more biblically related materials than they currently include? Could each parish put Bibles in every pew (just like hymnals)? Could a Bible (or the Book of the Gospels) be permanently enshrined or prominently displayed somewhere in each church (just like the Tabernacle and/or the Holy Oils)? Such proposals might at first sound "too Protestant" to many Catholic ears, or might seem too difficult and/or too expensive to implement. Yet we ought to consider them seriously if we really want to put our best theology into practice and overcome the age-old misconceptions that "Protestants read the Bible, while Catholics have the Mass."

If Catholics truly want to show that our Church is established upon the Word of God (*both* Jesus *and* the Bible, rather than a false either/or dichotomy), then we need to consider what we can do to ensure that the Sacred Scriptures are truly given the prominence and attention that they deserve in all aspects of pastoral life, not simply in the Lectionary readings at Mass or in the scattered Bible study groups that meet in only a few parishes.

Some Thoughts on Terminology

Words and phrases that may seem similar sometimes have very different connotations, and different effects. Although we might use the words *Bible* and *scripture* interchangeably, *scripture* is actually a broader term, which might refer to the "sacred writings" of other religions (Islam, Buddhism, Hinduism, etc.), whereas *Bible*, strictly speaking, refers only to the "Sacred Scriptures" of Jews and Christians.

Moreover, we should carefully consider what kind of groups we wish to establish in our parishes, since people's needs and inclinations differ, with important differences between studying, sharing, prayer, and reflection. Will the parish-based groups be called "Bible study" or "Scripture sharing"? Is the focus on "Biblical Literacy Training" or on "Scriptural Prayer"? Will the groups use a *Lectio Divina* approach or a different method for engaging the scriptures? Each of these designations has some advantages and disadvantages, which need to be assessed based upon the needs and styles of the particular community.

Although "Bible study" is probably the most common title, this designation places more emphasis on the academic nature of the enterprise, perhaps to the neglect of prayer and/or application. "Scripture sharing" highlights the group dynamics more explicitly, although possibly to the detriment of careful exegetical study. If a parish bulletin invites people to join a *"Lectio Divina"* group, many will not immediately know what kind of a group it is, since this Latin phrase is not yet in common usage today. Adding the word *Catholic* would make these titles a bit longer, but is probably necessary and important, in order to work against the popular misconception that Bible study is something that only Protestants do, as well as to highlight that we, as Catholics, have non-fundamentalist ways of reading the Bible.

The same considerations about terminology and titles apply not only to the names given to local parish groups but also to the diocesan-level program. Should it be called a Catholic Bible institute, or a school of Sacred Scripture, or a diocesan Bible literacy training program, or something else? Here I will not argue for or against the use of any of these names, but only suggest that it would be good for the local organizers to consider the terminology carefully, since the name you choose and the language you use will significantly affect the nature of the program, whether it be more academic or more pastoral, as well as who will be attracted to come and what these participants will expect.

Nature and Goals of a Diocesan Scripture Institute

The goal of a diocesan-level institute will certainly not be to train professional biblical scholars. That is better done by the master's or doctoral programs at various universities. Yet several different types of biblically related programs could be imagined under the rubric of a diocesan Scripture institute, each with slightly different goals.

Summer Scripture Courses and Bible Institutes

Several dioceses and various Catholic universities around the country already offer biblical courses for one or more weeks each summer. Some of these are stand-alone courses, while others are integrated into summer institutes, which might also include opportunities for residing on campus, prayer and liturgy, shared meals, and/or other communal activities. Some of these programs focus specifically on the Bible, while others provide a few biblical courses within a broader selection of theological and pastoral topics. These courses and institutes are generally open to the public and may even draw people from neighboring dioceses and states. Professors are recruited both from the local faculty and from around the country or even internationally. Although some participants may be fairly new to biblical studies, many have already received extensive prior training, yet desire to take further courses for continuing education or "updating" purposes, either for their own personal benefit and religious growth or also to improve their ability to facilitate local Bible study and Scripture-sharing groups.

Participants may include priests and deacons who wish to improve the biblical basis of their preaching, as well as lay ecclesial ministers (lectors, catechists, schoolteachers, and others) who wish to become even better in their respective ministries. Enrollment at such summer courses and institutes may be lower in recent years than it was a few decades ago, yet the need for such programs is ongoing, and it may be beneficial for even more dioceses or academic institutions to offer such programs in the future.

Brief Facilitator Training
for Particular Bible Study Programs

Some dioceses may wish to select a single Bible study program, such as the Little Rock Scripture Study program or the Six Weeks with the Bible series, and then recruit and train enough people to serve as facilitators of small Bible study groups in their local parishes. Due to the narrower focus of this goal, these training programs would be short-term, relatively inexpensive, and easier to organize and administer than a multi-year certificate program. Moreover, there could be some benefits to having all (or at least most) of the parishes within one diocese conducting the same program at the same time. The diocese could offer the brief facilitator training sessions one or more times each year to ensure a growing number of capable leaders, rather than expecting each parish to train its own facilitators. Each parish could then offer one or more Bible study groups at various times on different days of the week, but people would also be invited and welcome to participate in groups at neighboring parishes, if the meeting days and times fit better into their own schedules (just as many parishes around the country already publicize a schedule of Communal Reconciliation Services available at neighboring parishes during Advent and Lent). If coordinated well, opportunities for participating in a nearby Catholic Bible study group could be available on almost any weekday and weekend, both during the day and in the evenings, within the parishes of one cluster or deanery.

Multi-Year Certificate Programs

A few (arch)dioceses conduct longer and larger Bible-focused training programs, sometimes in conjunction with a local college or university that can provide Continuing Education Units (CEUs) or certification of some type for completion of the multi-year course of studies. In chapter 2, Dr. Renata Furst referred to these as "Flagship Programs," including the ones that have been offered for many years in Chicago, Dallas, and Los Angeles. These programs are of high academic quality, since they recruit well-known and capable professors, and many also pay attention to the spiritual and formational development of the participants. Yet they are unfortunately also relatively expensive, especially if they provide transportation, lodging, meals, and stipends for the visiting instructors. Although not all dioceses may be able to afford a larger program such as these, a few more (arch)dioceses may wish to establish one, so that more and more Catholic laity and religious can become more adept at reading the Bible, and can help others as well.

Since I have been personally involved as an instructor and core team member of two Catholic Bible institutes over the past twelve years (one in the Archdiocese of Los Angeles and one in the neighboring Diocese of San Bernardino), I will base the following remarks primarily on these institutes.[1] The Catholic Bible institutes in both dioceses are set up as three-year programs, with the first year focusing on the Old Testament, the second year on the New Testament, and the third year on the practical skills of how to facilitate small Bible study groups. Both Los Angeles and San Bernardino offer these institutes in English and in Spanish. Although the structures and contents of the programs in each language are fairly similar, the English-language and Spanish-language institutes are run almost totally separately from each other, led by different coordinators, taught by different instructors, and meeting on different dates. Each institute meets one Saturday each month (not including summers) from about 9:00 a.m. to 4:00 p.m. Participants are divided into small groups (six to eight people each) for small-group sharing, and each month one group prepares and leads a brief Opening Prayer and/or Closing Prayer. Participants are given reading assignments in advance (from the Bible and from textbooks), and are asked to write a short reflection paper each month, as well as one longer research paper each semester. The Los Angeles institutes recruit a different instructor for almost every month (with only a few instructors doing two sessions within a year), whereas the San Bernardino institutes use just two primary instructors in each language, one for the Old Testament year and the other for the New Testament year, respectively. In addition to the academic instructors, each institute has a "core team" of people who assist the participants, read and comment on their written work, and coordinate the overall program.

In the third year, or Practicum, the Saturday workshops introduce the participants to various biblical resources, and cover such topics as adult learning styles, small-group facilitation skills, conflict resolution, and so on. The participants also work in teams throughout the final semester and/or summer to plan and implement a short Bible study or Scripture-sharing program in their own parishes, which is supervised and evaluated by the core team members. Moreover, instead of training and requiring the participants to use the resources of just one particular Bible study program, these institutes introduce the participants to many different resources available from various publishers, since we wish to leave it up to the local facilitators and/or pastors to determine which approach and which resources will work best in the pastoral, cultural, and linguistic settings of their own parish.

These longer diocesan-level institutes are designed primarily to train laity (and some religious) as facilitators of local parish Bible study groups. Yet in addition to focusing on those who wish to lead (or already are leading) Bible-focused groups, the leaders of other *existing* groups in a parish (such as Cursillo, Charismatics, Lectors, or Knights of Columbus) might also be invited to participate, so they could use the Bible more regularly and effectively in all of their own activities, thereby affecting the great diversity of the Catholic community. Even more broadly, inviting anyone who is interested in learning more about the Bible to participate in the diocesan Scripture institute (with approval of his or her pastor, as necessary), might be the best approach, since these parishioners may well become more active pastoral leaders in the future.

How to Begin: Preparatory Steps

For a diocese to establish a new Catholic Bible institute, one of the first questions to ask is: Who will take the initiative? In some cases, the diocesan bishop himself might get things rolling by assigning this project to an individual or a diocesan office. Yet one need not wait for the local ordinary to take the first step. Although ecclesiastical support and approval (by the bishop, vicar general, office of religious education, etc.) is certainly necessary early in the process, almost anyone could take the initiative to propose the idea to the appropriate officials of the local diocese and/or a local academic institution. Rather than just one individual working alone, however, it would be good to gather a core group of interested persons as an organizing team. Ideally, this core group would include several leaders (clergy, religious, and laity) representing various constituencies, both pastoral and academic, such as the diocese's Office of Adult Faith Formation (or an equivalent), the Priests' Council, and/or the theology departments of any or all local Catholic universities, colleges, and high schools.

For example, the English-language Catholic Bible Institute in the Archdiocese of Los Angeles got started almost twenty years ago because two married couples, who had been attending summer Bible institutes in other dioceses for several years, asked themselves why something similar was not available closer to home. Soon they went beyond asking each other privately, and started asking people more publicly, including one of the regional auxiliary bishops. This bishop put them in touch with some officials at the archdiocesan Office of Religious Education and some administrators of the Continuing Education Division of Loyola Marymount University in Los Angeles. The project was soon organized through the cooperative efforts of the archdiocese and the university, but continued to be guided and inspired by the vision and efforts of the two lay couples. To this day, the English-language version of the Catholic Bible Institute continues to be officially cosponsored by the archdiocese and the university, with a core team still consisting of diocesan officials, university representatives, and lay leaders.

The Spanish-language version of the Catholic Bible Institute in Los Angeles had a slightly different history, since it was the archdiocesan Office of Religious Education itself that established the institute in Spanish, without the participation of the university. On the other hand, some administrators in the Division of Continuing Education of Loyola Marymount University took the initiative in establishing the very similarly structured Catholic Bible Institutes (one in Spanish and one in English) in the neighboring Diocese of San Bernardino, working in conjunction with the bishop and officials of that diocese. Smaller dioceses in which there is no Catholic college or university could do something similar, drawing upon the faculty of a Catholic high school and/or local priests, religious, or laypersons with sufficient training in biblical studies.

These examples show several different models for the possible relationships between a diocese and an academic institution in sponsoring or cosponsoring a Catholic Bible institute:

1. An institute cosponsored jointly by a diocese and a college or university
2. An institute sponsored primarily by a university, in cooperation with a diocese
3. An institute sponsored primarily by a diocese, drawing faculty from various diocesan or academic resources

Whether the initiative in establishing a Catholic Bible institute comes from the top down or the bottom up, whether the sponsorship is primarily diocesan or primarily from an academic institution, someone (an individual or a core group) clearly needs to be strongly invested in the success of this project, or else no one will take responsibility and invest the time and effort needed to make it a success. Since it is often financially unfeasible these days to have a full-time coordinator whose only responsibility is running such an institute, its success will likely depend on how dedicated the leaders can be, given their competing commitments to other programs and responsibilities.

Essential Emphases for a Catholic Bible Institute

A Catholic Bible institute should do much more than just give the participants an overview of biblical history and of the contents of the Old and New Testaments. A primary goal should also be that the participants understand the basic principles of a truly "Catholic" approach to the Sacred Scriptures, and that they learn to apply these principles in practice. Catholics need to learn to read the Bible as "sacred literature," recognizing the importance of both words of this phrase. The Bible is "sacred" or "holy" in that it is *God's Word* for us, it contains *Divine revelation*. On the other hand, it is also "literature," meaning that it was written by *humans* in specific historical, cultural, and linguistic *contexts*. When Catholics read and study the Bible, we also do so humbly, prayerfully, and ecclesially (not just as individuals, but in harmony with the Church community). These principles are explained quite succinctly in several magisterial documents, especially the Dogmatic Constitution on Divine Revelation *Dei Verbum* from the Second Vatican Council (1965), and very similarly in the section on Divine Revelation of the *Catechism of the Catholic Church* (2nd ed., 2000; § 51–141). Both of these documents first explain the concept of Divine Revelation, and then deal with the concept of Tradition or Transmission of that Revelation, before focusing more specifically on the Bible.[2] A more complex and detailed exposition of the principles and methods of Catholic biblical interpretation are in the document entitled "The Interpretation of the Bible in the Church" (Pontifical Biblical Commission, 1993).

In my own pastoral ministry and teaching about Catholic biblical interpretation, I often stress the following five principles, which are found in the aforementioned ecclesial documents, although presented in a different order here.

First, Catholicism uses a "both/and" approach in all aspects of theology, not just biblical interpretation, in contrast to the "one-sided" or "either/or" mentality of fundamentalism. Thus, for example, we recognize that the Bible is *both* the Word of God (written under divine inspiration) *and* authored by human beings (with limitations of human languages). It contains *both* the Old *and* the New Testaments. We *both* study it academically *and* read it prayerfully. We interpret it *both* literally *and* spiritually (christologically, morally, anagogically). However, in claiming to read the Bible "literally," we try to avoid misreading the texts overliterally or "literalistically" (as if everything recorded was merely "factual"), but instead realize that it is "literature."

Second, because the Bible is literature, we must pay close and careful attention not only to the meaning of individual words and phrases (in their historical and literary contexts), but must also recognize that the Bible contains a wide variety of literary genres, that it is not all merely history. Thus, biblical scholarship has helped us to recognize the many different categories or types of literature, each characterized by particular forms, styles, or contents (much as a newspaper contains many different sections written in different styles, not just with differing contents). Thus, the Bible is not just a single book, but a whole "library" of different books containing many different literary genres and subgenres.

Third, modern Catholic biblical interpretation makes use of both historical-critical exegesis and spiritual-theological hermeneutics, not just one or the other. Therefore, the historical-critical method is foundational and essential to our understanding of the Bible, although Catholic interpretation is not limited to historical-critical exegesis alone. Moreover, Catholics are not restricted to using just one official or preferred method of historical-critical exegesis; rather, we accept a wide variety of distinct exegetical methods, some of which are more historical, others more literary, while still others can be classified as canonical, ideological, and so on. We recognize the value and the limitations of each method, so we welcome the possible contributions of them all, rather than exclusively embracing only one of them. We analyze the biblical content on multiple levels (literal/historical content expressing the *original* meaning, and spiritual/theological content containing *enduring* meaning). We realize the essential role of context, both literary/canonical (the surrounding *texts*) and cultural/historical (the surrounding *world*). We are open to considerations of historical development within the Bible (from *oral* preaching/tradition to *written* texts/Scriptures), which expresses a growth in theological understanding and practical application over the centuries of biblical history.

Fourth, Catholic interpretation of the Bible stresses the importance of the *incarnational principle*, meaning that we stress that the pinnacle of God's self-revelation is a person (Jesus), rather than a book (the Bible). One could say, expanding upon Johannine terminology, "God sent his only-begotten Son, not his only-begotten book!" (cf. Jn 3:16). This incarnational focus contrasts with an overemphasis on the written text of the Bible by some other Christians, what could be called a type of "bibliolatry." Although we obviously recognize the Bible as "The Word of God," it is even more important to recognize that Jesus Christ himself is "The Word of God" as well as "The Word made flesh" (Jn 1:1–14).

Fifth, it is important to stress that Catholics read the Bible not just as individuals, but in the communal context of the Church, both locally and worldwide. We recognize and appreciate the role of ecclesial guidance to help steer us away from individualistic misinterpretations. We read and study the Bible within our families and in small groups; we hear the Scriptures proclaimed in our parish liturgies and explained in homilies. We learn from our pastors and teachers, from biblical scholars and bishops—not just those of today but also the writers and teachers from throughout the two-thousand-year history of Christianity.[3]

Considering the Hispanic context more specifically, at least briefly, one might also stress that the modern Catholic use of the Bible could also apply the principles of the pastoral circle: *ver*/see, *juzgar*/judge, *actuar*/act. Moreover, many Hispanic individuals and communities will inevitably read and interpret the Christian Scriptures from the experience of being immigrants in a new and different culture, providing new and rich interpretations that could supplement and enhance the more common biblical interpretations of the dominant American culture.

Finally, the Catholic use of the Bible does not limit itself to exegetical study and hermeneutical analysis. Rather, we read and apply our Sacred Scriptures in many concrete ways on a regular basis: in theological teaching and social action, in the Liturgy of the Hours and other forms of individual and communal prayer, and especially in the eucharistic liturgy and all the other sacraments. Thus, a Catholic Bible institute would do well also to include an introduction to the liturgical year and the Lectionary for Mass, as well as a survey of the use of the Bible in Catholic theology and pastoral praxis.

Organizational Details

Given the wide variety of social, demographic, economic, and ecclesial situations of the dioceses in the United States, it would be foolish for me to make very specific recommendations for how to run a Catholic Bible institute, as if one model would fit each diocese. Instead, this section will present several sets of questions that anyone who wishes to engage in such a project would do well to consider.

What: The Program

- Will the institute be offered only in English, or also in Spanish and/or in other languages?
- If provided in multiple languages, will the various groups meet in the same location at the same times, so that they can share some activities together (such as multilingual opening or closing prayers at each session, a multicultural Mass on occasion, or a multilingual graduation or commissioning ceremony at the end)?
- Will the institute be offered only at a single site (for geographically compact dioceses) or can videoconferencing be used to reach outlying areas of the diocese?
- Will the institute follow the "cohort" model (all participants go through a set sequence of courses together, starting and ending at the same time), or a "course" model (participants take the required courses and fulfill other requirements in any order they wish, like students completing a college major)?
- What will be the requirements for certification and/or CEUs (since there are not yet any national standards)? What is the total number of hours required for certification? (The institutes in Los Angeles and San Bernardino have about 150 hours total; other dioceses require courses totaling up to 250 hours.)

- What are the specific program requirements? What is the balance between "academic" components (exegetical courses) and "pastoral" requirements (practical projects)?
- How will the various aspects of the program (academic, spiritual, pastoral) be integrated?
- How much "homework" (required readings, written papers) will be assigned in advance and/or after each session? How much time can you reasonably expect the participants to put in?
- Will the written assignments be evaluated academically (with letter grades), or will feedback be given to the participants in other ways (to reduce the grade anxiety for the adult learners with varied abilities and academic backgrounds)?

How Long: The Schedule

- How many years and/or how many total hours will the program take to complete?
- If organized on the cohort model, will the program be subdivided into separate years or blocks (e.g., Year 1: Old Testament; Year 2: New Testament; Year 3: Practicum)? Or will the instruction be organized in a more integrated manner?
- If organized on the course model, how long will each course last? How many courses will be offered at the same time?
- When will the instruction primarily be offered: evenings? Saturdays? weekends? (This will partly depend on the geography of your diocese.)

Who: The Personnel

- Who will be the program directors or coordinators? Who will form the "core team"? Will they represent a variety of constituencies?
- Who will be the primary instructors or faculty? What level of biblical training must they have?
- Will you have one (or very few) instructors for the whole program (providing greater continuity overall), or will you use a variety of different instructors for each different course (providing greater variety of biblical and theological approaches)?

- Will you draw primarily on instructors available locally (with fewer transportation costs), or will you bring instructors in from farther away (having to pay airfare, lodging, meals)?
- Will the primary instructors also be responsible for reading/grading/commenting on the participants' written work, or will other "Readers" be hired or recruited to do this?
- If you are using videoconferencing, will you need extra staff or volunteers to serve as local site facilitators or small-group mentors?
- Who will provide the audiovisual (AV) technical support, and at what cost?
- Who will provide registration and other logistical support, and at what cost?

Where/When: Logistical Planning

- Where will the institute primarily be held? At a college or high school? In a parish or in a diocesan pastoral center?
- Does the host facility have large enough meeting spaces, prayer spaces, AV equipment?
- Is the facility able to accommodate adult learners, who may have physical disabilities or mobility issues more than younger learners?
- Can you secure the same facilities on a regular basis (to avoid the confusions caused by using multiple locations on an irregular basis)?
- Is the meeting space conducive to adult-learning styles? Can the participants sit in small groups around tables, or, if using individual desks in classrooms, can they be moved to allow for small-group interaction? (It is best to avoid classrooms or auditoriums with fixed seating that would inhibit such interactions.)
- Does the facility allow for food and drink (coffee breaks, refreshments, lunches)?
- What needs to be prepared in advance of each course or session (e.g., prayers, refreshments, environment, AV equipment)?
- What other learning resources will you need or provide: books, tapes/videos, online materials?

- Will the sessions be recorded to allow persons who are absent or who register late still to gain some benefit from anything they missed?

How Much: Finances and Budget

While most dioceses will probably wish to keep the costs of running a Catholic Bible institute as low as possible, so as to maximize the number of participants, the instructors and support staff should nonetheless be compensated fairly and justly, and material needs and administrative costs calculated realistically.

- Will the income be derived primarily from tuition or fees paid by the individual participants? Will the program also be supported by the participants' parishes?
- Will the diocese and/or a local academic institution subsidize the institute? Can donors be found who have a special interest in Scripture?
- Will scholarships be available for low-income participants? How many participants will be in need of financial assistance? Where will these funds come from?
- What are the institute's main expenses: facility rental, books/materials, printing and mailing of publicity materials, stipends for coordinators and instructors, AV equipment, refreshments, etc.? Can any of these be donated and/or subsidized by someone?

Publicity and Registration

- Who will be responsible for designing and distributing promotional materials: brochures, flyers, notices in diocesan newsletters or newspapers, inserts or notices for parish bulletins?
- What kind of publicity will you use (mailings, e-mails, faxes)? What costs are involved in these various modes of communication?
- Since personal contacts are usually most effective in recruiting new participants, who could help in the local recruiting efforts in parishes, schools, ecclesial groups, and organizations?

- Will the institute be open to anyone who wishes to register? (This may cause problems if "difficult" people enroll.) Or will there be an application process, possibly one in which pastoral approval is required (e.g., a letter from the local pastor)?
- How can diocesan offices (offices responsible for religious education, adult faith formation, liturgy/worship, ethnic ministries, parish life directors, deacons, or religious orders) help with recruitment? Can any of them be co-sponsors of the institute?
- How can other ecclesial groups help with publicity and recruitment (such as Cursillo, Charismatics, Knights of Columbus, St. Vincent de Paul)?
- If the diocesan goal is not merely to have Bible study groups in parishes, but also to promote the integrated use of the Bible in all parish activities, how will the leaders of such groups be recruited and encouraged to participate?

Special Considerations

- What level of general education and literacy can be expected from the majority of the participants? Will a minimal level of education be required of those who apply (high school diploma or G.E.D.)?
- How much emphasis will the institute place on reading and writing assignments? Will extra support be available for participants with lower academic skills?
- What are the different language needs of different generations of immigrants?

Graduation and Certification

- Where and when will some type of "graduation" ceremony will be held?
- Will this be in the context of a Mass, a Liturgy of the Word, or a more academic setting?
- Will the ceremony include a reception or a full meal? Who will pay for this?
- Who will preside: the local ecclesial ordinary and/or an administrator of the co-sponsoring academic institution?

- What kind of a certificate will the participants receive upon completing the course?

Follow-up and Conclusion

After the participants in a Catholic Bible institute "graduate" or complete the program, one would hope that most of them will become (more) involved in their parishes by facilitating some local Bible study or Scripture-sharing groups, possibly some existing groups or hopefully also new ones. These local facilitators would continue to benefit from regular opportunities for "updating" (through periodic courses or workshops available locally, online, or in summer institutes). They may also need some support and encouragement, not only from their local pastors but also from some diocesan-level offices or officials, who might provide some mentoring, resources, and contacts. Indeed, the diocesan institute might engage in very helpful self-assessment by regularly examining what its graduates are actually doing in their parishes and the overall quality of their ministry.

Yet who has the time and initiative to do all this? Since officials in most diocesan offices are already busy with many other projects and responsibilities, one may have to rely on a core group of volunteers (graduates of the diocesan Scripture institute?) to provide some ongoing support and encouragement of local parish facilitators.

There are obviously many questions to ask and many details to decide if a diocese wants to establish a Catholic Bible institute, but we can hope that at least a few more (arch)dioceses in the United States will do so, and that they will pay special attention to the involvement of Latino Catholics and other new immigrant groups when they do. Any such effort will do well to spell out the overall vision and pastoral goals first, before deciding on the detailed structure and content of the program. These goals will hopefully include the promotion of an authentically Catholic understanding and use of the Bible, one that is focused both on historical/exegetical study and on spiritual/pastoral application, one that remains humble, prayerful, and ecclesially focused, and one that enables more and more Catholics in all our parishes and dioceses to read the Scriptures more regularly and effectively. Most of all, may the Bible, which is God's Word written in human languages, help us continue to grow in our faith, hope, and love of God and of one another, no matter what culture(s) we come from or what language(s) we speak.

～

Notes

1. For more details, see http://www.lmu.edu/academics/extension/crs
    /certificates/cbi.htm and http://catholic-resources.org/CBI/index.html.
2. For a comparison of the structures and highlights of *Dei Verbum* and
    the corresponding section of the *Cathechism of the Catholic Church*, see
    http://catholic-resources.org/ChurchDocs/DeiVerbum.htm.
3. On these five principles, see also http://catholic-resources.org/Bible
    /Catholic-Interpretation.htm.

14

"He Explained the Scriptures to Us"

Rediscovering *Lectio Divina*

Ricardo Grzona, F.R.P.

~

Introduction

I write as a catechist. It has been many years since I felt the call to prepare myself to evangelize more effectively, and I have spent much of my life training catechists. Later, I came to understand that while training my brothers as catechists, I should dedicate myself to a very specific task, which is the "spirituality of the catechist." I have led workshops, courses, and retreats for catechists from most of the countries in the Americas, always seeking to encourage in them a greater spiritual depth in our service to the Church. The work of the catechist is not always adequately recognized.

Our challenge and ideal as catechists has always been to become spiritual persons, with our heart and all our knowledge focused on Jesus Christ: to understand his message for today, to transmit it today to our generation. But the message is not written theory; it is a person, living and active, and we should interact with this person. This is the center of our message. How can we interact today with the risen Jesus, the Christ, the one long awaited in all ages?

For an authentic Christian spirituality, a first step is to understand what we have just stated. Considerable confusion arises from words that people often take as synonyms: Jesus, Christ, Jesus the Christ. That confusion is seen within Christianity itself. Some believers forget that to say "Jesus Christ" is in itself a declaration of faith. That is to say, when we mention the historical Jesus, the Son of Mary, the one whose life we normally recognize as narrated in the Gospels, he is the very Son of God, the beginning and the end of everything and, above all other declarations, he is the long-awaited Christ, or Messiah. He is the "Lord of History"; he is the "*Alpha* and *Omega*." When we speak of history, we are not referring only to the history of humankind, but also to our personal history, in which the risen Jesus wants to be present, to save us and free us in our own history. Conversion is not a matter of intellectual understanding, but rather a complete change of life, understood from the outset as "*metanoia*," that is to say, a transformation.

In my humble appreciation of catechesis, I recognize that in many places there are different ways of understanding the evangelizing mission of the Church, and not all those ways are clearly Catholic. Catechesis (like an echo) is the echo of the Gospel that resounds in the life of persons, molding them, making them one with the Good News that is already an essential part of the life of the person making the proclamation. This is because our personal life is also a form of evangelization, our testimony. Therefore, we should not see catechesis merely as a group of formulas to learn and to know with the intellect. The formulas are important, as long as they reinforce our encounter with Jesus, the Christ, and as long as they help me to mold my life according to what I am understanding of Jesus, in my personal and community encounters with Jesus.

The encounter with Jesus, the Christ, the only Word that the Father has pronounced for our salvation, is that which essentially keeps us united in the Church. The Church, as mother and teacher, reminds us through its two-thousand-year history, in its rich tradition and magisterium, that the sources of catechesis are found principally in the Sacred Scriptures, where God speaks today.

> The Church has always venerated the Sacred Scriptures, just as it has the Lord's Body, not failing to take from the table and distribute to the faithful the bread of life, both the Word of God and the Body of Christ, above all, in the Sacred Liturgy. The Church has always considered and still considers them, along with the Sacred Tradition, as the supreme rule of its faith, since they are inspired by God and written once for all, they communicate unchangeably the very word of God, and cause the voice of the Holy Spirit to resound in the words of the prophets and the apostles. (*Dei Verbum* § 21)

Here we should take note of something very important that we cite from *Dei Verbum*: "Therefore, like the Christian religion itself, all the preaching of the Church must be nourished and regulated by Sacred Scripture" (*Dei Verbum* § 21).

Let us ask ourselves the big question: Have we read the documents of the Second Vatican Council? And if we have read them, then the other big question: Are we practicing their teachings? Have we understood that Jesus is the Christ? And does this understanding totally change our lives?

> After speaking in many and varied ways through the prophets, "now at last in these days God has spoken to us in His Son" (Heb 1:1–2). For He sent His Son, the eternal Word, who enlightens all men, so that He might dwell among men and tell them of the innermost being of God (see John 1:1–18). Jesus Christ, therefore, the Word made flesh, was sent as "a man to men." He "speaks the words of God" (John 3:34), and completes the work of salvation which His Father gave Him to do (see John 5:36; John 17:4). To see Jesus is to see His Father (John 14:9). For this reason Jesus perfected revelation by fulfilling it through his whole work of making Himself present and manifesting Himself: through His words and deeds, His signs and wonders, but especially through His death and glorious resurrection from the dead and final sending of the Spirit of truth. Moreover He confirmed with divine testimony what revelation proclaimed, that God is with us to free us from the darkness of sin and death, and to raise us up to life eternal. (*Dei Verbum* § 4)

Often, in the teaching and education of the faith, we find that those responsible for this evangelization are committed to different schools of spirituality. But not all groups have a spirituality that is completely of the Church. I can testify to this fact. All this reminds me of many of the products that we consume in our society that are known as "light," that is, lacking content and essence. Only the flavor is present. Just think of the cold drinks that have such a label. They look like the originals, but they are not. They look like the real thing! Today in our communities groups of diverse spiritualities abound that "look like" they are Catholic. But it is only in appearance. They don't offer true nourishment. They are a kind of spirituality "light," and we should take note. For the same reason, this phrase from the *Dei Verbum* comes to mind:

> The Christian dispensation, therefore, as the new and definitive covenant, will never pass away and we now await no further new public

revelation before the glorious manifestation of our Lord Jesus Christ
(see 1 Tim 6:14 and Tit 2:13). (*Dei Verbum* § 4)

This is where I want to situate myself as I begin this discussion. After having known a great variety of "schools" of evangelizers, of places and persons
that offer a "guarantee" to make us into spiritual persons, a long-awaited
moment arrived. The Church, thanks to the kindness of John Paul II as well
as Benedict XVI, calls on all believers to return their focus to its rich tradition. The Sacred Scriptures, read through the lens of tradition, under the
guidance of the magisterium, leads us to an encounter with Jesus, that God
might reveal himself to us, remove the veil that hid him and that we might
have a direct encounter with him. Thus Jesus, through his teaching, might
lead us to the community of the church, where we find our brothers and sisters who have also been invited by Jesus. This is where *Lectio Divina* enters
the scene, offered for today's world, for people of this new millennium, the
Church's method par excellence, to lead us as a Church to a living encounter
with the Lord of history. Thus we move from an encounter with the Word of
God, to an encounter with the God of the Word. We move from the Word
of the Lord, to an encounter with the Lord of the Word.

Many of these schools of spirituality have as an objective to awaken reflection and sentiments, as particular devotions that make people "feel good."
This kind of "modern devotion" has, among other things, the problem of
being anthropocentric and egocentric. Generally, an inner experience is
sought that leads us, with certain methods, to an intimate spirituality, not
born of revelation, but from a good feeling, that does not free us, but rather
enslaves us. Serious Christians should stay away from these methods, and
rather draw near to the authentic revelation and enter into communion
with God, who is the principal object of our spirituality.

For that reason our question is still valid: What is the right spirituality
for human beings today? What is the big difference between a solid spirituality that the Church offers us for living, and other forms of "spirituality
light" present in our communities? What should we do to drink clean water
directly from the spring?

So, finding myself among people thirsting for "clean water," I found that
the method of *Lectio Divina*, made available to today's Christian communities of Christian life today, continues to be a method valid for everyone.
To apply in our lives today what monks have been practicing for centuries
can change our way of thinking, bringing us closer to an understanding of

Jesus' message, that continues to be the same yesterday, today, and forever (see Heb 13:8).

The challenge we face today as Christians, and especially as catechists and pastoral agents, is how should we present "Salvation" in capital letters, in the midst of so many offers of "salvation" in lowercase?

Part 1:
Where Did *Lectio Divina* Originate?

Before dealing with the origin of *Lectio Divina*, it would be worthwhile to consider the origin of the Bible as we know it today. The texts were growing and becoming more significant among the people of Israel, until the fullness of time arrived with the coming of Jesus the long-expected Christ to save humanity. Therefore, the Sacred Scriptures are not just another group of sacred books, such as those of other religions, which serve especially to bring together people who share certain beliefs as well as to determine moral norms and common behavior. The Bible was inspired by the Holy Spirit in the totality of its texts, in which God reveals himself to us for our salvation. For that reason, these are different from other books that express great wisdom from the traditions of the peoples. The Bible is a collection of writings revealed by God himself, and therefore contains what we know as Sacred Scripture. To believe in God who reveals himself is also to profess our faith in the fact that God speaks to us from these texts.

When the Church formally decreed that there are seventy-three books that make up this body of God's Revelation for all humanity, there were already monastic communities which were responsible for reproducing them for other communities, as well as translating them.

The text, then, is a means of communication with the author. The sacred text is a proposal to get acquainted with the author who is God himself. Thus the Church understands that reading the Bible is for the purpose of communicating with the author, allowing the author to "manifest himself." In the Bible, the Author makes himself known. Thus the Church has always proclaimed that in the Bible, "the words contain the *Logos*," while understanding "contain" not as something derogatory, but rather referring to the fact of making known the *Logos*.

In the Bible, God presents himself to us as the "Logos-Word" in a familiar manner. The text itself refers to the preexistence of the "Logos-Word" (see Jn 1:1–14). Through incarnation, the Logos of God speaks to us of his "preexistence," that is to say, that he always was, he was never created, but from eternity he is God. Yet also in the incarnation God speaks to us of his "pro-existence," which is to say that the Logos of God, from the sacred text, becomes salvation in history. United with historic humanity, the Bible confronts us as the human face of God and, on the other hand, we as human beings, when we know him in life, we also encounter the face of the divine in human beings.

In this way, the preexistence of God speaks to us of his human vocation. God has a human vocation: to be a man, a human being, to become in all aspects like human beings. And in his pro-existence, we also find the divine vocation of human beings. For God, by becoming human, had a human face, and we, when we understand it, accept it, assume it, and live it, can also acquire a divine face.

Therefore, all of Sacred Scripture has a Christological dimension. The Word becomes an event. This Word is already the history of salvation and therefore *precedes* me and *exceeds* me. This word, which I can read in my own language, is in truth "inspired" by God, for me and for my salvation. Therefore, it cannot be considered the same as any other word or text. So it is that Church communities are born around the Word, to communicate it, but above all, to be able to read it in the Spirit. This spiritual dynamic causes Scripture to become a medium for communication. When we refer to mediation, we refer to two aspects: the divine and the human. Sacred Scripture is a medium between God and human beings.

Thus we can also say that the Bible is a gift from God. Yet at the same time it is a task for men and women. It is here, in the knowledge that human beings have of Sacred Scripture, that their heart begins to be purified, turning from idolatry and encountering God himself. To have a limited or incorrect knowledge of the Bible tends to encourage in Christians the possibility of dressing up the true God in idolatrous rags, which is a terrible and lamentable error that is altogether too common.

We also find that the Bible, because it is text (from the Latin *textus*, tissue), has an ecclesiological and pastoral dimension. That is to say, the word *evokes* our sentiments to call the attention of human beings and also *convokes* us to live in community. Believers in the eternal word, that *preexists* and *pro-exists*, together, are called together and form the Church.

This word that *evokes* sentiments, *convokes* to community, *provokes* mission. That is to say, vocation, broadly understood, is a matter of announcing this unique Word that has always existed and will always exist. It is to make known the incarnate Logos of God, for the salvation of all.

The recent synod had as its theme "The Word of God in the Life and Mission of the Church," and in its message to the people of God offered profound reflections that should be deeply received in the life of believers. One well-articulated theme is the unity between Christ and the Word, inasmuch as the written Word is the manifestation of the Logos-Word. This is, perhaps, the center of a process of biblical and theological discussion that remains open. Just as in Jesus there are two natures, so in the Sacred Scriptures something similar could be said to occur. Divine Word, human word. Completely divine, completely human:

> The eternal and divine Word enters into space and time and takes on a human face and identity. . . . Words without a face are not perfect, they do not fully complete the encounter. Christ is "the Word [that] was with God and the Word was God" (Jn 1:1). "He is the image of the unseen God, the first-born of all creation" (Col 1:15); but he is also Jesus of Nazareth.[1]

Yet in this same message that is shared with all the Church is recalled the tradition that places in near-equal conditions the Divine Word that becomes flesh with the Divine Word that becomes a book.[2]

> For the words of God, expressed in human language, have been made like human discourse, just as the word of the eternal Father, when He took to Himself the flesh of human weakness, was in every way made like men (*Dei Verbum* § 13).
>
> Christian tradition has often placed the Divine Word made flesh on parallel with the same word made book . . . the Second Vatican Council gathers this ancient tradition according to which "the body of the Son is the Scripture transmitted to us." . . . Indeed, the Bible is also "flesh," "letter" . . . the Bible is also the eternal and divine Word.[3]

We remember, then, that the communities that come into being around the Word not only do exegesis, but they also use it as media for their moments of spirituality. The Word becomes a perpetual memorial, unending, that helps human beings to read it and make it current. And in this "making it current," the Word is making history. Coming from eternity, where it lives with the Father, now this Word is introduced into our history. In reading the Bible, it is no longer just the human being that reads, rather he is "being read" from the eternal dimension, in his own history. Communities seek a comprehensive encounter with the Word, which offers the sense to judge the senses.

Thus, from a history that spans from Israel (who read while remembering), to those monastic communities that took the sacred texts into their custody, we can trace the development of a tradition. Taken from the Latin it is "reading from God" or "lesson from God," and we still call it *Lectio Divina* in Latin.

Lectio Divina as an exercise in the prayerful reading of the Sacred Scriptures is the most ancient practice that we know of making complete use of the Bible. If it is true that we can place it from the earliest centuries of Christianity, it was the year 1173, when the monk Guigo II, a Cartesian, wrote a letter to his pupil Gervasius about the contemplative life and taught him the traditional steps of *Lectio Divina*. From that time forward, we can affirm that this practice was maintained in the great majority of the monasteries, and it is on their writings that we base our understanding so as to share it.

This practice, quite common in the monasteries, is done with the conviction that *Lectio Divina* properly practiced offers the possibility of truly encountering, through the Scriptures, him who speaks, the living Word, God himself. This "prayerful reading" enables us to understand that from the biblical text, the living Word is seeking us, enlivens us, and models in us his image and likeness, providing orientation based on the demands of Christian faith. From that point it is up to us to follow, to practice it, and to live it out, which is always a great mystery.

Part 2:
What Forms Does *Lectio Divina* Take Today?

The practice of *Lectio Divina* has an important place in monasteries, and monks dedicate their lives to this exercise of prayerful reading. In many Christian communities on various continents it has also begun to occupy a place in the life of the faithful. In many parishes *Lectio Divina* is an exercise that has begun to gain popularity. One need only recall the crowded gatherings of young people in the Cathedral of Milan when Cardinal Carlo Maria Martini offered introductions to the practice of *Lectio Divina*.

That is to say, what was for centuries the patrimony of monks has now become a practice that the Church offers to all believers: approach the Sacred Scriptures to learn from them, to reflect on them, and to seek a vital and transforming encounter with the Lord. Blessed John Paul II, in his Apostolic Exhortation *Ecclesia in America* (1999), suggests:

> Jesus Christ is presented as the only way that leads to holiness. But the concrete knowledge of this journey is obtained principally through the Word of God that the Church announces with its preaching. This is why the Church in America should grant a significant priority to prayerful reflection on Sacred Scripture done by all the faithful. This reading of the Bible, accompanied with prayer, is known in the tradition of the Church by the name *Lectio Divina*, a practice that should be encouraged among all Christians. (*Ecclesia in America* § 31)

Perhaps the most important dimension of this text is its emphasis on all Christians, not only the clergy, religious vocations, and monks, but all communities and all the faithful. This implies a fundamental change, since the Scriptures are seen as both instrument and means to know, love, and follow Jesus, assuming his lifestyle, in holiness and commitment.

It was likewise John Paul II who, when initiating the new millennium in his Apostolic Letter *Novo Millennio Ineunte*, established a direct relationship between holiness and prayer with attentive listening to the Word of God:

> It is especially necessary that listening to the word of God should become a life-giving encounter, in the ancient and ever-valid tradition of *lectio divina*, which draws from the biblical text the living word which questions, directs and shapes our lives. (*Novo Millennio Ineunte* § 39)

It is worthwhile to underscore the expression: "life-giving encounter," which tells us that it is not a question of knowing much about the Bible, but rather that such knowledge should lead us to an encounter of the heart with the Lord, so that he might mold it, transform it, and leave "footprints" in our heart. Thus, with the practice of this exercise, it becomes a part of life, in such a way that "it is no longer I, but Christ who lives in me" (see Gal 2:20).

It is also good to see that the practice of *Lectio Divina* would appear to be more than important, perhaps even urgent, in these historic moments in which we live. Above all, when we see that there is a return to forms of "religiosity of that which is fascinating rather than the divine." Here we can observe that it is easier to run the risk that "God" and also "Jesus the Christ" would be words improperly used, losing their value and even becoming empty, hollow words for many people, which they then fill with projections of human desires. And it's here we wonder to what extent the "God" affirmed and confessed by Christians is the "living God" revealed by Jesus. Is it not rather a God who is the fruit of dreams and human expectations? It might be a God who satisfies the longings that we have. If that is so, it is necessary and urgent that we learn to "listen" to the living Word, so as to interpret it and pray with it. Otherwise, we might be speaking of God without "listening to" the Word. Are we not witnessing, especially through the mass media, that many speak in God's name, but not of the true God, but rather of the image they have of a god made to suit them?

> In a world of so many words, what is the Word that *reorients* the Christian's life in the perspective of eternity? What is the Word that *reassigns* the temporal occurrences on the horizon of eternal life? In a world saturated by multiple orientations and meanings it is easy to lose direction due to the seduction of so many proposals of apparent and easy fullness of life. The disciple of Jesus must turn his *open ears* to the Word of the Master and dispose his *heart liberated from idols* as good ground in which the Word can bear fruit. The Word of God offered to us in Sacred Scripture is the *divine proposal for orientation and meaning* to the lives of humans whose most profound vocation is the fellowship of life with the Father, by the grace of the redemption of Jesus Christ and the action of his Spirit.[4]

Thus *Lectio Divina*, as an exercise that comes down to us from the Church's great tradition, guides us so that the Sacred Scriptures are not reduced, on the one hand, to a "spiritualism" that seeks in the Bible to affirm certain emotions that negate history and take root instead in the culture of the one who seems to be "listening." On the other hand, that it not be a "fundamentalism" that reads directly from a translation, interpreting the letter just as it appears, while completely ignoring the context of the entire Bible. Therefore it is important to affirm here a phrase from popular tradition: "a text without a context is a pretext." This reminds us of what Origen himself tells us about the comprehension of all Scripture: "*Scriptura sui ipsius interpres*"[5] (Scripture is its own interpreter). This speaks to us of the "unity of the whole Bible" as well as that between unity and inspiration. We read the Bible with eyes of faith. The words lead us to "The Word." These words are "pneumatic," that is to say, they come from the Holy Spirit and therefore are "spirit and truth" (cf. Jn 6:1). They contain all the *dynamis* of the Spirit. This, then, leads us to an encounter that goes beyond the Scripture itself. As we said at the beginning, through *Lectio Divina* we reach the very author of the Bible, to enter into a dialogue in which he speaks to us.[6]

When we refer to a traditional method, the classical subdivision of memory, intelligence, and will is in fact quite ancient. Developed by Saint Augustine, especially concerning the memory, it then becomes a meditative process referred to the Scriptures or to a truth of faith.[7]

Following the Church's tradition, the patristic practice of *Lectio Divina* is divided into steps, and so we see a sequence. From the time of Guigo II to the present day, these steps are generally considered to be four, known in Latin as: *lectio, meditatio, oratio, contemplatio.* Pope Benedict XVI reminds us of these same steps in his address to the youth of the world:

> My dear young friends, I urge you to become familiar with the Bible, and to have it at hand so that it can be your compass pointing out the road to follow. . . . A time-honoured way to study and savour the word of God is *lectio divina,* which constitutes a real and veritable spiritual journey marked out in stages. After the *lectio,* which consists of reading and rereading a passage from Sacred Scripture and taking in the main elements, we proceed to *meditatio.* This is a moment of interior reflection in which the soul turns to God and tries to understand what his word is saying to us today. Then comes *oratio,* in which we linger to talk with God directly. Finally we come to *contemplatio.* This helps us to keep our hearts attentive to the presence of Christ whose word is "a lamp shining in a dark place, until the day dawns and the morning star rises in your hearts" (2 Pet 1:19). Reading, study and meditation of the Word should then flow into a life of consistent fidelity to Christ and his teachings.[8]

What is interesting about this method is that it has maintained for centuries these steps that constitute a stairway, which assures us that, if we follow it attentively, it will improve our communion with God. This is true even though today there are many steps, depending on the tradition that we follow.[9] The four traditional steps are the most used and the most basic. But if we read the pope's message to youth attentively, without saying so directly at the end he opens the door to a specific step that many actually include as part of the last step: *contemplatio / actio*. That is to say, *action* follows *contemplation* to accompany it as a testimony, commitment, and change (*metanoia*) in the life of whoever reads the Sacred Scripture. Today many of those who write about *Lectio Divina* not only use the four steps, but also add a fifth step. They do so to distinguish it from contemplation in the strictest senses, in reference to the monastic life, since the monks practiced their life in silence and work, putting into practice their "*ora et labora*" in this step, which is now added to reinforce the didactic element.

These steps are used to greater advantage now, with the modern understanding of psychology that also helps us to understand the biblical characters. We no longer speak of a human being as having a duality of body and soul. The human being is not something "given" as such; but rather is "being made," "being formed." Therefore, the fully human being has a spiritual soul, as an inner space that is being formed. Human beings are likewise situated in history, so that human beings must commit themselves to aligning themselves as closely as possible with the history that God wants us to live. Therefore, these exercises of *Lectio Divina* should lead us to history. From spirituality, we move on to Christian commitment for the transformation of society with the Word, so as to avoid falling into spiritualism.

Stage Zero: Invocation of the Holy Spirit

Lectio Divina is a spiritual exercise that begins with a conviction of faith. To open the Sacred Scriptures is an act of faith; therefore, before opening them, it is necessary to renew our faith in their author. Our recognition of proclaimed faith is that the Holy Spirit is the Bible's author. For that reason, and remembering that these writings have been placed there canonically, today they are *Verbum Domini*, the Word of God, and they continue to have validity today. For this reason it is important to recognize the authorship and presence of the Holy Spirit, invoking the Spirit's assistance in a brief and simple prayer so that our mind and heart might be opened to understand its message and put it into practice.

First Step: *Lectio* (Seek by Reading)[10]

In presenting this introduction, we follow the letter of Guigo to Gervasius in large part. We are working with a biblical text (we have already explained that *Lectio Divina* is to be used strictly for biblical texts and not other documents). There are many ways to choose the text. One way to engage in *Lectio Divina* is with the Psalms, for example, by following the order in which they appear in the Bible. One can do the same with a Gospel, or with one of Paul's letters. It can also be done following the liturgical lectionary with the texts used during the Eucharist, whether daily or weekly.

This step is the basis for everything that follows. A careful reading within the context of Sacred Scripture leads us to avoid pretexts. Therefore it is important to be well informed about what has been written about the text. For example, today there are many ways to discover how the text is related to the Fathers of the Church, to tradition, and to the magisterium.[11]

This step should lead us to answer questions that are essential for us to be able to move forward. In this case, after informing ourselves concerning the text, we will at last be prepared to respond to the following question: what does the text say? That is, when we have read it several times and, if possible, from various translations of the Bible,[12] how has this text reached us in our own language? It is important, then, to open our understanding to address this question. Then, when I understand that God speaks, I accept his Word, his message. I understand it in the context of Scripture, and I read it as many times as possible. Including, in some cases, we suggest underlining or placing some mark in the text (a question mark [?] for what is not clear to me, an exclamation point [!] for what catches my attention or appeals to me, an asterisk [*] when I am invited to pray, a word in the margin when I am challenged to action). In this way we are sure that we understand the passage.

Second Step: *Meditatio* (You Will Find by Meditation)

The second step in the exercise of *Lectio Divina* is meditation. Once I understand reasonably well what the text says, I know what the divine Author and the human author express in the text (reading), God himself directs his Word to me personally; he fixes his attention on my life, as if saying to me: "This is my message and now I bring it to your attention . . . in this way, come, let's review it in your life." We then move on to the second question. What does the text say to me today, personally, now that I have seen and understood the biblical text? That is to say, the second question involved in this step is to contextualize in my own life as a believer what the text says: what God wants to say to us, today, in our life, in our history, in our concrete situation. Here, the questions that actualize the text in our lives can be individual, or they can deal with the community. For those who undertake this exercise, it is convenient to ask questions that directly relate the text to personal situations. Thus we understand that it is the Bible that is reading our life, searching out all that we do and live. Meditation helps us to remember the text within the context of our life, to put the words of God into our hearts, so that they might resound directly there.

Third Step: *Oratio* (Call by Praying)

As we move on to this new step in the exercise of *Lectio Divina*, we recall the first two. If in the first two steps God speaks by giving us his message (*reading*) and he speaks to me in his personal search for me (*meditation*), the question that provides orientation for this step is: how do I respond to God who first speaks to me? That is to say, in the first two steps God is the protagonist who appeals to me and now I am responding directly to the questioning I sense. It is the step wherein I make myself known, where I speak to God concerning that about which he questions me. Perhaps this is the most important moment, since prayer is the greatest challenge that we humans have today. We should not confuse prayer with a recitation of petitions, with an innumerable list of things for which we are asking. When engaged in the exercise of *Lectio Divina* I am better prepared to under-stand—centered on the text and its message—what it is that I should ask of God. And, as we know, there are many kinds of prayer (praise, thanksgiving, request for forgiveness, supplication, surrender). Prayer may lead us to say something out loud, put some psalm to music that is related to the text, write a poem, or some other graphic or artistic expression.

Fourth Step: *Contemplatio*
(It Will Be Opened to You, Contemplating)

Contemplation is the fourth step in *Lectio Divina*. Acquired contemplation, which is an exercise to be practiced, is not that spiritual state that some saints had (infused contemplation), but something that we acquire over time. That is to say, through practice the person who contemplates seeks to become more and more conformed to the plan of the Lord who speaks through his Word. Therefore, the question we ask ourselves in this step is: how do I incorporate the message in my inner being?

Many people have difficulties when they reach this step, because they are accustomed to having everything served to them. In this step, it is the imagination, under the guidance of the Spirit of God, who helps us to "get into the scene," "become a part of the scene," and also to take a synthesis of the scene, that is to say, understand the central message of which I am a living part, and thus to become an "echo" where the Word resounds. Here there are no more rules: it is our spirit that develops a dialogue with the Lord, taking the substance of the text and assimilating it in our own lives.

Fifth Step: *Actio* (You Will Understand by Living)

This is a pedagogical step. It is not among the original four steps of the *Lectio Divina*. But we must understand that upon completing their prayer, monks would go in silence to contemplate and to work while they contemplated. Moreover, some authors understand contemplation as a twofold step that leads to action. I suggest that we consider it a fifth step, so as to distinguish it methodologically and so that it might be clear to the one who practices it that here the big question that we ask ourselves is: what is going to change in my life, after this experience of *Lectio Divina*? This is the moment at which we should seriously ask this of ourselves. If we read, meditate, pray, and contemplate a sacred text, but continue the same as before, without any change, then we are surely lying to ourselves. There was no such authentic exercise, for it did not produce in me any transformation. Just as every encounter with a friend whom we appreciate a great deal helps us to see ourselves from a different angle through in-depth dialogue, we are able to improve our attitudes. How much more is this so if this friend who helps us to find ourselves is Jesus, the Christ!

Lectio Divina in the Life of the Church

The Second Vatican Council's Dogmatic Constitution on Divine Revelation *Dei Verbum* provides us with a clear understanding of this process. We can synthesize its teaching in the following programmatic sentence: "Sacred Scripture . . . is the written Word of God . . . by inspiration of the Holy Spirit, and . . . entrusted to the Church for our salvation."[13]

Bishop Santiago Silva explains this synthesis of *Dei Verbum* in the following way:

Three affirmations of faith are underscored:

a) Written Word of God:

The Father who is in heaven "meets His children with great love
and speaks with them" himself and does so "through men and in
human language."

b) Inspired by the Holy Spirit:

These chosen men (or sacred writers) consign, assisted by the
Holy Spirit, the saving truth that God is pleased to reveal to us.

c) Entrusted to the Church for our salvation:

The Word of God which the Scriptures offer encourages and
directs the life of the Church which is sent to announce the
Good News of the Kingdom to all men and women throughout
the earth.[14]

After explaining these three affirmations of faith, he presents them in
a schematic diagram that can help to explain the process of *Lectio Divina*
from another perspective:

On the basis of this perspective on Sacred Scripture and from the
challenges to the church and to discipleship, we recognize the four
moments of *Lectio* Divina as presented in the following diagram:

Sacred Scripture is . . .			
Written Word of God	By inspiration of the Holy Spirit		Entrusted to the Church for salvation
Interpret the Word → *Dimension of wisdom or knowledge*	Actualize the Word → *Dimension of dialogue or communion*		Live the Word → *Dimension of testimony or mission*
❶ **READ** What does the Bible text *say*?	❷ **MEDITATE** What does the Lord *say to me* through his Word?	❸ **PRAY** What do we *say to the Lord* as we are moved by his Word?	❹ **CONTEMPLATE ACT** To what conversion and actions does the Lord *invite me*?
IN THIS WAY . . .			
God's message . . .	appeals to our life . . .	leads to prayer . . .	and leads us to conversion and action.

Each of the four moments of *Lectio Divina* (read, meditate, pray, and contemplate/act) has its own identity, but none of them can be understood apart from the others, and the first three reach their fullness in the last, contemplation of the Face of the Father, which is Jesus Christ, which translates into life (action) according to the model for the new humanity, Jesus.[15]

An Up or Down Stairway?

For some authors, the stairway ascends, beginning with our own human life, and leading us to God. Each step should move us upward in the exercise. Personal effort is required to move up, and the purpose of this exercise is accomplished in the person who undertakes it. In the tradition, some call it the "stairway of the saints."

True *religion* teaches us that "*re-ligare*" or reuniting that which was separated (divinity and humanity) cannot be the result of human action, but comes from God's revelation. In the theology of the Incarnation, which is the biblical basis for understanding the study of God and therefore spirituality, it is God who humbles himself. The Second Person of the Trinity is the one who "emptied himself" of his divine nature, so as to "clothe himself" with human nature. Being the eternal Word of God, he comes to us to speak to us in our language. The good news, then, is that the Second Person of the Trinity, without losing his divine condition, becomes totally human. Jesus is perfect God and perfect man (*hypostasis*).[16] The Logos (OT) becomes human (NT) to show us his full significance, "giving life to the Mosaic Law."

> *qui cum in forma Dei esset non rapinam arbitratus est esse se aequalem Deo, sed semet ipsum exinanivit formam servi accipiens in similitudinem hominum factus et habitu inventus ut homo.*[17]
>
> though he was in the form of God, [he] did not regard equality with God something to be grasped. Rather, he emptied himself, taking the form of a slave, coming in human likeness; and found human in appearance. (Philippians 2:6–7).

Therefore, in my own humble opinion, understanding these exercises from the perspective of the Incarnation of the eternal Word of God, the stairway of *Lectio Divina* is descending.

1. It begins with God who reveals himself: reading.
2. God continues to descend to the concrete life of the reader: meditation.
3. He awakens in the reader a concrete response: prayer.
4. He comes to be involved in our own life: contemplation.
5. He is incarnated in history by those who practice the exercise: action.

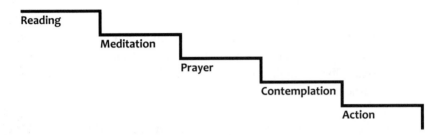

Therefore, *Lectio Divina* enables me to clearly understand that it is God who comes to encounter me, because I need him for my salvation, and not I who by my holiness seek him. Holiness, in this case, consists in "letting yourself be taken hold of" by God, who comes to seek each one of us. It is not I who love God out of my goodness. It is the other way around; holiness is a matter of being attentive to the Lord who reveals himself, who comes to meet us, who calls us by name. "You seduced me, Lord, and I was seduced" (Jer 20:7).

Part 3:
Where and How Is *Lectio Divina* Practiced and by Whom?

Every day *Lectio Divina* is becoming better known in the Church. It is no longer something confined only to monasteries. Entire religious communities use this method regularly and bring it to other communities, where both laypeople and religious participate equally. Throughout the Americas there are dioceses that invite all the faithful to prepare themselves in prayer using the method of *Lectio Divina*. Religious movements and biblical pastoral ministry offer it for all ages, lifestyles, and for diverse communities.

During the synod, Cardinal Oscar Rodríguez made note of some important themes that should be kept in mind:

At the interconfessional level, the United Bible Societies have provided much appreciated support to the Catholic Church. Both in translations done with Catholic biblicists and in new presentations of the Bible that support the pastoral work. The special relationship with CELAM has born as fruit several editions of the Sacred Scriptures that are much used in pastoral work. In the special relationship with CEBIPAL, we must mention the work with the youth preparing them to use *Lectio Divina*, those known as "lectionauts" who grow in number every day. And also, following Aparecida, *Lectio Divina* is working with children, known as "little disciples," and they are becoming very effective in catechesis and pastoral work with children.[18]

This work is not only done with children and youth. There are already many parish and diocesan communities that use this method for their times of prayer and discernment.

Part 4:
The Results in the Church

Lectio Divina in the Greater Continent-Wide Mission

In May 2007 the bishops of Latin America and the Caribbean met in their Fifth General Conference, to which were invited bishops of the United States and Canada with voice and vote as well. In Aparecida, Brazil, they worked for several weeks on a theme framed by the Vatican: "Disciples and missionaries of Jesus Christ, that our peoples might have life in Him." Their final document, commonly known as the Aparecida Document, is filled from beginning to end with references to the Sacred Scriptures, making it a model document based on the Bible.

The topic of *Lectio Divina* is not absent from the document, for in fact quite the contrary is true. This practice is mentioned on many occasions and it is recommended from many viewpoints and angles. But above all, besides insisting that pastoral planning be developed out of the prayerful reading of the Bible, the principal conclusion is that the great continent-wide mission to which the bishops are urgently called should have as its guideposts the knowledge of the Bible and instruction in *Lectio Divina*.

The Aparecida Document tells us that it is important to make clear that the biblical underpinnings of all pastoral work are crucial to the life of the

Church, so that the Bible is not a separate compartment among the episcopal conference's various pastoral activities identified as "biblical pastoral activity." Rather, the Bible is the unifying thread that orients every dimension of pastoral activity by focusing its principal reference to the Word. Thus the Word is the bedrock of the Church, as the inaugural discourse of Pope Benedict XVI to the gathering at Aparecida suggests: "To determine that the Word of God be the source that orients all pastoral activity in the Church." "The biblical orientation of pastoral work, having *Lectio Divina* as background, which is the integration of the Word of God with life; as the indispensable point of reference of the Constitution *Dei Verbum*, and as method and fundamental criterion, the reading based on our reality, has in its present and future horizon the defense of life and of Human Rights."[19]

In October 2008 Cardinal Oscar Rodríguez, S.D.B., addressed the synod in a speech called "The Bible and Its Comprehension in America." Toward the end he made reference to the theme of prayer, using the following words and quoting from Aparecida:

The Teaching of Prayer

Our experience is of a very distinctive popular religiosity, which provides considerable richness in those cultural contexts that have not lost their Christian traditions. However, we can observe the confusion of the faithful about the difference between reciting prayers (as the recitation of composed prayers, novenas, etc.)—that our devoutly faithful people practice with a certain affinity—and prayer as it is properly called, which is a response to God who communicates first through his Word. There is still much ground to cover in this subject of prayer and it is necessary that all our structures, beginning with catechism, be true schools of prayer. Its principal base is *Lectio Divina*, which is being developed and increasingly adapted to the needs of our children, youth, and adults. Prayer should be based on the Bible, and then, the reading of the Bible should be prayerful.

Lectio Divina cannot be just another proposal, and certainly not isolated from the rest of church life but, on the contrary, a proposal to guide all the forms and structures of our church, since it leads us to a coherent and concrete life of following Jesus and his Gospel. We should insist that *Lectio Divina* be the exercise of the whole church that listens to and obeys God who speaks to us. And for this there should be education of all the church even beyond catechetical matters.

Catechesis cannot be limited to a merely doctrinal formation; rather, it should be a true school of integral formation. Therefore, we should cultivate friendship with Christ in prayer . . . (Aparecida § 299).

We shall proceed to gradually introduce the young people to personal prayer and *lectio divina* (Aparecida § 229).

It becomes necessary, then, to propose to the faithful the Word of God as the Father's gift for a living encounter with Jesus Christ, the way of "authentic conversion and of renewed fellowship and solidarity." This proposal will be a means of encounter with the Lord if the revealed Word of God is presented, as contained in Scripture, as a source of evangelism. The disciples of Jesus want to be nourished with the Bread of the Word: they want Access to an adequate interpretation of the biblical texts, to use them as a means of dialogue with Jesus Christ, and that they be the soul of evangelism itself and the proclamation of Jesus to everyone. Therefore, the importance of a "biblical pastoral orientation," understood as biblical encouragement of pastoral work, that it be a school of interpretation or knowledge of the Word, of communion with Jesus or prayer with the Word, and of inculturated evangelization or of proclamation of the Word. This requires, on the part of bishops, presbyters, deacons, and lay ministers of the Word an approach to the Sacred Scripture that is not only intellectual and instrumental, but with the heart "hungry to hear the Word of the Lord" (Aparecida § 248).

Among the many ways of approaching Sacred Scripture, there is a privileged one to which all of us are invited: *Lectio Divina* or exercise of prayerful reading of Sacred Scripture. This prayerful reading, properly practiced, leads to an encounter with Jesus as Teacher, to the knowledge of the mystery of Jesus as the Messiah, to fellowship with Jesus as the Son of God, and to the testimony of Jesus as Lord of the universe. With its four elements (reading, meditation, prayer, contemplation), prayerful reading favors a personal encounter with Jesus Christ as seen in so many characters in the Gospel: Nicodemus and his search for eternal life (cf. Jn 3:1–21), the Samaritan woman and her desire for true worship (cf. Jn 4:1–42), the man born blind and his desire for inner light (cf. Jn 9), Zacchaeus and his desire to be changed (cf. Lk 19:1–10) . . . All of them, thanks to such an encounter, were illuminated and refreshed because they opened themselves to an experience of the Father's mercy that is offered through his Word of truth and life. They did not open their heart to something about the Messiah, but to the Messiah himself, the way of growth in "maturity conformed to his fullness" (Eph 4:13), process of discipleship, of brotherly fellowship and of commitment to society (Aparecida § 249).[20]

Lectio Divina in the Continent-Wide Mission of America

Following the meeting in Aparecida, where the bishops called for a continent-wide mission and a reaffirmation of the Church's missionary commitment, CELAM convened a team of experts to draft a brief document that, in keeping with the norms of Aparecida, following the norms of the Fifth General Conference, organized the key themes for this "Great Mission."

In the second part, identifying the means for the mission, they are quite clear:

> To drink from the Word, a place of encounter with Jesus Christ:
> If the central objective of the Mission is to lead people to a genuine encounter with Jesus Christ, the primary locus of any encounter with Him will be the profound and living knowledge of the Word of God, of the living Jesus Christ, in the Church that is our home (cf. Aparecida § 246).

Among the five goals that are proposed we find: "Formation in *Lectio Divina*, the exercise of prayerful reading of the Sacred Scriptures, and widespread promotion and diffusion of this practice" (cf. Aparecida § 248).

Reading through this document of the Continental Mission we discover ample evidence that the Church greatly desires that our peoples will encounter Jesus Christ through his Word in the Sacred Scriptures and that *Lectio Divina* is the privileged path toward realizing this encounter.

Lectio Divina during the Synod of "The Word of God in the Life and Mission of the Church"

A number of propositions of the October 2008 Assembly of the Synod of Bishops on the Word of God show us how often *Lectio Divina* was mentioned in the synod hall. I will simply quote from these propositions, leaving to the considered judgment of the reader their use and application, since these propositions were given to the Holy Father Benedict XVI so that he might prepare a post-synodal exhortation for the Church.[21]

Proposition 9:

Encounter with the Word in Reading Sacred Scripture

Taking up a thought shared by the Fathers, Saint Cyprian reminds: "Attend assiduously to prayer and to '*lectio divina.*'" When you pray you speak with God, when you read it is God who speaks with you" (*Ad Donatum*, 15).[22]

Proposition 22:

Word of God and Prayerful Reading

The synod proposes that all the faithful, including young people, be exhorted to approach the Scriptures through "prayerful" and assiduous "reading" (cf. *Dei Verbum* § 25), in such a way that the dialogue with God becomes a daily reality of the people of God.

Therefore, it is important:

- That the prayerful reading be profoundly related to the example of Mary and the saints in the history of the Church, as those who carried out the reading of the Word according to the Spirit;
- That it be ensured that pastors, priests, and deacons, and in a very special sense future priests, have adequate formation so that, in turn, they can form the people of God in this spiritual dynamic;
- That the faithful be initiated—in keeping with the circumstances, categories and cultures—in the most appropriate method of prayerful reading, personal and/ or community (*lectio divina*, spiritual exercises in daily life, "Seven Steps" in Africa and in other places, various methods of prayer, sharing in the family and in the grassroots ecclesial communities, etc.);
- That the practice of prayerful reading be encouraged, using liturgical texts that the Church proposes for the Sunday and daily eucharistic celebration, to better understand the relation between Word and Eucharist;

- That care be taken that the prayerful reading of the Scriptures, above all by the community, result in a commitment to charity (cf. Lk 4:18–19).

Conscious of the present widespread diffusion of "*lectio divina*" and of other similar methods, the synodal fathers see in them a true sign of hope and encourage all ecclesial leaders to multiply their efforts in this sense.[23]

Proposition 24:
Word of God and Consecrated Life

The synod highlights the importance of contemplative life and its valuable contribution to the tradition of "*lectio divina*." Monastic communities are schools of spirituality and give strength to the life of local Churches. . . .[24]

Proposition 32:
Formation of Candidates for Holy Orders

The formation of priests should include multiple approaches to Scripture. Prayerful reading of "*lectio divina*," both personal as well as in community, in the framework of a first reading of the Bible. It will be necessary to continue it during the whole process of formation, taking into account what the Church establishes in regard to retreats and spiritual exercises in the education of seminarians.[25]

Proposition 36:
Sacred Scripture and the Unity of Christians

To listen together to the Word of God, to practice the "*lectio divina*" of the Bible . . . is a path to follow to attain the unity of the faith, as response to the listening of the Word.[26]

Proposition 46:
Faithful Reading of Scripture:
Historical Authenticity and Fundamentalism

Faithful reading of Sacred Scripture, practiced since antiquity in the Tradition of the Church, seeks the truth that saves for the life of each faithful and for the Church. This reading acknowledges the historic value of the biblical tradition. It is precisely because of this value of historic testimony that it desires to rediscover the profound meaning of Sacred Scripture destined also for the life of today's believer.

Such a reading of Scripture differs from "fundamentalist interpretations," which ignore the human mediation of the inspired text and its literary genres. To use "*lectio divina*" fruitfully, the believer must be educated "not to confuse unknowingly the human limits of the biblical message with the divine essence of the message itself" (cf. Pontifical Biblical Commission, "The Interpretation of the Bible in the Church," I F).[27]

Conclusion

The title of this essay, following the text of the Emmaus narrative, is "He explained the Scriptures to us." Nothing could be more accurate: to allow Jesus, the eternal Word of the Father, to teach us "Words of God" with human words. When Jesus himself appeared to them on the road, the disciples who were on their way to Emmaus did not reject him, rather they allowed him to accompany them. This made them feel secure for their journey.

Just as he did on that Sunday of the Resurrection, Jesus himself appears on the pathways of our lives. He wants to share the journey with us. He wants to walk where we walk, and on that path he wants to explain the Scriptures to us himself, opening the Bible and giving us counsel in the ways of life. It is Jesus the Christ who comes to us! We do not seek him, but it is he who seeks us, to encounter us. These disciples were holy because they allowed him to accompany them, holy because they were not stubborn, but rather were docile to his teaching! They ceased to be "slow of heart" and opened themselves to the Master's teaching. While listening to the Master who explained the Scriptures, "their heart burned within them."

The practice of *Lectio Divina* is simply an exercise of docility that allows Jesus, the living Christ, to accompany us along the way. Through that revelation, he comes into our life, turning our pathway into a sharing of life, of walking with God. May we not be slow of heart, nor lacking in comprehension either. Holiness is docility for listening. Holiness is not rejecting the Master when he comes to us on the way and shares history with us and we allow him to open the Scriptures up for us.

"Speak, Lord, for your servant is listening!" (1 Sam 3:10).

~

Notes

1. Twelfth Ordinary General Assembly of the Synod of Bishops, "Message to the People of God," October 24, 2008, § 4, http://www.vatican.va/roman _curia/synod/documents/rc_synod_doc_20081024_message-synod_en.html.
2. Ibid., 5.
3. Ibid.
4. Santiago Silva Retamales, *Jesús Maestro, enséñanos a orar: teoría y práctica de la lectio divina* (Miami, FL: Fundación Ramón Pané, 2007), 5.
5. Origen, *Philocalia* 2,3.
6. See Enzo Bianchi, *Ascoltare la Parola: Bibbia e spirito: la lectio divina nella Chiesa* (Magnano, Italy: Qiqajon, 2008), 7.
7. See Saint Augustine, *De catechizandis rudibus.*
8. Benedict XVI, "Message of the Holy Father to the Youth of the World on the Occasion of the Twenty-first World Youth Day (April 9, 2006), http://www .vatican.va/holy_father/benedict_xvi/messages/youth/documents /hf_ben-xvi_mes_20060222_youth_en.html.
9. In his exercises, Cardinal Martini presents the steps in this order: *lectio, meditatio, contemplatio, oratio, consolatio, discretio, deliberatio, actio.* All of these are dependent on the four essential steps.
10. I will be using these ways of presenting the steps, as Guigo does in his letter to Gervasius (1:173).
11. The Congregation for the Clergy, in the Vatican, has developed an open-access web page (available in several languages), which I heartily recommend: http://www.bibliaclerus.org/index_eng.html.
12. During the synod on "The Word of God in the Life and Mission of the Church," Cardinal Oscar Rodríguez, S.D.B., presented the synthesis "The Bible and Its Comprehension in America" and recalled that there are at least twenty-six translations approved by the Catholic Church in Spanish, thirteen translations approved in Portuguese, nine translations in English, and eight translations in French.
13. See *Dei Verbum*, § 9, 11, 12, 21. Also see Pontifical Biblical Commission, "The Interpretation of the Bible in the Church," 102: "The Bible is a text inspired by God and entrusted to the Church to awaken faith and guide the Christian life."

14. Silva, *Jesús Maestro, enséñanos a orar*, 20.

15. Ibid., 28.

16. Literally, hypostatic union. This is the theological and magisterial expression, from the patristic era, which indicates the profound union of the divine reality with human reality in the person/subject of the eternal Son/Logos of God in Jesus Christ. This expression does not appear in the New Testament sources. Nonetheless, in the New Testament are found several confessional formulas about Jesus that serve as a basis for the subsequent explanation. The central object of the proclamation of faith of the New Testament is the man, Jesus of Nazareth, recognized as Lord, Christ, Son of God, God (cf. Mt 16:16; Mk 1:1; Acts 2:32–36; Phil 2:6–11; Rom 1:3, 10:9; Jn 1:14, 20:28, etc.). So it is that the New Testament clearly affirms the identity of a subject that belongs to two spheres of existence, the human and the divine, who lived as a human in humiliation/kenosis and presently lives in glory/*doxa*.

17. *Biblia sacra: Iuxta Vulgatam versionem* (Württemberg: Württembergische Bibelanstalt, 1969).

18. See the intervention of Oscar Andrés Rodríguez Maradiaga, "La Biblia y su comprensión en América" (October 9, 2008), http://www.zenit.org /article-28725?l=spanish. See www.lectionautas.com and also www .discipulitos.com.

19. See Diego Padrón (Bishop of Cumaná, member of the executive committee of the FEBIC), "La puesta en práctica de la *Dei Verbum* en América Latina y el Caribe: desafíos y perspectivas" (The Initiation of the Dei Verbum in Latin America and the Caribbean: Challenges and Perspectives), *La Palabra Hoy* 119 (2006), 45–51.

20. See Rodríguez Maradiaga, "La Biblia y su comprensión en América," http://www.zenit.org/article-28725?l=spanish.

21. Editor's note: The Post-synodal Apostolic Exhortation *Verbum Domini* had not yet appeared at the time this chapter was completed. It was promulgated by Pope Benedict XVI on September 30, 2010, http://www.vatican.va /holy_father/benedict_xvi/apost_exhortations/documents/hf_ben-xvi _exh_20100930_verbum-domini_en.html.

22. The English translation of this Synod Proposition is from ZENIT, December 3, 2008, http://www.zenit.org/article-24461?l=english.

23. The English translation of this Synod Proposition is from ZENIT, December 7, 2008, http://www.zenit.org/article-24497?l=english.

24. Ibid.

25. The English translation of this Synod Proposition is from ZENIT, December 10, 2008. http://www.zenit.org/article-24511?l=english.
26. The English translation of this Synod Proposition is from ZENIT, December 11, 2008, http://www.zenit.org/article-24532?l=english.
27. The English translation of this Synod Proposition is from ZENIT, December 16, 2008, http://www.zenit.org/article-24584?l=english.

15.

"Stay with Us"

The Word of God and the Future of Hispanic Ministry

Archbishop José H. Gómez

~

On March 10, 2009, Pope Benedict sent a very poignant and very personal letter to all the bishops of the world. In it he said:

> The real problem at this moment of our history is that God is disappearing from the human horizon, and, with the dimming of the light which comes from God, humanity is losing its bearings, with increasingly evident destructive effects. Leading men and women to God, *to the God who speaks in the Bible:* this is the supreme and fundamental priority of the Church and of the Successor of Peter at the present time.[1]

I believe our Holy Father is right. God *is* becoming more and more remote from the concerns and priorities of our culture. It's not as if God has withdrawn his presence. It's that *we* are moving away from *him*. More and more of our brothers and sisters go through their days without any awareness of his presence or their need for God in their lives. They don't hate God. They just don't think about him much anymore. It's as if he doesn't exist.

This includes more and more of our Latino brothers and sisters, I'm afraid. I'm not a big believer in polls that try to estimate people's religious faith. But every major study of Hispanics in the last few years has come to a consistent and disturbing conclusion—that between 10 and 12 percent of all Hispanics no longer practice any religion. And this number has doubled in the last decade.

This is the context for our ministry in the future. Our only priority can be what the pope said—to lead our brothers and sisters back to God. But not just to any "god," or to some vague spirituality, or to what some people call "cultural Catholicism." No. *Conducir a los hombres hacia Dios, hacia el Dios que habla en la Biblia.* To lead men and women to the God who reveals himself in the pages of the Sacred Scriptures. The God who has shown his face to us in Jesus Christ. Only this God can save us.

To take up the text that has set the theme for your weekend: the Gospel paints us a picture of the two disciples going down the road to Emmaus, all wrapped up in their hurt and disappointment, so shattered that all they can do is think about themselves. They say, "We had hoped that he was the one." *Nosotros esperábamos que sería él el que iba a librar a Israel.* This is one of the saddest moments in the Gospels. To see those who once believed lose hope. But why had they lost their hope? The text tells us very clearly. They had been hoping that Jesus was the one who would liberate Israel. *A librar a Israel.*

They came to Jesus expecting a political savior, a Messiah whose salvation would be expressed in political or sociological terms. A lot of people back then made the same mistake about Jesus. A lot of people still do. Those disciples had made Jesus in their *own* image. This is a problem with some of the hermeneutics in the Church today. With the best intentions and good faith, we try to read Jesus through the "lens" of our particular group and to interpret the Gospel in light of our group's needs. Of course Jesus speaks to the condition of every man and woman, and of course his Gospel has inevitable and radical political implications. But we can't make Jesus fit into our categories. We have to make ourselves fit into his. If we seek him and his kingdom, everything else will be added to us. We have to seek the true Jesus, not the Jesus of our imaginations and desires.

Those disciples in the Emmaus story had their own ideas about who Jesus *should* be, about what a Messiah should look like. This is an approach to Jesus that leads nowhere. It makes them blind. Jesus is walking right next to them and they can't see him. The Gospel says: *Pero sus ojos estaban retenidos para que no le conocieran.* "Their eyes were kept from recognizing him." Sometimes isn't this true of our theology, my friends? Too often we take the Jesus of the Gospels, who is meant to be an *icon*—the image of the invisible God and the firstborn of a new humanity—and we turn him into a *mirror*. All we can see in Jesus is ourselves. But our people want to see the real Jesus. They are like those folks who seek out the apostles in the Gospel.

They are coming to you and me because we are the so-called experts—the pastors, the scholars, the teachers. They are coming to us with that same simple request, "We wish to see Jesus" (Jn 12:21). *Queremos ver a Jesús.*

We have an obligation before God, and out of love for our neighbors, to show them the real Jesus. The Jesus of the Gospels. But we have to make sure we know the real Jesus ourselves. To do that we have to get rid of our preconceptions and read the Gospel in faith. At the Transfiguration, the apostles heard the voice from heaven say, "This is my beloved Son—*listen to him!*" (Mk 9:7). That's what we have to do. We have to listen to what Jesus says about himself and what is said about him in the Gospels. And we have to believe in the testimony of those who witnessed his rising from the dead, the testimony of the Church's great tradition.

We have a hard time today believing in the Gospel—even many of our professional exegetes, pastors, and teachers. We're so advanced, so scientific, that we think we're too sophisticated to believe in miracles like the ones we read about in the Gospel. But St. Paul is right: "If Christ has not been raised, then our preaching is in vain and your faith is in vain" (1 Cor 15:14). And if our faith is in vain, what are we living and working for? We see the roots of unbelief at Emmaus, too. The disciples refused to believe the witness of the women who discovered the empty tomb.

This theme runs through all of the Easter stories. The blindness caused by unbelief. We all remember "doubting Thomas." Remember what he said? "Unless I see . . . I will not believe" (Jn 20:25). In Mark's Gospel, Jesus criticizes the disciples *"because they had not believed those who saw him* after he had risen" (Mk 16:14). Jesus makes the same criticism in the Emmaus account. He calls the disciples there *"fools"*—*¡Oh insensatos y tardos de corazón para creer!* We have to watch out for the same temptation, my friends. None of us has *seen* the risen Christ either. We've never met anyone who can walk on water, or multiply loaves and fishes, or raise a man from the dead. We have no *"proof"* that Jesus is the one the Church says he is—the Son of God, the Savior of the human race.

For that kind of knowledge, we need the gift of faith. And this is what Christ draws near to give us. While they were walking, "Jesus drew near and went with them." *Jesús se acercó y siguió con ellos.* What great love our Lord has for us, my brothers and sisters! What a great gift he gives us, the gift of faith! Unless we believe, unless we have faith, Jesus will remain for us just another rabbi from ancient Israel. And again, if he is just a wise man, not the Son of God who rose from the dead, then he can't save anybody.

Then all our work is in vain. Practically speaking, we need the gift of faith to interpret the Scriptures properly and to proclaim them. The Scriptures were written by believers and they were written for the purpose of bringing others to that same faith, to the encounter with Jesus Christ.

We just celebrated the Year of St. Paul, the great evangelist. Paul said that God "was pleased to reveal his Son to me *in order that I might preach him*" (Gal 1:16). We need to have that same faith that Paul did. We need to believe that the biblical texts are inspired by God. We need to proclaim them as St. Paul did. "Not as the word of men but as what it really is—the Word of God" (1 Thes 2:13). *La Palabra de Dios.*

At Emmaus Jesus teaches us how we should read the New Testament, and how we should proclaim Christ. "Beginning with Moses and all the prophets, [Jesus] interpreted to them in all the Scriptures the things concerning himself." *Y, empezando por Moisés y continuando por todos los profetas, les explicó lo que había sobre él en todas las Escrituras.* Jesus explained his identity through the Old Testament, through the plan of God—what St. Paul and the Church Fathers called the "economy" of salvation. This is how he taught his disciples to proclaim him. That's why there is not a page of the New Testament that is not filled with allusions, citations, and quotations from the Old Testament. I worry sometimes that in our preaching we have become a little like Marcion, the early heretic who wanted to throw out the Old Testament. At Emmaus, our Lord himself tells us that if we want to know him then we need to know the Old Testament. We need to know how he is the fulfillment of all that Israel had hoped for.

The way we teach and preach about Christ should make the Word of God come alive. Our proclamation should make our people's hearts burn with the desire for conversion. The desire for a life that's more than just a surface existence. That is what happened to the disciples at Emmaus. "Did not our hearts burn within us while . . . he opened to us the Scriptures?" And they ask our Lord: "Stay with us." A simple request that reflects a profound conversion. *Quédate con nosotros.*

Through his interpretation of the Scriptures, Jesus has shown them that the Word of God, spoken of old through the prophets, in these latter days has become flesh, a living Person. As the book of Revelation says: "He is clad in a robe dipped in blood, and the name by which he is called is the Word of God" (Rev 19:13; cf. Heb 1:1). *Quédate con nosotros.* Jesus has come into their lives and they don't ever want him to leave. Now how does Jesus respond? He takes the bread, blesses it, breaks it, and gives it to them—just as he had done with the apostles at the Last Supper (Lk 22:14–20). The Word of God is meant to lead us to the table of the Lord. To the Eucharist. To the sacraments of the Church. In the Eucharist the story of salvation history continues. What the Scriptures proclaim, the liturgy makes real—the communion of God and his children. In the Eucharist, the disciples recognize Christ. "He was made known to them in the breaking of the bread"—which is what the early Church used to call the Eucharist. *Le habían conocido en la fracción del pan.*

And finally, we notice that the disciples, having met our Lord in Word and Sacrament, set out to proclaim him to their brothers and sisters in Jerusalem. The encounter with Christ in the Scriptures must lead our people to bear witness to him. To take their part in the mission that Christ gave to his Church: "Go therefore and make disciples of all nations" (Mt 28:19–20). Jesus said he came to "cast fire upon the earth" (Lk 12:49). This is the burning that the disciples felt in their hearts at Emmaus. The Word of God seeks to start that fire in the hearts of every man and woman. He wants to inflame our hearts with the desire to know him and to love him ever more deeply, with the zeal to bring other souls to love him too, with fervor to share his love with others. Let us then go out and proclaim this Word! Let us draw near to our brothers and sisters as they make their way down the road of life. Let us speak to them of our friendship with Jesus.

I pray that Our Lady of Guadalupe, who heard the Word of God and allowed it to dwell richly within her, will watch over you (cf. Col 3:16).

～

Note

1. Benedict XVI, "Letter to the Bishops of the Catholic Church Concerning the Remission of the Excommunication of the Four Bishops Consecrated by Archbishop Lefebvre," March 10, 2009, http://www.vatican.va/holy _father/benedict_xvi/letters/2009/documents/hf_ben-xvi_let_20090310 _remissione-scomunica_en.html.

PRAY WITH THE BIBLE.
MEDITATE WITH THE WORD.

Discover the exciting world of *Lectio Divina*.

The ancient Catholic method of *Lectio Divina* (Divine Reading) is a prayerful, reflective and responsive approach to engaging with Holy Scripture.

Help your parish experience the power of God's Word by teaching them about this powerful practice.

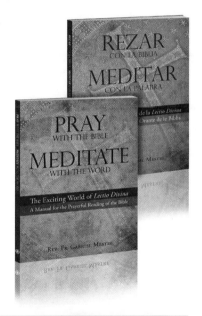

> "The diligent reading of sacred Scripture accompanied by prayer brings about that intimate dialogue in which the person reading hears God who is speaking, and in praying, responds to him with trusting openness of heart."
> — Pope Benedict

> "We join in partnership with the Catholic Church and are presenting *Lectio Divina* as the flagship program of American Bible Society for Catholics nationwide."
> — Mario Paredes, Presidential Liaision to Roman Catholic Ministry at American Bible Society

For more information in English contact:
Alicia DeFrange – ADeFrange@AmericanBible.org

or in Spanish contact:
Margaret Sarci – MSarci@AmericanBible.org

EVERYDAY IS A JOURNEY. GET SOME DIRECTION.

Discover hope, encouragement and direction offered in God's Word delievered right to you on your cell phone or online.

Lectio Divina Journey now available!

Using the USCCB's Roman Catholic lectionary calendar, prepare for liturgy of the Word on a weekly basis at **ABSJourneys.org**

JOURNEYS
something good every day

AMERICAN BIBLE SOCIETY